American White Pelican

Did You Know?

- The American white pelican is one of the world's largest birds, with a wingspan of almost 10 feet.

- White pelicans feed by skimming along the surface of the water and scooping up fish in their beaks.

- The bright orange pouch below a pelican's beak can hold up to three gallons of water.

Science

Macmillan
McGraw-Hill

Program Authors

Dr. Jay K. Hackett
Professor Emeritus of Earth Sciences
University of Northern Colorado

Dr. Richard H. Moyer
Professor of Science Education and Natural
 Sciences
University of Michigan–Dearborn

Dr. JoAnne Vasquez
Elementary Science Education Consultant
NSTA Past President
Member, National Science Board
 and NASA Education Board

Mulugheta Teferi, M.A.
Principal, Gateway Middle School
St. Louis Public Schools
St. Louis, MO

Dinah Zike, M.Ed.
Dinah Might Adventures LP
San Antonio, TX

Kathryn LeRoy, M.S.
Executive Director
Division of Mathematics and Science Education
Miami-Dade County Public Schools, FL

Dr. Dorothy J.T. Terman
Science Curriculum Development Consultant
Former K–12 Science and Mathematics Coordinator
Irvine Unified School District, CA

Dr. Gerald F. Wheeler
Executive Director
National Science Teachers Association

Bank Street College of Education
New York, NY

Contributing Authors

Dr. Sally Ride
Sally Ride Science
San Diego, CA

Lucille Villegas Barrera, M.Ed.
Elementary Science Supervisor
Houston Independent School District
Houston, TX

Dr. Stephen F. Cunha
Professor of Geography
Humboldt State University
Arcata, CA

**American Museum
of Natural History**
New York, NY

Contributing Writer

Ellen C. Grace, M.S.
Consultant
Albuquerque, NM

The American Museum of Natural History in New York City is one of the world's preeminent scientific, educational, and cultural institutions, with a global mission to explore and interpret human cultures and the natural world through scientific research, education, and exhibitions. Each year the Museum welcomes around four million visitors, including 500,000 schoolchildren in organized field trips. It provides professional development activities for thousands of teachers; hundreds of public programs that serve audiences ranging from preschoolers to seniors; and an array of learning and teaching resources for use in homes, schools, and community-based settings. Visit www.amnh. org for online resources.

RFB&D ◉
learning through listening

Students with print disabilities may be eligible to obtain an accessible, audio version of the pupil edition of this textbook. Please call Recording for the Blind & Dyslexic at 1-800-221-4792 for complete information.

C

The McGraw·Hill Companies

**Macmillan
McGraw-Hill**

Published by Macmillan/McGraw-Hill, of McGraw-Hill Education, a division of The McGraw-Hill Companies, Inc., Two Penn Plaza, New York, New York 10121.

Science Content Standards for California Public Schools reproduced by permission, California Department of Education, CDE Press, 1430 N Street, Suite 3207, Sacramento, CA 95814.

FOLDABLES is a trademark of The McGraw-Hill Companies, Inc.

Printed in the United States of America
ISBN 0-02-284378-7/4
3 4 5 6 7 8 9 (027/055) 11 10 09 08 07

Scientific Method

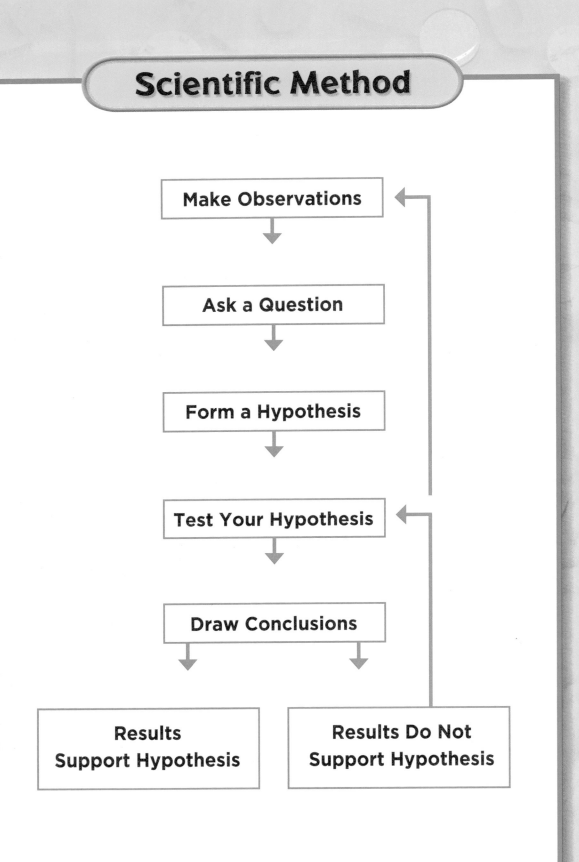

Make Observations

Ask a Question

Form a Hypothesis

Test Your Hypothesis

Draw Conclusions

Results Support Hypothesis

Results Do Not Support Hypothesis

Be a Scientist

Students make observations and record data. ▶

Life Science

▼ Antelopes travel together.

▼ **Coral reef ecosystems contain living and nonliving things.**

Earth Science

Feldspar is a mineral that makes ▶ up about half of Earth's crust.

▼ **Lava flows from an active volcano.**

Physical Science

▼ **Electrical power lines bring electricity to your home.**

▲ **Wind power is used to make electricity.**

Activities

Life Science

Earth Science

Activities

Physical Science

Reference

◀ **A hand lens is a tool that helps you observe.**

Safety Tips

In the Classroom

- Read all of the directions. Make sure you understand them. When you see "⚠ **Be Careful**," follow the safety rules.

- Listen to your teacher for special safety directions. If you do not understand something, ask for help.

- Wash your hands with soap and water before an activity.

- Be careful around a hot plate. Know when it is on and when it is off. Remember that the plate stays hot for a few minutes after it is turned off.

- Wear a safety apron if you work with anything messy or anything that might spill.

- Clean up a spill right away, or ask your teacher for help.

- Tell your teacher if something breaks. If glass breaks, do not clean it up yourself.

- Wear safety goggles when your teacher tells you to wear them. Wear them when working with anything that can fly into your eyes or when working with liquids.

- Keep your hair and clothes away from open flames. Tie back long hair, and roll up long sleeves.

- Keep your hands dry around electrical equipment.

- Do not eat or drink anything during an experiment.

- Put equipment back the way your teacher tells you to.

- Dispose of things the way your teacher tells you to.

- Clean up your work area after an activity, and wash your hands with soap and water.

In the Field

- Go with a trusted adult—such as your teacher, or a parent or guardian.

- Do not touch animals or plants without an adult's approval. The animal might bite. The plant might be poison ivy or another dangerous plant.

Responsibility

- Treat living things, the environment, and one another with respect.

Be a Scientist

Brown ant biting
a blade of grass

What Is
Science?

Science is a way of understanding the world around us. Scientists often ask questions about what they observe. They call on many skills to help them answer these questions. This process of asking and answering questions in science is called *inquiry*.

In this section you will see how scientists use inquiry skills to learn about ants.

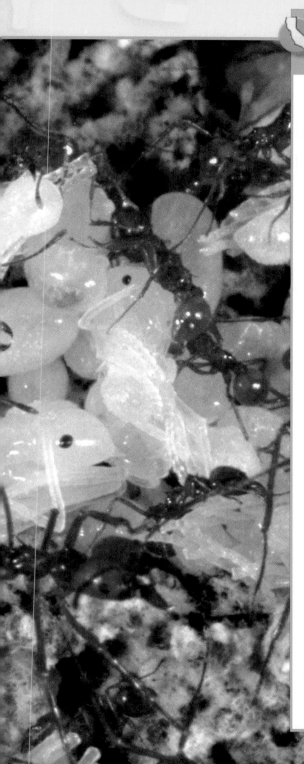

Investigation and Experimentation

6. Scientific progress is made by asking meaningful questions and conducting careful investigations. As a basis for understanding this concept and addressing the content in the other three strands, students should develop their own questions and perform investigations. Students will:

a. Differentiate observation from inference (interpretation) and know scientists' explanations come partly from what they observe and partly from how they interpret their observations.

b. Measure and estimate the weight, length, or volume of objects.

c. Formulate and justify predictions based on cause-and-effect relationships.

d. Conduct multiple trials to test a prediction and draw conclusions about the relationships between predictions and results.

e. Construct and interpret graphs from measurements.

f. Follow a set of written instructions for a scientific investigation.

Inquiry Skills

These are the inquiry skills scientists use. You can use these skills, too.

Observe

Infer

Classify

Measure

Use Numbers

Communicate

Predict

Record Data

Analyze Data

Form a Hypothesis

Use Variables

Experiment

Make a Model

Are you an observant person? You might look out the window to see if it is raining. You might even listen for rain on the windowsill. You make observations throughout your day. Observations on the world around us often raise questions.

The diagram on this page shows processes that scientists use to answer questions. Many call this the "scientific method." Scientists don't always use all of the steps. They may not use them in the same order.

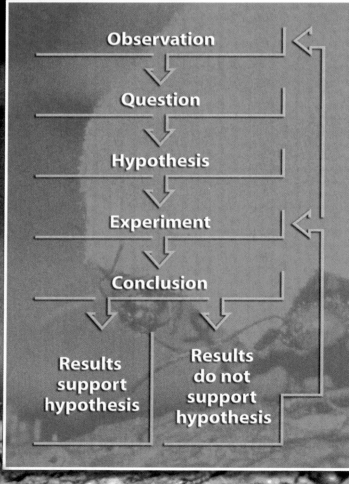

Observation

Question

Hypothesis

Experiment

Conclusion

Results support hypothesis

Results do not support hypothesis

Inquiry Skills

When you make observations, you use these skills.

Observe Use your senses to learn about an object or event.

Classify Place things that share properties together in groups.

Measure Find the size, distance, time, volume, area, mass, weight, or temperature of an object or an event.

Scientists are curious people who observe the world around them and try to understand it. To observe means to use your senses to learn about something. Scientists ask questions about the things they observe. You can too. When you ask questions about the things you see, smell, hear, taste, or feel, you are a scientist.

What do you think the ants in this photo are doing? Describe what you see.

Do you ask "why" questions when you are curious about things? The work of scientists often starts with an unanswered question. Scientists then suggest a possible answer that can be tested with an experiment. This is known as *forming a hypothesis*. A good hypothesis must:

▶ be based on what you observe.

▶ be testable by doing an experiment.

▶ be useful in predicting new findings.

The photo shows the entrance to an ant nest in the desert. Why do you think desert ants build their nests deep underground? Form a hypothesis to answer this question.

Inquiry Skills

When you ask questions and form hypotheses, you use these skills.

Infer Form an idea from facts or observations.

Form a Hypothesis Make a statement that can be tested to answer a question.

Scientists often do research before they experiment. They look in books, scientific journals, or Internet resources for information that other scientists have found. Scientists also know that they cannot rely on someone's opinion or claim unless it has been backed up by observations.

7

Now it's time to test your hypothesis with an experiment. In experiments you change one variable to see what happens with another variable. For example, you might vary the type of soil in an ant farm to see if it varies how many tunnels the ants build. It is important to change only one variable at a time. What would happen if you changed both the type of soil and the type of ant at the same time?

Experiments must be able to be repeated, too. Scientists describe the steps of their experiments and explain their results to the public. This allows other scientists to repeat the experiment. It also allows others to evaluate and compare each other's work. They can check their own work too! So a good experiment must:

▶ change only one variable at a time.

▶ be able to be repeated.

Before you test a hypothesis, you must have a plan. When scientists make a plan, they think about the variables they want to test. A variable is something that can be changed or controlled. It is important to change or control only one variable at a time. Keep all other parts of the experiment the same. That way you will know what caused your results.

After they determine their variables, scientists decide what materials they will need. Then they write a procedure. A procedure is a series of numbered steps that tell what to do first, next, and last.

After scientists have developed their procedure, they predict what will happen when they follow it. To predict means to tell what you think will happen.

Inquiry Skills

When you experiment, you use these skills.

Experiment Perform a test to support or disprove a hypothesis.

Use Variables Identify things in an experiment that can be changed or controlled.

Predict State possible results of an event or experiment.

Make a Model Make something to represent an object or event.

What's one important part of a science experiment? Collecting and recording good data! When data are collected, they may then be explained, or interpreted. Collecting and interpreting data often requires working with numbers. This scientist uses numbers to record her observations.

When scientists follow their procedure, they make observations and record data. Data is information. Measurements are a type of data. Scientists use measurements whenever they can to describe objects and events. Scientists measure such things as length, volume, mass, temperature, and time.

Scientists repeat their procedure several times. This helps them know if their results are correct. They often compare their results with other scientists. Other scientists will repeat the procedure to see if they get the same results.

Inquiry Skills

When you collect and interpret data, you use these skills.

Use Numbers Order, count, add, subtract, multiply, and divide to explain data.

Measure Find the size, distance, time, volume, area, mass, weight, or temperature of an object or an event.

Record Data Accurately arrange and store information collected in science investigations.

Analyze Data Use the information that has been gathered to answer questions or solve a problem.

You've collected and interpreted data. Now what? It is time to draw a conclusion. A conclusion states whether your data support your hypothesis.

But what if your data do not support your hypothesis? Perhaps different experiments are needed. Perhaps a new question will result.

Scientists also share with others what they have found. This allows scientists around the world to stay informed. And it allows scientists to check each others' work.

Scientists also share what they have learned with the public. Dr. Edward O. Wilson shares his knowledge of ants and other insects through books and lectures.

12

Inquiry Skills

When you draw conclusions and communicate results, you use this skill.

Communicate Share information.

Scientists organize and analyze their data to see if the results support or disprove their hypothesis. They determine if their prediction matched their results. They draw conclusions and try to explain their results. When you draw conclusions, you interpret observations to answer questions.

Sometimes the results of an experiment lead to new questions. These questions can be used to form a new hypothesis and perform new tests. The process starts all over again. This process of asking and answering questions is called the scientific method.

Forming a Hypothesis

Most science experiments start with an unanswered question. To design a good experiment you must keep a few important details in mind. Here is a sample question that two students wanted to explore. Take a good look at it. See if there is anything about it you would change.

Question

- Would more ants be attracted to an unpeeled piece of fruit or to a piece of fruit that was peeled?

  The students turned the question into a statement they could test. This statement is called a **hypothesis**. A *hypothesis* is an "if... then..." statement. Here is the hypothesis proposed by the students:

Hypothesis

- If fruit is peeled, then more ants will be attracted to it.

  Can this hypothesis be tested?

Defining Variables

The next step is to make a plan to test your hypothesis. The test for your hypothesis is your experiment.

You need to decide what you are testing and what you are not testing. These are your *variables*.

Controlled variables are not being tested. They are used to control the experiment so it can be repeated.

In this experiment the controlled variables will be:

- the type and ripeness of the fruit .
- the place where the fruit is placed.
- the time of day you make your observations.

The only factor that will change is what you are testing. This is the *independent variable*. The best experiments test one variable at a time.

In this experiment the independent variable will be:

- whether the fruit is peeled or left unpeeled.

In an experiment, the factors you measure are called the *dependent variables*. They change based on the independent variable.

You will be counting the number of ants on the fruit. The dependent variable in this experiment will be the number of ants on the fruit.

What other variables can you identify?

Designing an Experiment

Then design your experiment to test your hypothesis. Here is one student's design.

Procedure

1. Find a spot such as under a tree, where there will likely be ants.

2. Place one unpeeled banana and a peeled banana on the ground one meter apart from each other.

3. Predict which piece of fruit ants will be more attracted to.

4. Leave both bananas on the ground. Check to see if there are any ants on them. Check back after one hour; after two hours; after three hours.

5. Make a data table like the one below. Fill in for each banana the number of ants after one hour; after two hours; and after three hours.

	Peeled Fruit	Unpeeled Fruit
Start of experiment	0	0
Hour 1	15	4
Hour 2	25	9
Hour 3	30	15

6. Repeat the experiment on another day.

7. Did your results match your prediction?

8. Compare your results with other students' results to confirm your findings.

4 IE 6.f. Follow a set of written instructions for a scientific investigation.

16

Analyzing Data

To communicate your results, set up your data clearly. The students used the data table to set up a line graph. They grouped the numbers in their data table using the scale: fewer than 10; 10–20; more than 20.

See the students' results on the graph below.

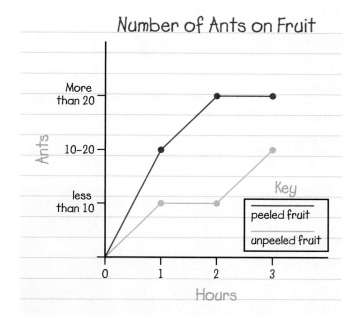

Number of Ants on Fruit

Ants

More than 20

10–20

less than 10

Key

peeled fruit

unpeeled fruit

0   1   2   3

Hours

Explain how you think the line graph makes the results clear.

Once scientists have done an experiment, they repeat the experiment. Why is this important?

4 IE 6.d. Conduct multiple trials to test a prediction and draw conclusions about the relationship between predictions and results.
4 IE 6.e. Construct and interpret graphs from measurements.

Forming New Questions

The exciting thing about doing experiments is that you find out new things and may have new questions. After doing their experiment, the students wrote down new questions they wanted to study:

- What if you placed the fruit in another location?

- What if you used a different kind of fruit or food?

- What if you did the experiment during a different time of day or a different season?

- What if you did the experiment in different weather?

Use one of the above questions or another one that you think of. Set up a hypothesis and experimental plan to test it.

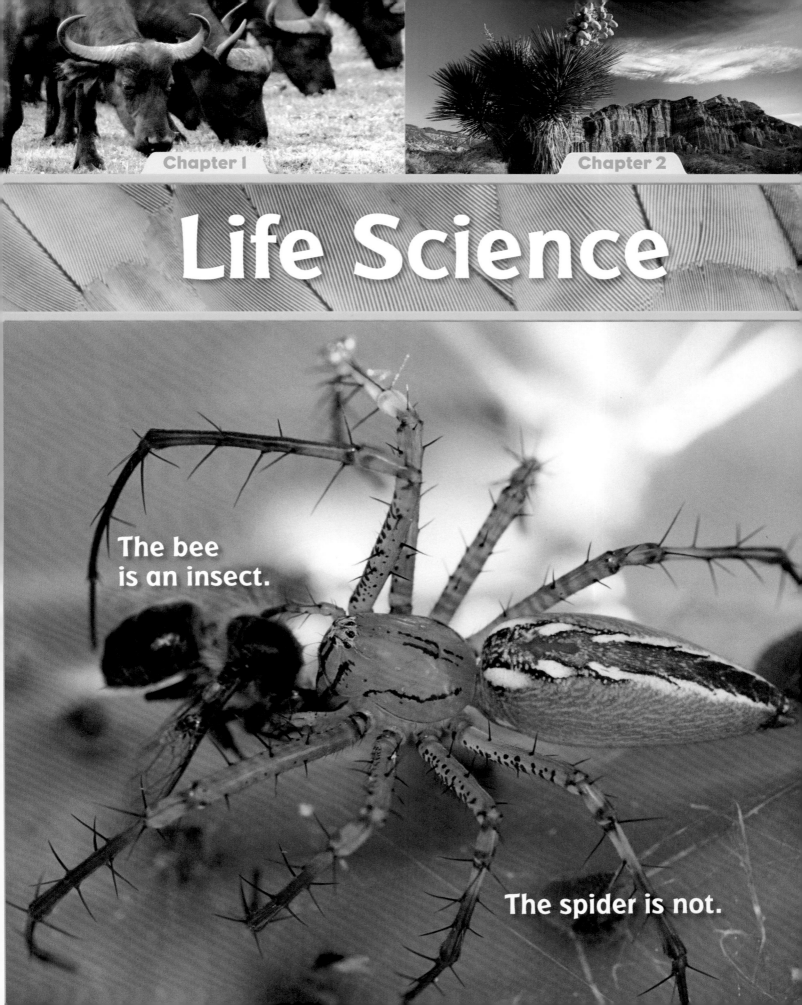

Life Science

The bee
is an insect.

The spider is not.

Living Things Need Energy

How do living things
get energy to live and grow?

4 LS 2. All organisms need energy and matter to live and grow.

21

Literature
Poem

ELA R 4.3.2.
Identify the main events of the plot, their causes, and the influence of each event on future actions. **ELA W 4.2.1.** Write narratives.

grasshopper

The Story Goes On

by Aileen Fisher

Here's where events
will unroll one by one.
With quick drops of rain.
With warm rays of sun . . .

The seed breaks its skin
with nary a sound.
A shoot seeks the air.
A root hugs the ground.

A plant starts to grow
and soon, to be brief,
there's a stalk with a green
little fluttery leaf.

Now enter a bug
who's looking for dinner.
He stops.
Ho! A leaf,
a tender beginner.

He climbs the short stalk
to nibble, not knowing
an enemy lurks
where some grasses are growing.

 Write About It

Response to Literature The poet brings to life a sequence of events that happens every day in nature. What do you think the poet is describing? Write a story that tells what might happen next in the poem.

 e-Journal Write about it online @ **www.macmillanmh.com**

Plants and Sunlight

Look and Wonder

Have you ever wondered where food comes from? You might say, "The supermarket!" But where does food really come from? The story begins with the Sun and leaves. What do leaves have to do with making food for a whole community?

4 LS 2.a. Students know plants are the primary source of matter and energy entering most food chains.

How are leaves different from each other?

Make a Prediction

How can leaves from different plants differ from each other? Write a prediction.

Test Your Prediction

1 **Observe** Use the hand lens to observe both leaves carefully. What do you notice?

2 **Communicate** Record your observations in a chart like the one shown. How are the leaves different?

Leaf Trait	Leaf A	Leaf B
Texture		
Color		
Size		
Shape		

Draw Conclusions

3 **Infer** Tell what each leaf trait on the chart is for. For example, you might infer that fuzzy leaves are for catching rain. Colored leaves might be for attracting insects. Record your ideas.

Explore More

What leaf traits do both leaves have in common? Tell what each shared leaf trait is for. Make a plan to test your idea.

Materials

- **leaves from two plants**
- **hand lens**

Step 1

 4 IE 6.f. Follow a set of written instructions for a scientific investigation.

Read and Learn

Main Idea 4 LS 2.a

Plants use the Sun's energy to make food energy through a process called photosynthesis.

Vocabulary

photosynthesis, p. 28

solar energy, p. 28

environment, p. 32

biomass, p. 32

LOG ON e-Glossary
@ www.macmillanmh.com

Reading Skill

Compare and Contrast

Different   Alike   Different

What are plants?

Plants are living things. They do much more than just add beauty to our world. Plants give us the food we eat and some of the clothes we wear. They even give off a gas that we breathe, called *oxygen* (OK•suh•juhn). Without plants, Earth would be an empty place. With plants, our planet is bursting with life.

Plants come in all sizes, shapes, and colors. Some are so small you can barely see them. Others can be as tall as skyscrapers. The giant California redwoods are the tallest living things on Earth. Some are 112 meters (367 feet) tall. That is taller than the Statue of Liberty!

◄ How long does it take a tree to grow this tall? Some redwood trees are over 2,000 years old!

This pinecone is from a redwood tree. ▼

Amazing Plants

PLANT NAME/FACT	PLANT	DESCRIPTION
castor bean plant the most dangerous plant	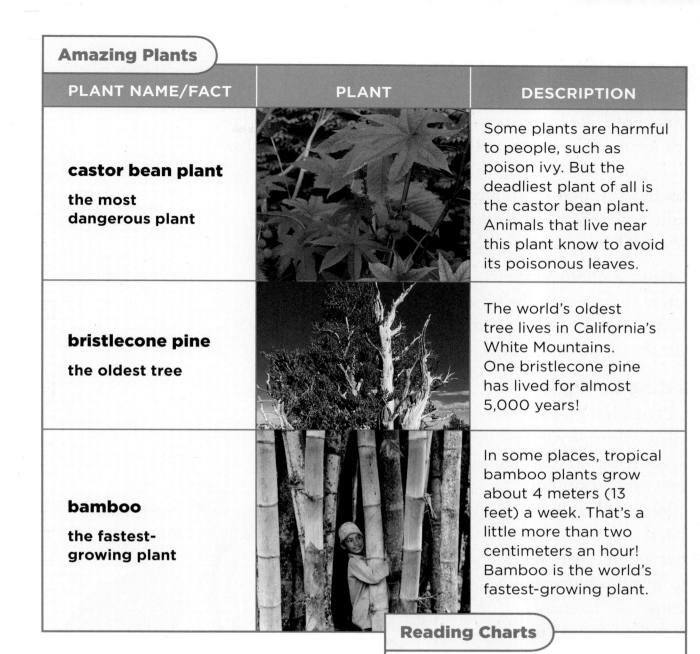	Some plants are harmful to people, such as poison ivy. But the deadliest plant of all is the castor bean plant. Animals that live near this plant know to avoid its poisonous leaves.
bristlecone pine the oldest tree		The world's oldest tree lives in California's White Mountains. One bristlecone pine has lived for almost 5,000 years!
bamboo the fastest-growing plant		In some places, tropical bamboo plants grow about 4 meters (13 feet) a week. That's a little more than two centimeters an hour! Bamboo is the world's fastest-growing plant.

In all, there are about 400,000 different kinds of plants. Each one is different. Yet most plants share some basic parts. *Roots* anchor the plant to the ground. They also take in water and nutrients from the soil. *Stems* hold the plant upright. They move water and nutrients throughout the plant. *Leaves* connect to the stem and collect light from the Sun.

Reading Charts

Which plant is found in California?

Clue: Scan the chart for the word "California." Find the plant name that matches that description.

 Quick Check

Compare and Contrast What structures do most plants share?

Critical Thinking How does a plant's leaves differ from its roots?

How do plants get energy?

Although plants differ in their shapes and sizes, all plants are alike in one way. They make their own food in a process called **photosynthesis** (foh•toh•SIN•thuh•suhs). All organisms, or living things, need energy to grow, stay healthy, and reproduce. *Reproduce* means to make more of one's own kind. Plants get the energy they need from the food they make.

During photosynthesis, plants take in sunlight, water, and a gas in the air called *carbon dioxide*. Plants use these things to make sugar, which is a plant's source of food and energy.

Getting Sunlight

Plants have a material called *chlorophyll* (KLAWR•uh•fil) that helps them take in sunlight. Chlorophyll is the material that gives plants their green color. With the help of chlorophyll, plants take in energy from the Sun and use it to produce sugar. Energy from the Sun is called **solar energy**.

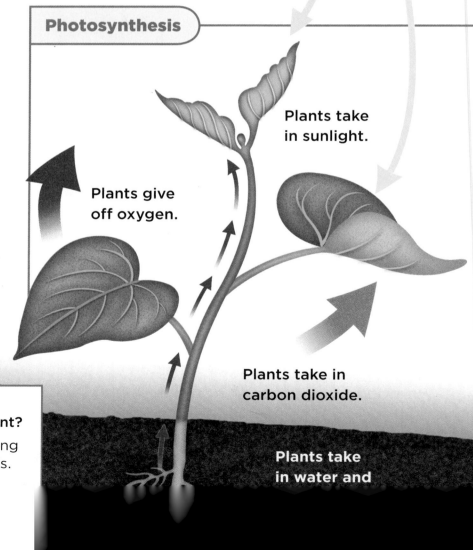

Photosynthesis

Plants take in sunlight.

Plants give off oxygen.

Plants take in carbon dioxide.

Plants take in water and

Reading Diagrams

Which gas is made by the plant?

Clue: Follow the arrows pointing out of the plant. Read all labels.

Getting Water and Carbon Dioxide

Getting water is easy for some plants. For example, moss leaves soak up water straight from the ground. In other plants, such as oak trees, water has to travel a long distance to get from the plant's roots to its leaves. Most large plants have a system of tubes throughout the plant. These tubes carry water and nutrients from the bottom of the plant to the top.

Carbon dioxide is part of the air all around us. Plants take in carbon dioxide through tiny holes on the bottom of their leaves. These tiny holes are called *stomata* (STOH•muh•tuh).

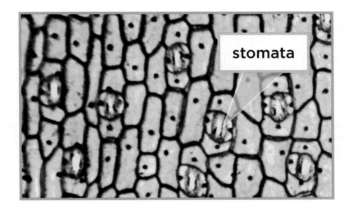

stomata

✓ Quick Check

Compare and Contrast How are plants alike? How do they differ?

Critical Thinking What might happen to a plant that gets sunlight but no water?

Quick Lab

Photosynthesis

1. Label two identical plants "Plant A" and "Plant B." Wrap each leaf of Plant A with aluminum foil. Keep the leaves of Plant B uncovered. Put the plants on a sunny windowsill. Make sure each plant gets the same amount of sunlight and water.

Plant B

Plant A

ALUMINUM FOIL

2. **Predict** What do you think will happen to each plant?

3. **Observe** Uncover Plant A after four days. Record your observations about each plant in a chart.

4. **Infer** Why do Plant A and Plant B differ after four days?

5. **Draw Conclusions** Where on a plant does photosynthesis take place? How can you tell?

Why are plants important?

Plants need photosynthesis to survive and grow. Did you know that you need photosynthesis too? In fact, most animals depend on plants making their own food. Why?

Animals cannot make their own food the way plants can. Instead they must eat other organisms to get the energy they need. Plants provide the energy that travels from one organism to another. Plants capture energy from the Sun to make their own food. They use most of their food energy as they grow and reproduce. They also store some energy in their roots, stems, leaves, and other structures. When an animal, such as a grasshopper, eats a plant, stored energy passes from the plant to the animal. The animal uses most of this energy to grow and reproduce. It also stores some energy. When an animal, such as a bird, eats the grasshopper, stored energy passes to the bird. In this way, most animals depend on plants for energy.

Animals depend on plants for food energy. ▼

cattle grazing, Big Sur, California

horseback riding, Mackerricher State Park, Mendocino, California

▲ Plants give off oxygen into the air. When you breathe in air, your body gets the oxygen it needs.

In addition to providing animals with energy, plants also provide animals with the oxygen they need. Most animals cannot survive without oxygen for more than a few minutes. They need oxygen to carry out life processes. Most of the oxygen we breathe comes from plants and plant like living things that make their own food.

Plantlike living things in the ocean, such as this kelp, produce much of the oxygen you breathe. ▼

 Quick Check

Compare and Contrast
How does the way plants get energy differ from the way animals get energy?

Critical Thinking Would animals be able to live without plants? Why or why not?

▲ Compare the number of plants to the number of animals you see in this picture. Plants make up most of the biomass in this rain-forest environment.

Where do plants grow?

Plants can be found all over Earth. They live in a variety of environments from oceans to deserts. An **environment** is everything that surrounds a living thing. Plants live in any environment where they can get water, carbon dioxide, sunlight, and nutrients.

Plants make up most of the biomass in an environment. **Biomass** is a measure of the amount of living things in an environment. There are more plants in most environments than any other living thing. Plants are the main source of matter and energy in an environment. The animals in an environment use plants as a source of food and energy.

✔ Quick Check

Compare and Contrast
How does the number of plants in an environment compare to the number of animals?

Critical Thinking How would an environment's biomass change if plants could not carry out photosynthesis?

Summarize the Main Idea

Plants are living things. Most plants have roots, stems, and leaves. (pp. 26–27)

Green plants carry out **photosynthesis** to make food energy from sunlight, water, and carbon dioxide. (pp. 28–31)

Plants make up most of the **biomass** in an environment. (p. 32)

Make a FOLDABLES™ Study Guide

Make a layered look book. Use it to summarize what you learned.

Plants and Sunlight

Plants

Photosynthesis

Biomass

Think, Talk, and Write

1 **Main Idea** How do plants use energy from the Sun?

2 **Vocabulary** What is photosynthesis?

3 **Compare and Contrast** How are the roles of a plant's leaves and roots different? How are they alike?

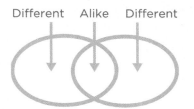

Different   Alike   Different

4 **Critical Thinking** Suppose you were starting a space colony on a planet with no oxygen. Why would it be a good idea to bring green plants with you?

5 **Test Practice** A plant uses all of the following to carry out photosynthesis EXCEPT

A sunlight

B oxygen gas

C carbon dioxide gas

D water

Writing Link

Write an Essay
Suppose we lived in a world without plants. Write an essay about what life might be like. Explain why life would be like this.

Health Link

Plants as Medicine
Research plants that are used as herbs and medicines. Make a chart to list what the herb or medicine is used for. List the plant that it comes from.

Observe

You just read about plants, including ways they use water. You read that water travels from the roots of a plant up its stem. How do scientists know this? They **observe** plants!

① Learn It

When you **observe**, you use one or more of your senses to learn about the world around you. Although scientists know a lot about plants, they continue to observe them. Scientists are always learning new things about plants. They record their observations so they can share information with others. They use their observations to try to understand things in our world. You can, too.

② Try It

In this activity you will **observe** how water moves through a plant. Remember to record your data as you observe.

▶ Pour 100 mL of water into a jar. Add a few drops of blue food coloring to the cup and stir with the measuring spoon.

▶ Use scissors to cut about 3 cm off the bottom of a fresh celery stalk. Put the stalk in the water. Record the time that you did this.

4 IE 6.a. Differentiate observation from inference (interpretation) and know scientists' explanations come partly from what they observe and partly from how they interpret their observations.

▶ Observe the celery for a half hour. Record your observations. Use your observations to describe how water moves through a plant.

③ Apply It

▶ Now **observe** how water travels through other plants. Repeat the investigation using a white flower, such as a carnation. Record your observations so you can share them with classmates.

What I Did	What I Observed

Food Chains

Look and Wonder

Animals need energy to live and grow. Where do you think this energy comes from? Where do you get the energy you need to live and grow?

4 LS 2.a. Students know plants are the primary source of matter and energy entering most food chains. •**4 LS 2.b.** Students know producers and consumers (herbivores, carnivores, omnivores, and decomposers) are related in food chains and food webs and may compete with each other for resources in an ecosystem. •**4 LS 2.c.** Students know decomposers, including many fungi, insects, and microorganisms, recycle matter from dead plants and animals.

How much energy do living things use?

Purpose

Find out how much energy passes to living things as food energy.

Procedure

1. **Make a Model** Working in groups of four, make labels that read "Sun," "Plant," "Plant Eater," and "Meat Eater."

2. **Measure** Cut out a 1 m strip of butcher paper. Mark off ten 10 cm sections. This represents energy that can be used by living things.

3. Each student should take a label. The "Sun" starts by passing the energy strip to the "plant." The plant cuts off 10 cm from the strip. The plant holds the larger section and passes the smaller section to the plant eater. This represents the passing of food energy.

4. **Measure** The plant eater cuts off 1 cm from the strip and passes it to the meat eater. The plant eater holds onto the larger section.

Draw Conclusions

5. **Infer** Why do you think the energy strip gets ripped before it gets passed on?

6. Why is the smallest amount of energy passed to the meat eater?

Explore More

What might happen if the plant could not make its own food energy? Design a test to find out.

4 IE 6.f. Follow a set of written instructions for a scientific investigation.

Materials

- **markers**
- **butcher paper**
- **meter stick**
- **scissors**

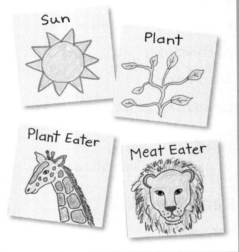

Sun

Plant

Plant Eater

Meat Eater

Step 3

Main Idea

4 LS 2.a
4 LS 2.b
4 LS 2.c

Food chains describe the flow of matter and energy among living things in an environment. A complete food chain includes producers, consumers, and decomposers.

Vocabulary

food chain, p. 38

producer, p. 38

consumer, p. 38

decomposer, p. 39

herbivore, p. 40

carnivore, p. 42

omnivore, p. 43

LOG ON ⓔ-Glossary
@ www.macmillanmh.com

Reading Skill

Sequence

First
Next
Last

What is a food chain?

You know that living things need energy to live and grow. They get energy from food. A **food chain** shows how energy passes from one organism to another as food. First, a plant uses the Sun's energy to make its own food. Next, an animal such as an insect eats the plant. Then, another animal, such as a bird, eats that insect. Energy passes from the Sun, to the plant, to the insect, to the bird.

Green plants in a food chain are called **producers**. They are called this because they make, or produce, their own food. Animals are called **consumers**. Animals cannot make their own food. They must eat, or consume, plants or other animals for food.

Mountain Food Chain

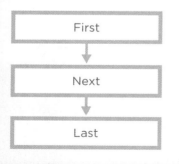

Solar energy is the main source of energy for life on Earth.

A mustard plant takes in energy from the Sun to make its own food. ▼

Energy in Food Chains

Most food chains are similar in a few ways. Sunlight is at the beginning of nearly all food chains. A plant, or producer, is next in the chain. Then, an animal eats the plant. Next, an animal eats the plant eater. The chain continues until tiny living things break down organisms and return nutrients to the soil. These tiny living things are **decomposers**. The nutrients they return to the soil are used by new plants, and the chain begins again.

With each step of the food chain, matter and energy pass from one organism to another. Because organisms use most of the energy in food to live and grow, only a small amount of energy is passed from organism to organism.

✔ Quick Check

Sequence What is the first step of a food chain?

Critical Thinking How are a producer and a consumer different?

Reading Diagrams

How does energy move through this food chain?
Clue: Arrows help show a sequence.

A mountain lion eats the weasel. ▶

▲ A gopher eats the mustard plant.

A weasel eats the gopher. ▶

When the mountain lion dies, its body is broken down by decomposers. ▶

What are herbivores?

The gopher in the mountain food chain is an example of a herbivore (HUR•buh•vawr). **Herbivores** are animals that eat mainly plants. They are also known as primary consumers because they are the first consumers in a food chain. Examples of herbivores include deer, rabbits, grasshoppers, squirrels, and cows.

These are just a few examples of animals that eat plants as their main food source. ▶

caterpillar

mountain goat

Many herbivores, such as these antelope, travel together to stay safe from predators.

chipmunk

elephant

Wide Varieties

Herbivores can be found in most environments on Earth. They live in oceans, forests, deserts, and grasslands. They even live in the cold arctic environment that surrounds the North Pole. Herbivores live in every environment where plants grow.

Herbivores can be big or small. The African elephant, Earth's largest land animal, is a herbivore that eats mainly grasses. An adult elephant eats between 100 and 200 kilograms (220 and 440 pounds) of plant matter every day! In North America's grasslands, herbivores can include animals from tiny insects to very large buffaloes.

Passing Along Energy

Herbivores can be food for other animals. An animal that is hunted by another animal for food is called *prey*. An animal that hunts another animal for food is called a *predator*. Both predator and prey are consumers because they both must eat food to survive.

✔ Quick Check

Sequence Which comes first in a food chain, a herbivore or a producer?

Critical Thinking How might traveling together help hervivores stay safe?

What are carnivores and omnivores?

You know that animals that eat mainly plants are called herbivores. What are animals that eat mainly other animals called? How about animals that eat both plants and animals? Each group has a name to describe it.

Carnivores

Animals that eat other animals are called **carnivores**. Examples of carnivores include cats that eat mice and hawks that eat other birds. Frogs that eat insects and snakes that eat rabbits are also carnivores. In some cases, carnivores eat other carnivores. Hawks, for example, often eat snakes. Herons eat frogs, and lizards eat spiders.

◀ An orca whale is a carnivore.

▲ A heron is a carnivore.

Omnivores

Some animals, such as bears, seem to eat everything! They eat such living things as fish, berries, leaves, mice, and squirrels. Are bears carnivores because they eat animals? Are they herbivores because they eat plants? In fact, bears are called omnivores. An **omnivore** is an animal that eats both plants and animals.

Other examples of omnivores include raccoons, pigs, dogs, and chickens. Some insects, such as wasps and flies, will eat both plants and animals. Most people are omnivores, too. People eat from a wide mix of plant and animal food groups. Both omnivores and carnivores are called secondary consumers.

◄ A hornet is an omnivore. It eats both plants and animals.

✔ Quick Check

Sequence What eats a primary consumer in a food chain?

Critical Thinking Can an omnivore and carnivore be in the same food chain? Explain.

Quick Lab

Find a Food Chain

1. Take a walk with a partner around the schoolyard. Make a chart to list the plants and animals that you see.

2. **Classify** Which organisms are producers? Why?

3. **Classify** Which organisms are consumers? Why?

4. **Communicate** Circle organisms that might belong to the same food chain and link them together. What organisms are in your food chain?

Producers	Consumers

A bear is an omnivore. ►

What are decomposers?

Each fall and winter, thousands of leaves fall to the forest floor. Some trees also fall down. Yet some of this plant material is gone by the following spring. There are fewer dead leaves on the ground. The fallen trees are rotting away.

Who, or what, is responsible for this cleanup? It is decomposers that do this important job for an environment. Decomposers break down organisms that are no longer living. They break them down into nutrients that can be used again by new plants.

◀ Vultures eat rotting animal matter and get rid of it as waste. This helps decomposers break down matter faster.

▲ The decomposers growing on this log are called fungi. They slowly break down this fallen log.

▲ Most earthworms eat plant life that has already died. Earthworms pass nutrients from dead plants to the soil.

Special Jobs for Decomposers

There are many types of decomposers. Each breaks down a special type of organism. For example, earthworms break down plants only. Plantlike organisms called *fungi* (FUN•jigh) break down rotting wood and other plant parts. Still other decomposers break down what is left of dead animals. Decomposers that consume dead matter are also consumers.

Decomposers work together to break down organisms completely. The once-living material may become part of the soil. This material adds nutrients to soil that help plants to grow well. Now the food chain can start all over again!

Some insects, like this beetle, are decomposers. Other insect decomposers include flies and wasps. ▼

Quick Check

Sequence Why does a food chain start again after a decomposer does its job?

Critical Thinking How do decomposers help an environment?

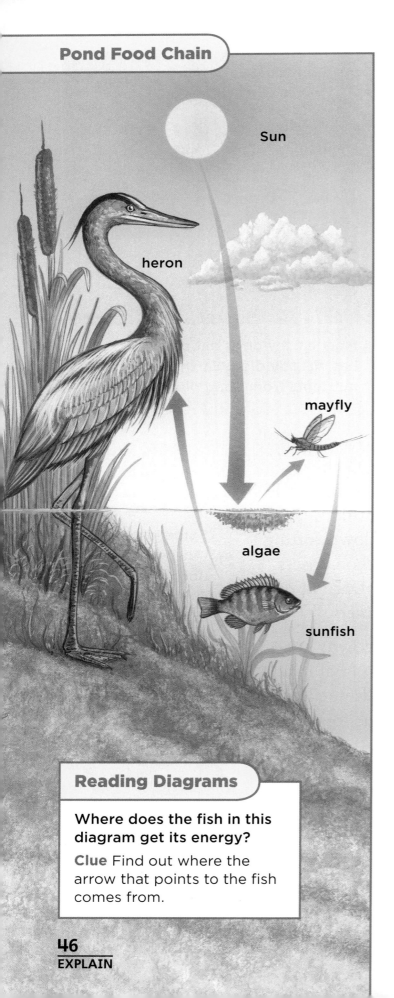

Pond Food Chain

Sun

heron

mayfly

algae

sunfish

Reading Diagrams

Where does the fish in this diagram get its energy?

Clue Find out where the arrow that points to the fish comes from.

What are some examples of food chains?

Every environment has its own food chains. However, the same basic parts of each are the same. Here are some examples of food chains you might find in California. Can you identify which organisms are the producers and consumers in each?

A pond food chain might start with a plantlike producer called *algae* (AL•jee). These algae float in the water collecting sunlight. They are food for young mayflies, which eagerly gobble them up. The mayflies swarm near the surface of the water and become food for sunfish. The sunfish are then eaten by the blue heron. Finally, decomposers break the heron down after it dies.

In the California desert, seed pods of the mesquite tree are food for harvester ants. The ants live in large colonies of thousands. The ants become food for the horned lizard. These lizards, in turn, are eaten by larger animals such as coyotes.

✔ *Quick Check*

Sequence What is the order of a California desert food chain?

Critical Thinking Can one environment have more than one food chain?

Lesson Review

Summarize the Main Idea

A **food chain** is made of **producers**, consumers, and decomposers. (pp. 38–39)

Consumers can be herbivores, carnivores, or omnivores. (pp. 40–43)

Decomposers break down organisms that are no longer living. (pp. 44–45)

Make a FOLDABLES™ Study Guide

Make a layered look book. Use it to summarize what you learned about food chains.

Food Chains

Producers

Consumers

Decomposers

Think, Talk, and Write

① **Main Idea** Why is a food chain important to an environment?

② **Vocabulary** What is an omnivore?

③ **Sequence** List the order of organisms through which energy flows in a food chain.

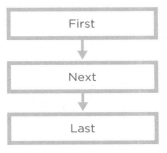

First

↓

Next

↓

Last

④ **Critical Thinking** Can a primary consumer eat a secondary consumer? Explain.

⑤ **Test Practice** Which type of organism makes its own food?

  A producer
  B primary consumer
  C secondary consumer
  D decomposer

Writing Link

Write a Paragraph
Choose an animal and write a paragraph to explain what it eats. Explain whether that animal is a herbivore, omnivore, or carnivore. Also, include which animals, if any, eat that animal.

Social Studies Link

Research an Environment
Use a map of California to highlight where you live. What is the environment like? What kinds of food chains exist in your area? Research and plot the information on a map. Compare maps with a partner.

Be a Scientist

Materials

index cards

tape

research tools

scissors

markers

Inquiry Structured

Can an environment have more than one food chain?

Form a Hypothesis

Energy from the Sun helps grasses grow. A mouse eats the grass. A coyote eats the mouse. Is this the only food chain that can be found in a grassland? What happens when one environment has many producers and consumers? Write a hypothesis in the form, *"If different producers and consumers can be found in an environment, then . . ."*

Test Your Hypothesis

1. **Make a Model** Write "Sun," "grass," "mouse," and "coyote" each on an index card. Use tape to connect the cards in the order of a food chain.

   Step 2

2. Use books and the Internet to research another grassland food chain. Find a new producer, herbivore, and carnivore that can be linked together in a food chain.

   Step 3

3. Write the names of the new organisms on index cards. Find pictures of each plant and animal to put on the cards, or draw your own pictures.

4. **Make a Model** Assemble the second set of index cards in the order of a food chain. You will now have two separate food chains.

   Step 4

Draw Conclusions

5 Did your results support your hypothesis? Why or why not?

6 What does this activity tell you about the number of different food chains in one environments?

7 **Compare** How are the food chains alike? How are they different?

Inquiry Guided

How can food chains change?

Form a Hypothesis

What might happen to the organisms in your food chain if the producer is taken out of the chain? Answer in the form, *"If the producer is taken out of the food chain, then . . ."*

Test Your Hypothesis

Design an experiment to investigate what might happen if the producer is removed from a food chain. Write out the steps you will follow. Record your results and observations.

Draw Conclusions

Did your test support your hypothesis? Why or why not? Compare your results with a classmate's.

Inquiry Open

What else would you like to learn about organisms and food chains? For example, what happens if a new consumer is added to the environment? Determine the steps you will follow to answer your question. Keep a record of any materials you used in your investigation.

Remember to follow the steps of the scientific process.

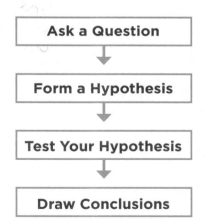

Ask a Question
↓
Form a Hypothesis
↓
Test Your Hypothesis
↓
Draw Conclusions

---

 4 IE 6.f. Follow a set of written instructions for a scientific investigation.

Food Webs

Look and Wonder

This bird is catching its dinner. What kind of fish will it have today? How can one animal be part of two different food chains?

 4 LS 2.b. Students know producers and consumers (herbivores, carnivores, omnivores, and decomposers) are related in food chains and food webs and may compete with each other for resources in an ecosystem.

How can living things be part of more than one food chain?

Make a Prediction

Can an animal be a part of more than one food chain?

Test Your Prediction

1. Use the chart to make organism cards. On each card, list an organism and what it eats.

2. Draw a "Sun" card. Tape the card to the top of your poster board. Tape cards of organisms that depend on it for food directly underneath it. Draw arrows to show the flow of energy between the organisms.

3. Continue to add cards to the poster. Draw arrows to link each card to the organisms it directly depends on for food.

Draw Conclusions

4. **Analyze Data** How many food chains does the spotted skunk belong to?

5. What can you conclude about food chains from this poster?

Explore More

What might happen if the pocket mouse were taken off the poster? Make a prediction and make a plan to test your prediction.

 4 IE 6.c. Formulate and justify predictions based on cause-and-effect relationships.

Materials

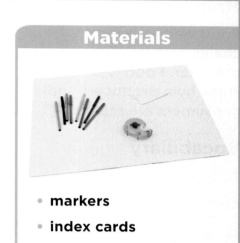

- **markers**
- **index cards**
- **poster board**
- **tape**

Step 2

What Animals Eat

Organism	How It Gets Food
California poppy	makes own food from sunlight
mustard plant	makes own food from sunlight
yucca plant	makes own food from sunlight
caterpillar	leaves
California quail	insects, seeds
pocket mouse	seeds
pocket gopher	yucca plant
spotted skunk	mice, birds, insects
gopher snake	rodents such as gophers
fence lizard	insects

Main Idea 4 LS 2.b

Food webs are food chains that are linked together. Food webs show how producers and consumers are related.

Vocabulary

food web, p. 52

competition, p. 53

population, p. 54

energy pyramid, p. 58

LOG ON e-Glossary
@ www.macmillanmh.com

Reading Skill

Summarize

Summary

What is a food web?

One morning a sparrow eats a worm. The next day it eats a juicy green caterpillar. What food chain is the sparrow part of? Is it part of the worm's food chain or the caterpillar's? It is part of both food chains. Many food chains in an environment can overlap with each other. A **food web** shows how a group of food chains are linked together.

The arrows in the food web show the direction that energy flows from one living thing to the next. ▼

Food Web

Look at the food web diagram below. It shows several overlapping food chains. You can see that the mouse belongs to two separate food chains. In one food chain the plant is eaten by the mouse. Then the mouse is eaten by the coyote. Can you find the second food chain the mouse could be part of?

A food web can tell you a lot about the living things in an environment. For example, the diagram tells you that the mouse eats grass. It also shows that two different carnivores compete for mice. They are the coyote and rattlesnake. **Competition** (kohm•pi•TISH•uhn) is the struggle of several organisns for the same resource. There is more competition for the mouse than any other animal in this food web.

✔ Quick Check

Summarize What is the importance of a food web in an environment?

Critical Thinking Why do organisms in a food web compete for food?

Reading Diagrams

Name two food chains that end with the hawk.

Clue: Find the hawk on the food web. Then follow each set of arrows with your finger.

How can food webs change?

Living things in a food web depend on one another. Suppose the population of one organism in a food web changes. A **population** is all the members of a single type of organism in an environment. When one population changes, all the other populations in the food web can be affected also. This is what happened in the ocean's kelp forests. Kelp is a type of seaweed. Kelp forests are home to thousands of ocean creatures. Some kelp forests were greatly changed by just one animal. That animal was the sea otter.

Sea otters eat several animals in their ocean food web. They eat sea stars, sea urchins, mussels, crabs, and large fish. The kelp forest was almost destroyed when the sea otter population changed about two hundred years ago.

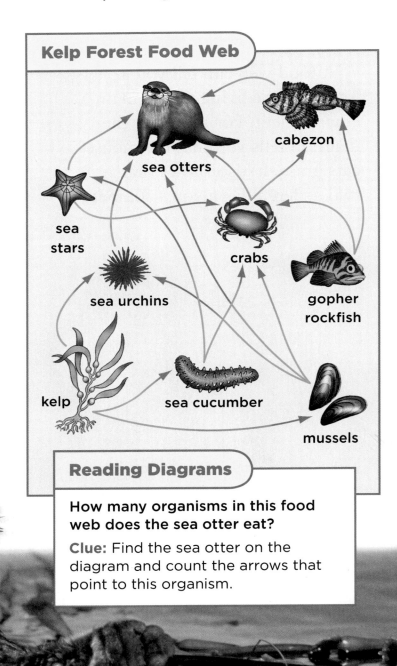

Kelp Forest Food Web

cabezon

sea otters

sea stars

crabs

sea urchins

gopher rockfish

kelp

sea cucumber

mussels

Reading Diagrams

How many organisms in this food web does the sea otter eat?

Clue: Find the sea otter on the diagram and count the arrows that point to this organism.

Sea otters make up one population in a kelp forest. ▼

▲ Many ocean animals depend on kelp to survive.

A Sea Without Sea Otters

What happened to the kelp forest? In the 1800s, too many sea otters were hunted for their fur. Without sea otters, fewer sea urchins were eaten. Soon, too many sea urchins were being born. Smaller fish could not survive because sea urchins ate their supplies of kelp. These fish were food for sea stars and crabs. The sea stars and crabs began to die out.

Mussels also depend on kelp to stay alive. Fewer mussels meant fewer crabs and large fish that depend on mussels for food. After a while, even decomposers could not survive. Without the sea otter to help control the size of the sea urchin population, the kelp forest almost disappeared.

In the 1900s, many countries agreed to stop hunting sea otters. The kelp forest food web became balanced again. Now, new food web changes are putting kelp forests in danger again.

≡ Quick Lab

Changes in Food Webs

1. Copy or trace the kelp forest food web shown on page 54.

2. Put an X through each organism that was affected by the change in sea otter populations.

3. **Analyze Data** Copy your new food web. How many organisms are left?

4. **Communicate** How can a change in one population affect other populations in a food web?

5. **Draw Conclusions** What does your new food web tell you about why it is important to protect environments?

✔ Quick Check

Summarize What can happen when one organism is removed from a food web?

Critical Thinking Is one organism in a food web more important than others? Why or why not?

How do new organisms change food webs?

Every living thing in an environment is part of a food web. What can happen to a food web when a new organism moves into an environment?

Australia's Sugarcane Fields

In 1935, Australia's sugarcane fields were being destroyed by two insects. One insect was the greyback cane beetle. The other was French's cane beetle. Local scientists decided to bring in cane toads as predators to eat these beetles. Scientists thought the cane toads would eat both types of beetles. They also thought lizards and birds would eat the toads. They hoped this would keep the toad population from growing too fast. Do you think the scientists were right? Did everything go as planned in Australia's sugarcane fields?

Unexpected Results

The cane toads did not do what scientists hoped they would. The toads did not eat the beetles at all. Instead they ate just about everything else in sight. They ate frogs, rodents, birds, lizards—even pets!

▼Sugarcane is a crop used to make sugars and syrup.

Birds and lizards did not eat the toads as expected. The toads were poisonous to these animals. Instead the toads ate the birds and lizards! Without any predators, the cane toad population grew and grew. The whole food web was changed by just one new organism.

The cane toads have been in Australia's environment for 70 years. They are still causing problems for local farmers.

✔ Quick Check

Summarize What can happen to a food web when a new organism is brought into an environment?

Critical Thinking Why couldn't scientists tell what would happen when the cane toad was brought to the sugar cane fields?

▲ The greyback cane beetle became a pest in Australia's sugarcane fields in the 1930s.

The cane toad was brought to Australia's sugarcane fields to eat beetles. Something unexpected happened instead. ▼

▲ The highlighted area on this map shows the location of Australia's sugarcane fields.

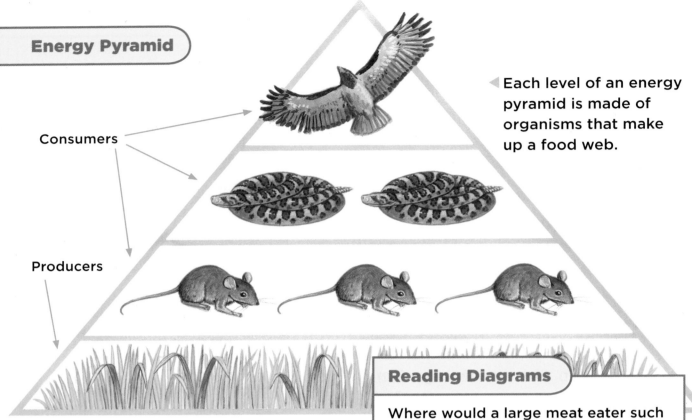

Consumers

Producers

◀ Each level of an energy pyramid is made of organisms that make up a food web.

Reading Diagrams

Where would a large meat eater such as a lion fall in the energy pyramid?

Clue: Look at what kind of animal is on each level of the pyramid.

What is an energy pyramid?

An **energy pyramid** is a model that shows how much energy flows through a food web. Producers are at the bottom level of the pyramid. Plants get energy from the Sun. They use about 90 percent of this energy to live and grow. They store the other ten percent in parts such as stems and leaves.

The next levels of the pyramid are consumers. Primary consumers, or herbivores, must eat many plants to stay alive. Why? Only the ten percent of energy that the plants stored passes to the animal. Omnivores and carnivores both make up the

next levels of the pyramid. These consumers get energy from the organisms in the level below them. Only ten percent of the energy from one level is passed on to the next. Animals at the top of the pyramid must eat a lot of food to get the energy they need to survive. Food webs have more producers than consumers.

✔ Quick Check

Summarize What does an energy pyramid tell us about food webs?

Critical Thinking Why are producers at the bottom of the pyramid?

Lesson Review

Summarize the Main Idea

A **food web** is a group of linked food chains. Each member of a food web can belong to more than one food chain. (pp. 52–53)

Even small **changes to a food web** can affect the food web greatly. (pp. 54–57)

An **energy pyramid** shows how much energy is passed to living things in a food web. (p. 58)

Make a FOLDABLES™ Study Guide

Make a three-tab book. Use it to summarize what you read.

Food Web

Changes to a Food Web

Energy Pyramid

Think, Talk, and Write

1 **Main Idea** How is a food web important to an environment?

2 **Vocabulary** What is competition?

3 **Summarize** How is a food web different from a food chain?

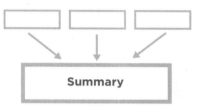

Summary

4 **Critical Thinking** You know that a single organism can be a member of two different food chains. Can a single organism also be a member of two different food webs? Give an example.

5 **Test Practice** Which member of a food web supports the most organisms?

   A producer
   B primary consumer
   C secondary consumer
   D decomposer

Math Link

Solve a Problem
Ninety percent of the energy a plant gets from the Sun is used for it to grow. Ten percent gets stored in the plant. If you start with 100 units of energy, how many units are stored? Now try it with 1,000 units.

Art Link

Make a Mobile
Create a food web mobile for the classroom. Draw and hang plants and animal cutouts from several food chains in an environment. Connect the food chains with string or crepe paper.

Good persuasive writing

▶ clearly states the writer's opinion about a topic

▶ tries to persuade readers to agree with the writer's opinion

▲ The mission blue butterfly uses the lupine flower as food for its young.

A Call for Help

Think of a field of beautiful blue flowers called lupines. Mission blue butterflies perch on the lupines. The butterflies lay their eggs on lupines. When the eggs hatch, the caterpillars eat the flowers. The caterpillars then become butterflies.

The mission blue butterfly, once common in the San Francisco area, is slowly disappearing. Why? Lupine flowers grow in grassland and rocky areas. Recent building activities in these areas have disturbed the butterflies' habitat. The flowers are quickly disappearing. The loss of lupine flowers means that fewer mission blue butterflies can survive.

When an animal's source of food is disturbed, the whole food web is affected. Today, thousands of animals throughout the world are in danger of disappearing forever. There is still time to help. If we protect environments, we can protect the organisms that live there.

Write About It

Persuasive Writing Write a persuasive letter to a community leader. Convince him or her that it is important to protect environments and living things in your area.

LOG ON e-Journal Write about it online @ **www.macmillanmh.com**

  ELA W 4.1.1. Select a focus, an organizational structure, and a point of view based upon purpose, audience, length, and format requirements.

How Many Monarchs?

Each winter about 180 to 280 million monarch butterflies travel from the north to California for the warmer climate. Changes in the monarch's food chain have caused many million fewer butterflies to make the journey each year. Monarchs are having more trouble finding enough milkweed plants to stay alive. This plant is the butterfly's main source of food.

Place Value

A place value chart can help you record values of large whole numbers.

hundred millions	ten millions	millions	hundred thousands	ten thousands	thousands	hundreds	tens	ones
1	0	5,	8	3	7,	5	0	9

▲ This number reads: one hundred five million, eight hundred thirty-seven thousand, five hundred nine.

 ## Solve It

A population of monarch butterflies is now one million, nine hundred fifty-eight thousand, thirty-three. Use a place value chart to write this number.

 MA NS 4.1.1. Read and write whole numbers in the millions.

Microorganisms

Look and Wonder

Are these creatures from outer space? No. There are millions of these living things on Earth. But you can only see them if you look through a microscope. Tiny living things such as these do many important jobs. What jobs do they do?

4 LS 2.c. Students know decomposers, including many fungi, insects, and microorganisms, recycle matter from dead plants and animals. •**4 LS 3.d.** Students know that most microorganisms do not cause disease and that many are beneficial.

How can tiny living things change plant material?

Make a Prediction

How can tiny living things change an apple? Write a prediction.

Test Your Prediction

1. View a piece of apple under a microscope. Record what you see.

2. **Predict** What do you think will happen to a piece of apple if it is left out for one week? Record your predictions.

3. Put a piece of apple in each of three plastic bags. Seal the bags.

4. **Observe** Leave the apples in the bags for one week. Observe them every day. Do all three apples change in the same way?

5. **Observe** Your teacher will prepare a slide of your apples. View them under a microscope. Record what you see.

   ⚠ **Be Careful.** Do not remove the apples from the plastic bags.

Draw Conclusions

6. What happened to the apples after one week? Did your results match your predictions?

7. **Infer** What caused the apples to change?

Explore More

How do you think a slice of bread might change after a week? Make a plan to find out.

 4 IE 6.d. Conduct multiple trials to test a prediction and draw conclusions about the relationships between predictions and results.

Materials

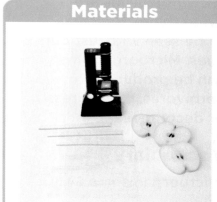

- **three peeled pieces of apple**
- **plastic bags**
- **microscope**

Step 3

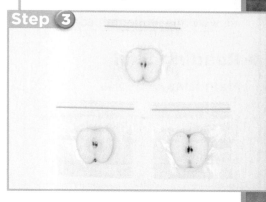

Step 5

Main Idea
4 LS 2.c
4 LS 3.d

Microorganisms are living things too small to be seen with just our eyes. Microorganisms can be producers, herbivores, carnivores, or decomposers.

Vocabulary

microorganism, p.64

bacteria, p. 65

protist, p. 65

fungi, p. 68

LOG ON e-Glossary
@ www.macmillanmh.com

Reading Skill

Main Idea

Main Idea	Details

SCIENCE QUEST Explore microorganisms on Science Island.

What is a microorganism?

You cannot see them, but there are tiny living things every place you look. They are on the food you eat. They are on the book you are holding now. They are inside and outside your body. You will find them in oceans, lakes, ponds, and rivers. You will even find them in puddles.

What are these tiny creatures? They are microorganisms (migh•kroh•AWR•guh•niz•uhms). **Microorganisms** are living things too small to be seen with just our eyes. Many microorganisms are made of only one *cell* (SEL). Cells are the smallest units of life. Plants and animals are made of many cells.

Most microorganisms can be seen through a tool called a *microscope*. A microscope shows an enlarged view of an object. Many classroom microscopes magnify objects 30 to 60 times their normal size.

eye piece

focus knob

lens

handle

◀ This photo shows what a protist looks like under a microscope.

mirror

base

▲ Washing and covering cuts and scrapes can keep harmful bacteria out of our bodies.

Bacteria

There are many kinds of microorganisms. One of the smallest is called **bacteria** (bak•TEER•ee•uh). Bacteria can be both helpful and harmful to human life. Harmful bacteria can cause illness. Helpful bacteria aid humans in swallowing and digesting food. They can even help to fight disease.

Protists

Protists (PROH•tists) are another group of microorganisms. Like bacteria, some protists can be helpful or harmful. Some protists eat bacteria. This helps to keep harmful bacteria under control. Other protists cause disease. Many harmful protists are found in ponds and lakes.

How do protists compare to bacteria? They are much larger than bacteria. They also have structures that do special jobs. They have parts for making and using food. They even have parts for making new protists.

✓ Quick Check

Main Idea What are microorganisms? Name two kinds.

Critical Thinking How can microorganisms be helpful to humans?

Which microorganisms are producers and which are consumers?

Some microorganisms act like plants. They get energy from the Sun and make their own food. These microorganisms are producers. They are helpful to us because they carry out photosynthesis and give off oxygen. They are not plants because they do not have true roots, stems, and leaves.

Other microorganisms act much like animals because they move to get their own food. These microorganisms are consumers. Some eat plants, some eat animals, and others eat both. This means that microorganisms can be herbivores, carnivores, or omnivores.

These microorganisms are called radiolaria. They are consumers.

◄ Algae can be found in water, such as in ponds and oceans. They are producers.

Producers

Algae (AL•jee) are a type of protist that live in water. Algae are producers. They act a lot like plants because they carry out photosynthesis. Have you ever noticed something green at the top of a pond or lake? This may be algae. Like most microorganisms, one algae can reproduce to form a colony. A colony is a group of algae. Algae make up most of the biomass in the ocean. They are an important part of ocean food webs.

Consumers

An *amoeba* (uh•MEE•buh) is a protist that acts like an animal in most ways. Unlike an animal, however, it changes its body shape to catch food. The amoeba flows all around the food until it surrounds it.

Producer and Consumer

Euglena (yew•GLEE•nuh) is one kind of protist found in ponds and streams. It acts like both a plant and an animal. How? In bright sunlight, euglena carries out photosynthesis like a plant. In the dark, euglena acts like an animal. It whips a body part that looks like a tail. This helps it move to get food.

 Quick Check

Main Idea What makes a microorganism a producer?

Critical Thinking Why is euglena not a plant if it gets energy through photosynthesis?

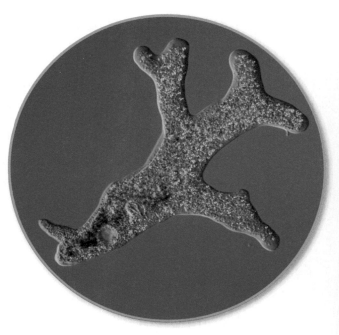

▲ An amoeba moves to get food by flowing its body in one direction.

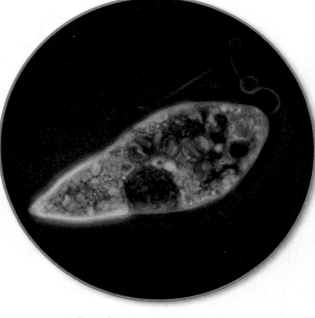

▲ Euglena is a protist that is both animal-like and plantlike.

Which microorganisms are decomposers?

A tree falls down in the forest. Billions of microorganisms start to break it down. These decomposers are the last step in the food chain. What part do microorganisms play in getting rid of the fallen tree?

Fungi

Fungi is one kind of decomposer. In a forest, colonies of fungi are the first decomposers to attack a tree when it falls down.

Mold is a type of fungi. You may have seen mold grow on foods. In a forest, molds cling to dead wood and start to break it down.

Bacteria

From there, bacteria might take over. There may be billions of bacteria in a gram of soil. Most of them are decomposers. Different types of bacteria consume different nutrients in the tree. Almost nothing is wasted. Once the tree is decomposed and part of the soil, new plants use the nutrients to grow.

▼ Sometimes a fungus will develop a structure called a mushroom. This shows decomposers are at work.

▲ Molds, like the ones growing on this apple, grow faster in warm temperatures.

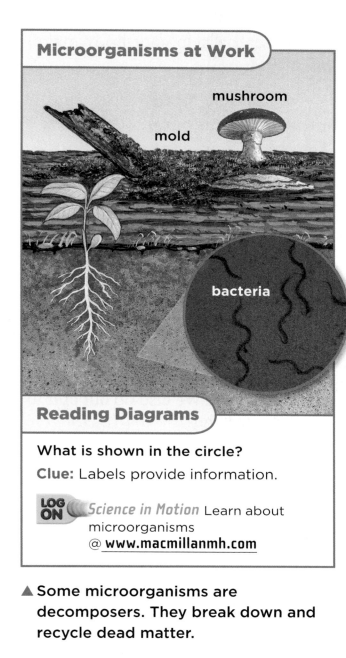

mushroom

mold

bacteria

Reading Diagrams

What is shown in the circle?

Clue: Labels provide information.

LOG ON *Science in Motion* Learn about microorganisms @ **www.macmillanmh.com**

▲ Some microorganisms are decomposers. They break down and recycle dead matter.

Natural Recyclers

Just as you recycle cans or bottles, decomposers recycle plant and animal matter. Plant and animal decomposers take matter that was once alive and change it into something new. Organisms become part of the soil. The soil is then used to grow new plants.

Quick Lab

Observing Decomposers

1 Put soil on the bottom of a plastic tub. Add food scraps such as bread crusts, banana peels, or other fruits.

2 Add leaves and place a few earthworms in the tub. Cover the tub and leave it outside.

3 **Predict** What do you think will happen to the food scraps and leaves?

4 **Observe** Use a hand lens to observe the mixture over the next few days. Record what you see.

5 **Infer** What do the results tell you about decomposers?

✔ Quick Check

Main Idea Which microorganisms help decompose a tree after it falls?

Critical Thinking Some molds can look like a plant. How do you know mold is not a plant?

How do microorganisms work in our bodies?

Your body contains many microorganisms. More live in your mouth than people live on Earth! Many microorganisms keep you healthy. Some make you sick.

Natural Protection

Many helpful microorganisms live in liquids in your body. Tears in your eyes and mucus in your nose keep out harmful microorganisms. How does your body break down food after you eat it? With help from billions of bacteria! Some of these same bacteria help your body make its own vitamins.

We can do a lot to keep harmful microorganisms out of our bodies. The chart shows how people can stay healthy from diseases caused by microorganisms.

✔ Quick Check

Main Idea Are most microorganisms in your body helpful or harmful? Give examples.

Critical Thinking If some microorganisms help fight disease, why should we also do our part to keep healthy?

Do Your Part to Prevent Disease

Disease	Microorganism	Prevention
tooth decay	tooth bacteria	brush and floss to remove food
Lyme disease	bacteria in ticks	wear long pants on hikes
dysentery	amoeba-like protist	drink clean water
malaria	protist in mosquitoes	use anti-malaria medicine
food poisoning	salmonella bacteria	cook and handle food properly

Reading Tables

How can you prevent microorganisms from making your teeth decay?

Clue: Look for the row that talks about teeth. Follow the row across to the "prevention" column.

◀ This girl is keeping healthy by brushing her teeth and using clean water.

Lesson Review

Summarize the Main Idea

Bacteria and protists are two examples of **microorganisms**. They can be helpful or harmful. (pp. 64–65)

Microorganisms can be **producers**, **consumers**, or **decomposers**. (pp. 66–69)

Microorganisms in your body help you **stay healthy**. You can help keep harmful bacteria out of your body. (p. 70)

Make a FOLDABLES™ Study Guide

Make a three-tab book. Use it to summarize what you read about microorganisms.

Microorganisms

Producers, Consumers, and Decomposers

Staying Healthy

Think, Talk, and Write

1. **Main Idea** How are microorganisms both helpful and harmful?

2. **Vocabulary** What is a protist?

3. **Main Idea** How do microorganisms fit into a food chain? Give examples.

Main Idea	Details

4. **Critical Thinking** In which places in your home would you expect to find microorganisms?

5. **Test Practice** Which microorganism is the smallest?

   A protist
   B bacteria
   C euglena
   D amoeba

+6 Math Link

Make a Bar Graph
There are 4 billion bacteria on a leaf. There are 3.5 billion bacteria on an animal. There are 2 billion bacteria on a phone. Show these numbers in a bar graph.

Health Link

Research Diseases
Choose a disease from the chart on page 70. Research the disease and write a report about it. Explain how it affects the human body. Share your report with the class.

▲ Susan is a microbiologist. That is a scientist who studies microorganisms.

Meet Susan Perkins

Susan Perkins knows that the smallest things can be the most important. She is a scientist at the American Museum of Natural History who studies microorganisms.

Microorganisms are found all over Earth—in soil, air, and water. They are found from the poles to the deserts. There are millions of them in just one drop of ocean water.

▲ These microorganisms cause malaria, a blood disease that causes severe fever in humans.

AMERICAN MUSEUM OF NATURAL HISTORY

ELA R 4.2.1. Identify structural patterns found in informational text (e.g., compare and contrast, cause and effect, sequential or chronological order, proposition and support) to strengthen comprehension.

Some microorganisms live inside the animals they attach to and cause disease. Susan studies the microorganisms that live in the blood of lizards and cause a disease called malaria.

How does Susan investigate these tiny creatures? She starts by taking blood from a lizard. Then she takes the blood to a lab and studies the microorganisms. This helps her understand the relationship between the microorganisms and the lizard it lived inside.

Next, Susan tries to understand how different kinds of malaria are related to each other. She studies why these microorganisms are found in different parts of the world and how they react to different medicines. Susan's research is then applied to humans and helps scientists to fight the disease.

▲ **Susan studies microorganisms that cause malaria. She stores her samples in a refrigerator in her lab.**

Susan studies anole lizards. ▶

Write About It

Sequence Reread the article with a partner. Make a sequence-of-events chart, to describe what Susan does first, next, and last in her research. Then use your chart to write a summary about her work.

LOG ON **e-Journal** Write about it online @ **www.macmillanmh.com**

A sequence
▶ gives events in order
▶ uses time-order words such as *first*, *then*, and *next*

Summarize the Main Ideas

Plants turn the Sun's energy into food energy through photosynthesis. (pp. 24–33)

Food chains describe the flow of energy among living things in an environment. (pp. 36–47)

Food webs show how producers and consumers are linked together in an environment. (pp. 50–59)

Microorganisms can be seen under a microscope. They can be producers, consumers, or decomposers. (pp. 62–71)

Make a FOLDABLES Study Guide

Tape your lesson study guides to a piece of paper as shown. Use your study guide to review what you have learned in this chapter.

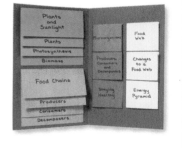

Fill each blank with the best word from the list.

competition, p. 53

consumer, p. 38

decomposer, p. 39

food web, p. 52

herbivore, p. 40

microorganism, p. 64

photosynthesis, p. 28

producer, p. 38

1. Several food chains that are linked together is a _____. 4 LS 2.b

2. An organism that does not make its own food is a _____. 4 LS 2.b

3. The struggle between different organisms for the same resource is called _____. 4 LS 2.b

4. An animal that eats only producers is called a _____. 4 LS 2.b

5. An organism that can be seen through a microscope is called a _____. 4 LS 3.d

6. Plants make their own food in the process of _____. 4 LS 2.a

7. An organism that recycles matter from dead plants and animals is a _____. 4 LS 2.c

8. An organism that makes its own food is a _____. 4 LS 2.a

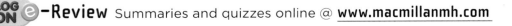

LOG ON e-Review Summaries and quizzes online @ **www.macmillanmh.com**

Answer each of the following in complete sentences.

9. **Sequence** Describe the sequence of events that takes place in photosynthesis. Include all materials that plants take in and give off. 4 LS 2.a

10. How can a primary consumer belong to two different food chains? 4 LS 2.b

11. **Persuasive Writing** Write a letter to a newspaper that explains why most bacteria are not bad for the environment. 4 LS 3.d

12. **Observe** Take a look at the closest natural environment to you. Describe a food web that exists in your environment. Draw a diagram. 4 LS 2.b

13. **Critical Thinking** The Moon has no known life forms. Predict what would happen if a sandwich were left in a sealed plastic bag on the Moon. 4 LS 2.c

 How do living things get energy to live and grow?

CHAPTER 1

Report on Changing Food Webs

Investigate a changing food web. Use newspapers, magazines, or the Internet as research tools.

- Find information on a food web that has been disturbed because of a plant or animal that was introduced to the environment. Some examples include kudzu, bullfrogs, bittersweet, and purple loosestrife.

- When you have chosen your plant or animal, write a summary of how that organism affected its new environment.

- Share your summary with a classmate. Explain what parts of the food web changed.

Food Webs

1 Which of the following are the main source of energy in a food chain? 4 LS 2.a

A producers

B herbivores

C carnivores

D omnivores

2 Which organism in the illustration below is both a consumer and a decomposer? 4 LS 2.b

A tree

B earthworm

C mammal

D bird

3 Which of the following recycles matter from dead plants and animals? 4 LS 2.c

A fungus

B grass

C cactus

D gopher

4 Which gas produced by photosynthesis do animals need to survive? 4 LS 2.a

A carbon dioxide

B helium

C hydrogen

D oxygen

5 Which organism can help fight disease in humans? 4 LS 3.d

A bean seeds

B caterpillar

C bacteria

D cane toad

6 Which organism gets energy directly from the Sun? 4 LS 2.a

A earthworm

B bee

C tree

D hawk

7 Which animal would compete with the coyote in this food web? 4 LS 2.b

A gopher

B lizard

C rattlesnake

D tortoise

8 What do microorganisms help humans do? 4 LS 3.d

A digest food

B walk and run

C hear sounds better

D see better at night

9 Students charted how many birds were in an environment on the bar graph below. Which prediction can they make for year 5? 4 IE 6.e

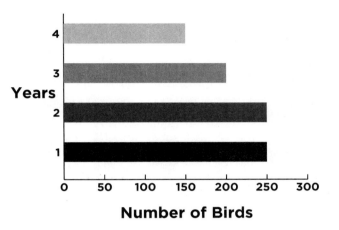

Number of Birds

A The number of birds will go up in year five.

B The number of birds will stay the same in year five.

C The number of birds will go down in year five.

D It is not possible to predict what will happen in year five.

10 A mushroom helps cause a log to decompose into the soil. What do you predict will happen to the soil in the area? 4 IE 6.c

A It will grow new plants well.

B It will not grow new plants well.

C It will decompose also.

D It will become polluted.

CHAPTER 2

Living Things and Their Environment

⭐ How do living things depend on one another and their environment?

Red Rock State Park, California

4 LS 3. Living organisms depend on one another and on their environment for survival.

Literature
Poem

ELA R 4.3.5. Define figurative language (e.g., simile, metaphor, hyperbole, personification) and identify its use in literary works. ELA W 4.2.1. Write narratives: c. Use concrete sensory details.

▲ Sonoran Desert

bobcat in the
Sonoran Desert

From *Welcome to the Sea of Sand*

Sea of Sand

by Jane Yolen

Welcome to the sea of sand,
a hot sea,
a dry sea,
a rock and stone and sky sea,
where mountains rise like islands
high
above the waves of sand.

But this sandscape
is not just a tan scape!
It's a wash of blue sky,
the splash of terra-cotta sunrise,
the dash of a speckled roadrunner,
a cache of kangaroo rats busy in their burrows,
a scuttle of tarantulas,
a muddle of centipedes,
a huddle of ocelots at noon
in the shadow of a cave,
a slither of green lizards,
the dither of butterflies
hovering over the desert
surprise
landscape after rain.

Write About It

Response to Literature The poet uses similes and metaphors to describe a desert environment. Why do you think she describes the desert as a sea of sand? What details does she use to paint a picture of a desert? Use similes and metaphors to paint a word picture of your own environment.

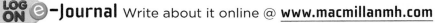

Ecosystems

Look and Wonder

Environments are made of both living and nonliving things. What living things do you see in this environment? What nonliving things do you see?

4 LS 3.a. Students know ecosystems can be characterized by their living and nonliving components.

What are some living and nonliving things in your environment?

Make a Prediction

What living and nonliving things might you find in your environment? Write a prediction.

Test Your Prediction

1. **Measure** Mark off an area of ground that is about 1 m square. Stick a clothespin in the ground at each corner. Wrap yarn around the tops of the clothespins.

2. **Observe** Use your hand lens to look at the living and nonliving things in this area.

3. **Record Data** Use a chart to record what you see. Label each object as living or nonliving.

4. Share your findings with a classmate. Compare the environments each of you observed.

Draw Conclusions

5. **Analyze Data** How many different kinds of living and nonliving things are in your environment? What did you see most of?

6. Choose one living thing you observed. What are the characteristics of this organism?

Explore More

How do the living things in the environment use the nonliving things in the environment?

4 IE 6.f. Follow a set of written instructions for a scientific investigation.

Materials

- tape measure
- 4 clothespins
- ball of yarn
- hand lens

Step 1

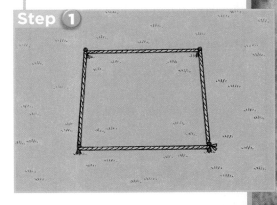

Step 2

What is an ecosystem?

Plants make their home in soil. Birds may use grasses to make nests. Bacteria in the soil break down leaves. Living and nonliving things interact every day. An **ecosystem** (EK•oh•sis•tuhm) is all the interacting parts of an environment. An ecosystem can be large, such as a redwood forest, or small, such as a pond.

Large or small, ecosystems are made up of living and nonliving things. The living things that shape an ecosystem are called **biotic factors** (bigh•OT•ik FAK•tuhrz). Plants, animals, and microorganisms are biotic factors.

Pond Ecosystem

1. Many plants find space to live along the water's edge. They get water and nutrients from the soil.

2. Birds use pond plants to make their nests.

3. Frogs feast on the insects they find around the pond.

4. Turtles come to the water's surface to get air and warmth from the Sun.

The nonliving things that shape an ecosystem are called **abiotic factors** (ay•bigh•OT•ik FAK•tuhrz). Temperature, rainfall, snow, ice, sunlight, and soil are abiotic factors.

Life in a Pond

Think of a pond ecosystem with only its abiotic factors. You might think of water and soil. Now add the biotic factors in and around the pond. Both of these factors together make up the ecosystem.

The biotic and abiotic factors of an ecosystem work together. For example, plants in a pond need a lot of water. They also need a certain kind of soil to grow well. Pond animals need a special climate (KLIGH•mit). *Climate* describes the typical weather patterns of an area over time.

✔ Quick Check

Compare and Contrast What is the difference between biotic and abiotic factors?

Critical Thinking What kinds of abiotic factors might you see in an ecosystem that is cold all year?

Reading Diagrams

How do living and nonliving things in this pond interact?

Clue: Look at the picture and read each caption.

What is a desert ecosystem?

Suppose you are in a mysterious place somewhere in the world. How can you identify the ecosystem you are in? You look around for clues. You notice that the soil is dry and crumbles in your hands. There are few plants and animals around. Where are you? You are in a desert!

There are many desert ecosystems around the world. Although all deserts are dry and similar in some ways, each one is different from the next. Some deserts are hot. Others are cold. Some are home to many living things. Others are almost lifeless. The Mojave Desert in California is a hot desert. It is more than 40,000 square kilometers (25,000 square miles). It is home to hundreds of plants and animals. Each one must live on very little water. Why? The Mojave Desert gets an average of only 13 centimeters (5 inches) of rain each year.

California's Mojave Desert is hot and dry. Plants and animals that make their home in this ecosystem can survive well in these conditions. ▼

Life in a Desert

Deserts like the Mojave are home to many birds, snakes, lizards, and other animals. They survive well in desert conditions. The fennec fox, for example, gets most of the water it needs from the food it eats. It can also go without water for a long time. The small animal lives in a hole, or burrow, under the ground. It stays here during the hot days and comes out at night for food.

The desert tortoise also spends most of its time underground. This protects the tortoise from the harsh temperature changes of the desert. In summer, temperatures can reach 120°F (49°C) during the day. They can drop below 50°F (10°C) at night.

✓ Quick Check

Compare and Contrast How does a desert ecosystem differ from a pond ecosytem?

Critical Thinking Explain why soil is an important abiotic factor in an ecosystem.

house finch

fennec fox

desert tortoise

The abiotic and biotic factors in a rain forest are different in each of the four layers.

What is a rain-forest ecosytem like?

Suppose you are in an ecosystem with dense forests and a hot, damp climate. You may be in a tropical rain forest. It rains a lot in this ecosystem, and the soil is very thin and poor in nutrients. However, there is more life here than any place on Earth. Rain forests cover less than six percent of Earth's surface. Yet they are home to 50 to 70 percent of all life on Earth!

The tall trees of the rain forest give the ecosystem different layers. The tops of the tallest trees are called the *emergent* layer of the rain forest. This layer gets a lot of sunlight but also can have high temperatures and winds.

Just below the emergent layer of the rain forest is the *canopy*. Most rain-forest animals live here because there is a lot of sunlight and food. Snakes, tree frogs, and toucans can be found in this layer.

▲ Squirrel monkeys are part of the biotic factors in the rain-forest canopy.

The *understory* is the area beneath the rain-forest canopy. Not much sunlight reaches this layer because the canopy provides so much shade. Leopards, jaguars, frogs, and many insects live in the understory.

The *forest floor* is even darker than the understory level. Not many plants grow here because there is very little sunlight. Decomposers work quickly in this layer. A leaf that falls to the forest floor might decompose in less than two months. In another climate this process could take a whole year.

A tropical rain forest can get up to 457 centimeters (180 inches) of rain each year. Compare that to the 13 centimeters (5 inches) of rain in the Mojave Desert!

◀ Iguanas live high in the rain-forest canopy. To escape predators, they drop into streams below and swim away.

≡Quick Lab

Ecosystem Soils

① **Observe** Examine clay, sandy soil, and topsoil carefully. Record your observations in a table.

② Place about 8 cm of each soil in a pot. Have a partner hold the pots over the pan.

③ **Measure** Pour 120 mL of water into each pot. Measure how long it takes the water to start draining from the pots. Then measure how much water dripped out of each pot.

④ **Infer** Which soil held water better? How might this affect plant growth?

✓ Quick Check

Compare and Contrast How do the abiotic factors of a rain forest differ between the canopy and the forest floor?

Critical Thinking Why might a toucan prefer to stay in the canopy layer?

Reading Photos

What biotic factors do you see in this ecosystem?

Clue: Classify the things in the photo as biotic or abiotic factors.

What is a coral reef ecosystem?

Coral reefs can be found in warm, shallow water. They are often in tropical areas. The water in these ecosystems usually stays between 70 and 85°F (21 and 29°C) all year. This temperature range allows many fish and eels to live here.

Coral reefs are formed from organisms that are no longer living. Coral polyps (POL•ips) are tiny animals that live in large groups.

When they die they leave behind hard skeletons that form coral reefs. The reefs are home to many ocean animals. Although coral polyps were once living, coral is an abiotic factor of the reef ecosystem.

✓ Quick Check

Compare and Contrast How does a coral reef ecosystem compare to a rainforest?

Critical Thinking What might happen to the fish in a coral reef if the water became colder?

Summarize the Main Idea

The living and nonliving things that interact in an environment make up an **ecosystem**. (pp. 84–85)

Ecosystems are shaped by their **biotic** and **abiotic factors**. (pp. 84–85)

Deserts, rain forests, and coral reefs are just a few **examples of ecosystems**. Each has a different climate, soil, and organisms. (pp. 86–90)

Make a Study Guide

FOLDABLES™

Make a layered-look book. Use it to summarize what you learned about ecosystems.

Investigating Ecosystems

Ecosystems

Biotic and Abiotic Factors

Examples of Ecosystems

Think, Talk, and Write

1 **Main Idea** What kinds of living and nonliving things make up a desert ecosystem?

2 **Vocabulary** What is an abiotic factor?

3 **Compare and Contrast** How are the abiotic factors of a dry ecosystem different from the abiotic factors of a moist ecosytem?

Different   Alike   Different

4 **Critical Thinking** You plant a seed from a rain-forest ecosystem in desert soil. The plant does not grow. Why?

5 **Test Practice** In which ecosystem would it rain less than 13 cm (5 in.) each year?

   A pond

   B rain forest

   C desert

   D coral reef

+6 Math Link

Solve a Problem

A redwood forest can get 76–127 cm (30–50 in.) of rain a year. A tropical rain forest can get 203–457 cm (80–180 in.) of rain a year. If each ecosystem gets the maximum centimeters of rainfall, what is the difference in rainfall?

Social Studies Link

Humans and Ecosystems

Choose an ecosystem to research. Find out how the biotic and abiotic factors influence the people of the area. How do the people use the land? What kinds of foods are grown there? How does the climate affect people's lives?

LOG ON **e-Review** Summaries and quizzes online @ **www.macmillanmh.com**

Predict

Scientists observe and analyze things to understand why they happen. For example, scientists know that plants depend on soil, sunlight, and water. With this information they can **predict** what might happen when they experiment with plants and their needs.

① Learn It

When you **predict**, you state the possible results of an event or experiment. First, you tell what you think will happen. Then, you experiment and record your observations and results. That information can tell you if your prediction was correct.

② Try It

How well do you **predict** a seed will grow in polluted soil? Use what you have learned about plants and ecosystems to make your prediction. Write your prediction. Then experiment to see if your prediction is correct.

▶ Mark two milk cartons "A" and "B." Place a cup of soil in each milk carton and plant 5 bean seeds in each. Water the soil in each container until it is just moist. Mix 80 mL of vinegar with red food coloring. Pour it into carton B to model polluted soil.

▶ Place the boxes near a sunny window. Water the soil over the next few days if it gets too dry. Observe both cartons every day. Write your observations in a chart like the one shown.

Carton A	
Day	**Observations**
Day 1	
Day 2	
Day 3	
Day 4	
Day 5	
Day 6	
Day 7	
Day 8	
Day 9	
Day 10	
Day 11	
Day 12	

Carton B	
Day	**Observations**
Day 1	
Day 2	
Day 3	
Day 4	
Day 5	
Day 6	
Day 7	
Day 8	
Day 9	
Day 10	
Day 11	
Day 12	

In which box did the seeds grow better? Compare your prediction to your results. Was your prediction correct?

Use a spoon to dig up the polluted soil. Can you still see the vinegar and food coloring? What does this tell you about pollution?

③ Apply It

Now that you have learned to think like a scientist, make another prediction. How do you **predict** different amounts of water will affect a plant's growth? Plan an experiment to find out if your prediction is correct.

4 IE 6.c. Formulate and justify predictions based on cause-and-effect relationships.

Living Things Need Each Other

Look and Wonder

This salamander lives among forest plants in California. How does the salamander use the plants in its environment to help it survive?

4 LS 3.c. Students know many plants depend on animals for pollination and seed dispersal, and animals depend on plants for food and shelter.

How do plants and animals depend on each other?

Materials

- **terrarium kit**
- **spray bottle and water**
- **tape measure**
- **hand lens**

Purpose

Find out how plants and animals use each other in their environment.

Procedure

1. **Make a Model** Place about 8 cups of soil in the container. Place the plants in the soil. Put the animal in the container and place the terrarium in a lighted area. Avoid direct sunlight. Spray the terrarium each day with a small amount of water.

2. **Measure** Carefully measure the organisms. Record the information in a data table.

3. **Observe** Use the hand lens to observe the ecosystem. How do the organisms depend on each other?

4. **Measure** After a week, measure the plants and the animal again. Record the information on your data table.

Step 1

Draw Conclusions

5. **Analyze Data** Draw a diagram of your terrarium. Draw arrows to show how the organisms depend on one another.

6. **Infer** What are the living and nonliving things in your terrarium?

Explore More

How might another animal use plants as food and shelter? How might you test your ideas?

4 IE 6.b. Measure and estimate the weight, length, or volume of objects.

▶ Main Idea 4 LS 3.c

Animals depend on plants for food and shelter. Plants depend on animals to pollinate flowers and spread seeds.

▶ Vocabulary

pollination, p. 98

seed dispersal, p. 100

 **ⓔ-Glossary**
@ www.macmillanmh.com

▶ Reading Skill

Summarize

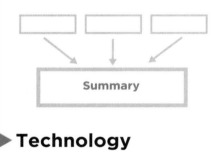

▶ Technology

SCIENCE QUEST Explore how living things interact on Science Island.

How do animals depend on plants?

Animals depend on plants in many ways. Animals breathe in oxygen that is produced by plants. They depend on plants for food. They also use plants for shelter and protection.

Plants as Food

Every part of a plant is food for some animal. Caterpillars and rabbits eat mainly plant leaves. Other animals, such as beetles, eat plant roots and stems. Animals such as earthworms and some snails eat plants that are no longer living. Bears, birds, bats, monkeys, and some lizards eat fruits and seeds.

Even meat eaters depend on plants for food. Remember, plants are the main source of energy entering food chains. Meat eaters depend on plant eaters. Plant eaters depend on plants. Directly or indirectly, all animals need plants for food.

Caterpillars eat leaves as a source of food energy. ▼

Squirrels use nuts as a source of food energy. ▶

▲ The bird uses twigs and plant material to build its nest.
Nests provide a safe place where birds can feed their young.

Plants as Shelter

Animals make nests, dens, burrows, and other shelters from plants. Squirrels move into tree holes and line them with soft moss and leaves. Many birds collect twigs and sticks and weave them into a tight nest. Birds use these nests to keep their eggs safe and care for their young.

An animal senses danger ahead. What can it do? Hide! Leafhoppers and garter snakes hide in the grass for shelter and safety. A rabbit or bird stays out of sight in the bushes. Fish sneak among thick seaweed beds in the ocean. Plants help keep animals safe from harm.

Grass as Protection

Reading Photos

How does the grass help the snake hide from predators?

Clue: Look at the color of the snake and grass.

✓ Quick Check

Summarize What are some ways that animals use plants?

Critical Thinking Why might a rabbit want to hide in the bushes?

How do some plants depend on animals to reproduce?

Flowering plants reproduce when male cells are transported to female cells in a flower. This process is called **pollination** (POL•uh•nay•shuhn). After pollination a seed develops. The seed can then grow into a new plant.

Look at the diagram of the flowers. The *stamen* (STAY•muhn) holds the male cells. The *pistil* holds the female cells. Flower parts cannot move by themselves. How then do male and female cells join together?

▲ After pollination, the ovary, at the base of the pistil, turns into a fruit.

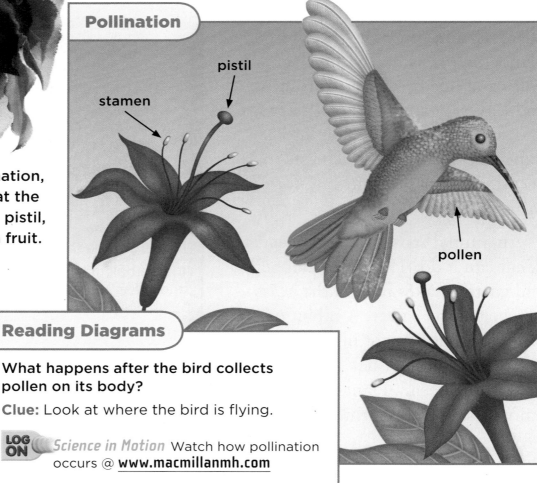

Pollination

pistil

stamen

pollen

Reading Diagrams

What happens after the bird collects pollen on its body?

Clue: Look at where the bird is flying.

LOG ON *Science in Motion* Watch how pollination occurs @ **www.macmillanmh.com**

▲ When a bee lands on a flower, pollen collects on its body.

Moving Pollen Around

Some animals help flowers with pollination. Animals such as bees, hummingbirds, wasps, butterflies, and bats travel from flower to flower. They collect a sweet drink inside the flowers called *nectar* (NEK•tuhr). As an animal visits a flower, a powdery material called *pollen* (POL•uhn) rubs off the flower and onto the animal's body. Pollen is located in a flower's stamen. It holds the male cells. When the animal visits another flower, some of this pollen rubs off on the flower. The animal does not know this, but the powder helps the flower reproduce.

Pollination helps both plants and animals. Animals get nectar, a source of food, from the plants. The plants can reproduce.

Quick Lab

Flower Parts

1 Use a hand lens to carefully observe the parts of a flower. Make a drawing of the flower and label each part you see.

⚠ **Be Careful.** Do not do this activity if you are allergic to flowers.

2 Use tweezers or toothpicks to open the ovary at the base of the pistil. Draw what you observe.

3 Make a list of the plant parts. Label which parts are "male" and which are "female" parts.

✔ Quick Check

Summarize How does pollen get from the male part of a flower to the female part?

Critical Thinking Why do you think many fruit growers keep beehives near their growing flowers?

▲ This iguana is eating a punta cactus fruit. The seeds inside the fruit are dispersed in the animal's waste.

How do plants depend on animals to carry seeds?

How do the seeds inside fruit get planted in the ground? **Seed dispersal** (SEED di•SPUR•suhl) is the process of spreading seeds. During this process, seeds are left in a place where they can grow into new plants. Animals play an important part in dispersing, or spreading, seeds.

An animal eats a fruit and its seeds. The seeds are later left on the ground in the animal's waste. The seeds may grow into a new plant.

Some plants have very sticky seeds. These seeds can easily stick to an animal's fur. When the animal moves to a new place, the seeds rub off. They fall to the ground. Here they may grow into new plants.

✓ Quick Check

Summarize How can an animal help spread fruit seeds?

Critical Thinking Do you think all seeds from a fruit grow into new plants? Explain.

Lesson Review

Summarize the Main Idea

Many animals depend on plants for **food** and **shelter**. (pp. 96–97)

Many plants depend on animals to help **pollinate flowers**. (pp. 98–99)

Many plants depend on animals to **spread seeds**. (p. 100)

Make a **FOLDABLES**™ Study Guide

Make a four-tab book. Use it to summarize what you learned about ways plants and animals depend on each other.

Plants as Shelter and Protection

Plants as Food

Animals Pollinate Flowers

Animals Spread Seeds

Think, Talk, and Write

1 **Main Idea** Name some ways that plants and animals depend on each other.

2 **Vocabulary** What is pollination?

3 **Summarize** How do some animals use plants as shelter?

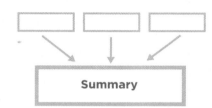

Summary

4 **Critical Thinking** Suppose fruit-eating animals disappeared from an ecosystem. How would this affect the ecosystem?

5 **Test Practice** What food do animals get from flowers?

A stamens
B ovaries
C honey
D nectar

 Writing Link

Write a Story
Write the story of a seed and its travels. You might explain how the seed sticks to an animal's fur and then grows in a new place.

+6 **Math Link**

Solve a Problem
Six different bees from a hive visit 250 flowers each to collect nectar. How many different flowers did the bees visit in all?

LOG ON e-**Review** Summaries and quizzes online @ **www.macmillanmh.com**

101
EVALUATE

The Moth That Needed the Tree

The yucca moth of the Mojave Desert visits flowers of yucca trees and picks up pollen. Then the moth does an extraordinary thing. When it visits the next yucca flower, it pokes a hole in the ovary. Then it places its own eggs into the flower! The moth leaves pollen on the flower as well so that the plant can reproduce.

The moth's eggs and the tree's seeds develop at the same time. The seeds become food for the moth's hatched larvae. All of this happens inside the flower! The larvae get the food they need and they stay safe from predators. The yucca moth and yucca flower depend on each other.

Good expository writing

▶ presents the main idea and supports it with facts and details

▶ may organize facts and details to show causes and effects

▶ draws a conclusion based on the information presented

▲ The yucca tree and the yucca moth depend on each other.

Write About It

Expository Writing Write a report that shows how the yucca tree and yucca moth depend on one another. Include facts and details that you have learned from this chapter and from your own online research. At the end, draw a conclusion about how the organisms help each other.

LOG ON **e-Journal** Write about it online @ **www.macmillanmh.com**

ELA W 4.2.3. Write information reports: a. Frame a central question about an issue or situation. b. Include facts and details for focus. c. Draw from more than one source of information (e.g., speakers, books, newspapers, other media sources).

Math in Science

Parts of a Whole

How many new plants grow from a flower's seeds? Each flower is different, and each type of flower is different. Only a fraction of seeds will grow into new plants. A fraction is a part of a whole.

Suppose a sunflower plant and a yellow star thistle plant make 100 seeds each. One-fourth ($\frac{1}{4}$) of the sunflower's seeds grow into new plants. Two-fifths ($\frac{2}{5}$) of the yellow star thistle's seeds grow into new plants. Which plant made the most new plants from 100 seeds? Use fraction strips to find out.

Fractions

Fraction strips can show how a whole and a fraction are related.

▲ This fraction strip shows $\frac{2}{5}$ is greater than $\frac{1}{4}$.

 Solve It

A tomato and a pepper each have 100 seeds. Two-thirds ($\frac{2}{3}$) of the tomato seeds grow into new plants. Two-fifths ($\frac{2}{5}$) of the pepper seeds grow into new plants. Which grows more plants?

 MA NS 4.1.5 Explain different interpretations of fractions, for example, parts of a whole, parts of a set, and division of whole numbers by whole numbers; explain equivalents of fractions.

Changes in Ecosystems

Look and Wonder

It looks like it hasn't rained here in years! A period of little or no rain is called a drought. How can living things in this ecosystem survive when their ecosystem has changed so much?

4 LS 3.b. Students know that in any particular environment, some kinds of plants and animals survive well, some survive less well, and some cannot survive at all.

How can changes to ecosystems affect living things?

Materials

Form a Hypothesis

How can a drought affect living things?

Test Your Hypothesis

1. Write "hawk" on a yellow card, "lizard" on a green card, and "fox" on a red card. Write "prey" on the rest of the cards.

2. Give each player a predator card. Then mix ten of each color prey cards and put them on the table. Put the other prey cards aside.

3. **Make a Model** Take turns drawing a prey card. Keep only the cards that match the color of your predator card. Return the others to the bottom of the pile. After every three turns, add a new prey card to the deck. This represents new growth. Play for 12 rounds. Count the cards left in the pile.

4. **Experiment** A drought has killed half of the prey in the ecosystem. Remove three prey cards of each color. Play again. After every six turns, add a prey card to the deck. This shows slower growth after a drought.

- **18 green index cards**
- **18 yellow index cards**
- **18 red index cards**

Step 1

lizard hawk fox

Draw Conclusions

5. How was the game different with each trial?

6. **Infer** What can happen to living things when an ecosystem changes?

Step 3

Explore More

What might happen if you changed the number of prey cards? Try it.

4 IE 6.c. Formulate and justify predictions based on cause-and-effect relationships.

▶ Main Idea 4 LS 3.b

When an ecosystem changes, plants and animals in that ecosystem can be harmed. Some organisms survive changes better than others.

▶ Vocabulary

accommodation, p. 108

endangered, p. 109

extinct, p. 109

LOG ON ⓔ-Glossary
@ www.macmillanmh.com

▶ Reading Skill

Predict

My Prediction	What Happens

How can ecosystems change?

You learned that living and nonliving things in an ecosystem work together. Plants and animals need the right amount of water, sunlight, and soil to live. When a biotic or abiotic factor changes, the whole ecosystem can be affected.

It may be hard to notice, but ecosystems are always changing. Over time, ecosystems can become warmer or colder, wetter or drier. Over millions of years, the land itself can change. Mountain ranges can be built up and broken down. Lakes can dry up or fill in. Some changes affect living things and make it difficult for them to survive.

Lake Tahoe in California has changed slowly over thousands of years to look the way it does today. It also changes from season to season as the weather changes. ▼

Natural Events Change Ecosystems

Weather and climate changes affect ecosystems. Lightning storms can start fires that can turn a forest to ash. Hurricanes and tropical storms can change coastlines in a single day. In a drought, some living things cannot find enough water to live.

Humans Change Ecosystems

Activities such as farming or building can affect many plants and animals. Cutting down forests and digging for resources in Earth's surface can change ecosystems. Many human activities cause pollution and make living things sick.

 Quick Check

Predict What might happen to living things if there is too much rain in an ecosystem?

Critical Thinking How are natural changes and human changes to an ecosystem different?

▲ Hurricanes and tropical storms bring strong winds and heavy rains that can change ecosystems quickly.

▲ Pollution can make it difficult for plants and animals to live.

What happens when ecosystems change?

A deer perks up its head to sniff the air. The smell of fire fills the forest. Flames rush through the ecosystem. The struggle for survival begins. How do living things survive ecosystem changes?

Some Organisms Survive Well

Some living things can survive changes by changing their behaviors and habits. An **accommodation** (uh•kom•uh•DAY•shuhn) is an individual organism's response to change. For example, the main food supply of some animals may be wiped out after a fire. Some animals will change what they eat in order to survive. They may also survive with less food by being less active. Some animals will use new plants or materials as shelter.

A fire can change a forest ecosystem quickly. Some organisms can survive through ecosystem changes.

Reading Photos

How do the two photos show a cause and effect?

Clue: Describe the events taking place in each photo.

Some Move to New Places

Not all animals can accommodate to ecosystem changes. Food and clean water may be hard to find after a fire. Some animals must find a new place to live. There they will look for the food, water, and shelter they need.

Some changes can be good for an ecosystem. A fire can keep an ecosystem from becoming too crowded. Overcrowding can keep plants and animals from meeting their needs for survival.

Some Do Not Survive

Some living things that do not move after an ecosystem change can slowly die out. An animal or plant that has very few left of its kind is **endangered** (en•DAYN•juhrd). Some endangered plants and animals can become **extinct** (ek•STINGKT). This means there are none left of their kind.

Quick Check

Predict A forest can grow again after a fire. Do you think some animals that left the area will return?

Critical Thinking After a fire a bird rebuilds a nest with new materials. Is this an accommodation? Explain.

Quick Lab

Crowded Ecosystems

1. **Make a Model** Drop ten paper clips into a small box. This shows the room needed for a population in an ecosystem. How many of the paper clips are touching each other?

2. Repeat step 1 three times.

3. **Predict** What might happen if the ecosystem becomes crowded?

4. **Make a Model** Toss 20 paper clips into the box. This shows a population in a crowded ecosystem. How many of the paper clips are touching?

5. Repeat step 4 three times.

6. **Infer** What happens when organisms are crowded in an ecosystem? How might this affect how a population meets its needs?

How can humans protect ecosystems?

Human activity has harmed many ecosytems. However, people can also do a lot to protect ecosystems. People make laws to limit pollution. Laws also make hunting certain animals or picking certain plants illegal.

The California condor is an endangered animal. Its ecosystem was destroyed by human activities. Not long ago there were only 22 of these birds left. With the help of many people, there are now over 200. Scientists and volunteers help raise these birds in a safe environment. Some are returning to the wild.

Humans have helped to bring back the California condor. ▶

You don't have to be a scientist to help save ecosystems. You don't even have to be an adult. Everyone can do something. The chart below lists just a few things people can do to help. The more people help, the better an ecosystem will survive.

✔ Quick Check

Predict What might happen if people stopped helping the California condor?

Critical Thinking Why should humans save ecosystems?

Saving Ecosystems

What Can I Do?	How Will It Help?
Turn off water while brushing your teeth.	saves water, a natural resource
Recycle more and reuse items when possible.	cuts down on trash and uses fewer new resources
Walk or ride a bike when possible.	cuts down on oil, a natural resource used in cars
Do not litter.	keeps water, land, and air clean

Reading Tables

How does reusing an item help save ecosystems?

Clue: Find the row about reusing items. Read across to the second column.

Lesson Review

Summarize the Main Idea

Natural events and **human activities** can cause ecosystems to change. (pp. 106–107)

When ecosystems change, some organisms survive and others are harmed. (pp. 108–109)

Humans can help **protect ecosystems**. (p. 110)

Make a FOLDABLES™ Study Guide

Make a trifold book. Use it to summarize what you learned about ecosystems and change.

Think, Talk, and Write

1. **Main Idea** What are some ways that plants and animals respond to changes in their ecosystem?

2. **Vocabulary** What does *endangered* mean?

3. **Predict** Suppose mice leave an area to escape damage from a storm. What could happen to the foxes that rely on them for food?

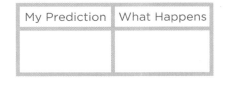

My Prediction	What Happens

4. **Critical Thinking** How can a fire both help and harm an ecosystem?

5. **Test Practice** Which is an example of accommodation?

   A A plant becomes endangered.

   B An animal finds a new food supply.

   C An animal eats the same foods.

   D A plant becomes crowded out of an ecosystem.

Writing Link

Write a Letter
Choose one change that humans make to ecosystems. Write a letter to a newspaper to convince people that the change is harming plants and animals. Tell why you think it is important to protect ecosystems.

Math Link

Make a Graph
An ecosystem gets 20 cm of rain each month for the period of January through August. Then there is a drought for the rest of the year. Graph the year of rainfall data for this ecosystem.

III
EVALUATE

MAIL CALL

Scientists at the American Museum of Natural History collect stories from people around the world to learn about local environments.

Dear Museum Scientists,

My name is Clara. I live in a small town in Southern California. The hills around our town are covered with evergreen shrubs. The land is very dry and there are not a lot of trees. This environment is called chaparral.

We didn't get a lot of rain here last summer. In August, a lightning storm started a wildfire in the chaparral. When I walked through the area after the fire, all I saw were gray ashes and dead shrubs.

a chaparral environment

AMERICAN
MUSEUM OF
NATURAL
HISTORY

ELA R 4.2.1. Identify structural patterns found in informational text (e.g., compare and contrast, cause and effect, sequential or chronological order, proposition and support) to strengthen comprehension.

It's April now, and I hiked through the burnt chaparral last week. I brought my field guide with me so I could look up the plants and animals I saw. The chaparral has changed so much! There are fields of wildflowers blooming everywhere. I found a hillside monkey flower and scarlet larkspur. My guidebook told me that these flowers have seeds that can stay dormant for several years. They need fire, heat, or smoke to sprout. The wildflowers have attracted insects like honeybees. The birds and animals are back, too! I saw a cactus wren and jackrabbits. My guidebook explained that the low bushes provide shelter for jackrabbits and nesting for cactus wren.

I can't wait to go back to see how the chaparral will change even more!

Your friend,

Clara

When you predict, you

▶ use what you know to tell what might happen

▶ use what you read to tell what might happen

 Write About It

Predict Read the letter again. Predict what the chaparral will be like next year. What might happen if a drought were to affect the chaparral environment? Write your prediction in the form of a paragraph.

LOG ON **e-Journal** Write about it online @ **www.macmillanmh.com**

Adaptations

Look and Wonder

This hummingbird has the perfect "tool" for getting nectar from flowers. What do you think this tool is? Why do living things have the right parts for doing different jobs?

  4 LS 3.b. Students know that in any particular environment, some kinds of plants and animals survive well, some survive less well, and some cannot survive at all.

How does the shape of a bird's beak affect what it eats?

Form a Hypothesis

Why do some bird beaks pick up some foods better? Write a hypothesis.

Test Your Hypothesis

1 **Predict** The first five materials represent different shapes and kinds of bird beaks. Which "beaks" do you think will work best for picking up rice grains? Foam chunks? Water? Record your predictions.

2 **Experiment** Try picking up each "food" with each type of "beak." Record your results and observations in a chart like the one shown.

- **chopsticks**
- **empty cup**
- **spoon**
- **fork**
- **straw**
- **rice grains**
- **large foam packing material**
- **water**

My Results				
"beaks"	rice	foam	water	observations
chopsticks				
empty cup				
spoon				
fork				
straw				

Draw Conclusions

3 **Infer** Were your predictions correct? What kinds of bird beaks might be best for picking up small, hard things? Large things? Explain.

Explore More

Are different claw shapes better for catching different prey? How would you test your ideas?

 4 IE 6.c. Formulate and justify predictions based on cause-and-effect relationships.

Step 2

Read and Learn

Main Idea 4 LS 3.b

An adaptation is a special feature or behavior that helps an organism survive in its environment.

Vocabulary

adaptations, p. 116

camouflage, p. 117

mimicry, p. 117

genetics, p. 117

LOG ON e-Glossary
@ www.macmillanmh.com

Reading Skill

Compare and Contrast

Different   Alike   Different

Dragonflies are some of the fastest insects. They can catch prey more than half their body weight. ▼

What is an adaptation?

Why is a giraffe's long neck just right for reaching high branches? Why are a dolphin's fins and tail great for swimming? Are these organisms just lucky to have these body parts?

In fact, necks, fins, and tails are examples of adaptations. **Adaptations** are special features or behaviors that help living things survive in their environment. A fish's gills, a dragonfly's wings, and an eagle's sharp eyesight are also adaptations. Adaptations can help animals move, catch food, and live in certain climates.

Strong, sharp beaks and good eyesight are just two of many adaptations that help bald eagles to survive and catch prey. ▼

Adaptations

Reading Photos

What adaptation helps the eagle catch fish?
Clue: Find the fish in the photo.

Adaptations can also help living things protect themselves. For example, some animals hide by blending into their environment. This adaptation is called **camouflage** (KAM•uh•flahzh). Some animals hide by looking like other organisms. This adaptation is called **mimicry** (MIM•i•kree).

Can one plant or animal adapt for survival on its own? No. Think of a giraffe's long neck. This trait was passed from the parent to the next generation. Long ago many giraffes' necks were much shorter. The tallest giraffes that reached leaves in trees could get more food. These giraffes survived. Over time giraffes with shorter necks died out. The study of how organisms pass traits from one generation to the next is called **genetics** (juh•NET•iks).

◀ A giraffe's long neck helps it to reach leaves and see predators.

▲ Can you find the Indian leaf butterfly in this picture? Mimicry helps it hide in plain sight.

✔ Quick Check

Compare and Contrast How are an eagle's claws and a giraffe's neck similar?

Critical Thinking Is escaping a forest fire an adaptation? Explain.

What are some adaptations of desert plants and animals?

Deserts are dry environments. Less than 25 centimeters (10 inches) of rain falls in a desert each year. That is less rain than some places get in one month! How do desert plants and animals survive in such a dry environment?

creosote bush

Special roots Creosote bushes have mainly shallow roots. This helps them take in the little rain that falls.

barrel cactus

Storing water The barrel cactus has thick, waxy skin and a thick, round stem. These adaptations help it store water.

ocotillo

Leaves This plant drops its leaves during very dry times to avoid losing extra water. The leaves grow back again when it rains.

wildflowers

Seeds Desert wildflowers bloom during the very short rainy season. This is when they spread their seeds for the next season.

Desert plants and animals have adaptations that help them survive with little water. Adaptations also help them stay cool and safe. A few of these adaptations are shown below.

✔ **Quick Check**

Compare and Contrast How are a desert jackrabbit's ears and a lizard's belly alike?

Critical Thinking Would an animal with thick fur survive well in a desert? Explain.

great horned owl

Nightlife Some desert animals are nocturnal. They sleep during the day and are active at night when it is cooler.

chameleon

Temperature control To cool down, this lizard raises its belly off the hot desert ground. The sand can be 40° F (22° C) warmer than the air.

jackrabbit

Large ears The jackrabbit has extra long, thin ears to keep cool. When warm blood flows through the animal's ears, it loses extra heat.

kangaroo rat

Kidneys Many animals have body parts called *kidneys*. The kangaroo rat's kidneys help it to store water in its body.

What are some adaptations of arctic plants and animals?

The arctic tundra is a harsh, cold environment. Living things here have special adaptations to help them survive the cold.

ptarmigan

Feathers The ptarmigan has feathers on its feet. The feathers help the bird walk on snow without sinking in.

polar bear

Skin and fur Waterproof outer fur keeps a polar bear dry. Thick inner fur keeps the bear warm. Black skin helps the bear absorb heat from the Sun.

musk ox

Large size The smaller an animal's body size, the more quickly it loses heat. The musk ox's large body helps it to keep warm.

arctic fox

Camouflage In winter, the arctic fox has a thick white coat that matches the snow. In summer, its coat is short and brown.

Quick Check

Compare and Contrast How is a polar bear's fur similar to an arctic fox's fur? How is it different?

Critical Thinking How do you think the arctic fox's camouflage helps to protect it?

arctic willow

Plant parts The arctic willow has fuzzy hairs to keep in heat. Its shallow roots grow near the surface where the ground thaws out in the summer.

yellow saxifrage

Height and color Yellow saxifrage grows low to the ground, protecting it from winds. Its bright color attracts animals it depends on for pollination.

≡ Quick Lab

Absorbing Heat

1. **Predict** Which color do you think will take in heat best—black, green, or white? Write your prediction.

2. Place black, green, and white construction paper side by side on a windowsill. Use sheets of paper that are the same size.

3. After a while, feel each piece of paper with your hand. Put the papers in order from warmest to coolest.

4. Record your results. Was your prediction correct?

5. **Infer** How do you think color affects heat absorption?

Reading Photos

How does this plant's color help it survive in its environment?

Clue: Labels and captions give information.

What are some adaptations of living things in the ocean?

For many animals, the ocean would be a cold and difficult place to live. However, it is the only place some organisms can survive.

Like land organisms, ocean organisms have adaptations that help them survive in their environment. Some adaptations help them breathe underwater. Others help them stay warm or safe. A few of these adaptations are shown on this page.

✔ Quick Check

Compare and Contrast How are a whale and leafy seadragon similar? How do they differ?

Critical Thinking In what other ecosystem might an animal with blubber survive well? Why?

whale

Blubber A thick layer of fat called blubber keeps a whale's body warm in cold ocean water.

giant kelp

Floating parts Giant kelp survives in the ocean because of delicate parts that help it float.

leafy seadragon

Mimicry Is this a plant or an animal? The leafy seadragon confuses its predators by looking like seaweed.

Summarize the Main Idea

Adaptations are features or behaviors that help living things survive in their environment. (pp. 116–117)

Desert and **arctic** plants and animals have adaptations that help them survive in their ecosystems. (pp. 118–121)

Ocean plants and animals have adaptations that help them survive underwater. (p. 122)

Make a **FOLDABLES™** Study Guide

Make a four-tab book. Use it to summarize what you learned about adaptations.

Adaptations
Desert Life
Arctic Life
Ocean Life

Think, Talk, and Write

1. **Main Idea** How do adaptations help plants and animals survive in an environment?

2. **Vocabulary** What is mimicry?

3. **Compare and Contrast** How are the adaptations of a desert plant different from those of an arctic plant?

Different   Alike   Different

4. **Critical Thinking** Could a desert animal survive in the Arctic? Explain.

5. **Test Practice** Which adaptation will help an organism find food?
   - **A** a sense of smell
   - **B** a shell
   - **C** thick fur
   - **D** blubber

Writing Link

Write a Report
Think about a turtle's shell. What do you think this adaptation is for? Research and write about it. Tell how it helps the animal survive.

Art Link

Hidden Artwork
Research an animal that uses camouflage. Draw a poster of that animal hidden in its environment. When you are finished, have a partner locate the animal.

Be a Scientist

Materials

craft sticks

glue

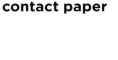

contact paper

scissors

basin of water

How are some animals adapted to swimming?

Form a Hypothesis

Adaptations help plants and animals survive in their environments. Animals such as ducks and penguins have webbed feet. How do webbed feet help these animals? Write your hypothesis in the form, *"If an animal has webbed feet, then . . ."*

Test Your Hypothesis

1. **Make a Model** Spread out three craft sticks in a fan shape. Secure the sticks in place with glue. This is the frame for your foot structure.

2. Make another foot structure identical to the first.

3. **Use Variables** Cover the top and bottom of the first foot structure with contact paper to make a webbed foot. Cut the paper to the correct size around the outside of the foot. Leave the second foot uncovered.

4. **Experiment** Test each foot in a basin of water to see how it could be used for swimming. Write your observations in your science journal.

Step 1

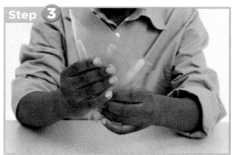

Step 3

Step 4

Draw Conclusions

5 **Compare** Which foot structure moves more water?

6 **Infer** Which foot structure works best for swimming? Why?

7 Did the results of your experiment support or reject your hypothesis? Explain.

Inquiry Guided

How do teeth help us eat different foods?

Form a Hypothesis

As humans, our front teeth are shaped differently from our back teeth. How does the shape of our teeth help us eat different foods? Write a hypothesis.

Test Your Hypothesis

Design an experiment to tell how the different shapes of human teeth are suited for eating different foods. Compare different foods, such as an apple and a cracker. Write out the steps you will follow. Record your results and observations.

Draw Conclusions

Did your experiment support your hypothesis? Why or why not?

Inquiry Open

What other questions do you have about adaptations? Design an experiment to answer a question you have. Your experiment must test only one variable, or one item being changed. Your experiment must be written so that another group can complete the experiment by following your instructions.

Remember to follow the steps of the scientific process.

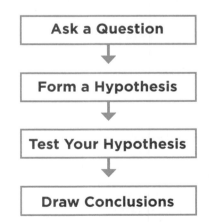

Ask a Question

↓

Form a Hypothesis

↓

Test Your Hypothesis

↓

Draw Conclusions

---

4 IE 6.a. Differentiate observation from inference (interpretation) and know scientists' explanations come partly from what they observe and partly from how they interpret their observations.

Summarize the Main Ideas

An ecosystem is made up of the living and nonliving things that interact in an environment. (pp. 82–91)

Animals depend on plants for food and shelter. Plants depend on animals to spread seeds and pollinate flowers. (pp. 94–101)

When an ecosystem changes, living things are affected. Some organisms survive changes better than others. (pp. 104–111)

Adaptations are special feature that help organisms survive in their environment. (pp. 114–123)

Make a FOLDABLES Study Guide

Tape your lesson study guides to a piece of paper as shown. Use your study guide to review what you have learned in this chapter.

Fill each blank with the best word from the list.

abiotic factors, p. 85

adaptations, p. 116

camouflage, p. 117

climate, p. 85

ecosystem, p. 84

extinct, p. 109

genetics, p. 117

pollination, p. 98

1. Some organisms use _____ to blend in with their environment. 4 LS 3.b

2. The study of traits that are passed on from generation to generation is called _____. 4 LS 3.b

3. Temperature, sunlight, and soil are examples of _____ in an ecosystem. 4 LS 3.a

4. Animals such as bees help flowers reproduce in the process of _____ . 4 LS 3.c

5. The long-term weather patterns of an area is called _____. 4 LS 3.a

6. Living and nonliving things interact in an _____. 4 LS 3.a

7. When there is no longer any plant or animal left of its kind, the organism is _____. 4 LS 3.b

8. A giraffe's long neck and a dragonfly's wings are examples of _____. 4 LS 3.b

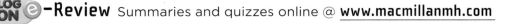

LOG ON **e-Review** Summaries and quizzes online @ **www.macmillanmh.com**

Answer each of the following in complete sentences.

9. **Infer** What kind of land animals might benefit from having blubber? 4 LS 3.b

10. Look around your local environment. What plants and animals do you see? What abiotic factors are important in your environment? Make a chart to record your observations. 4 LS 3.a

11. **Expository Writing** Explain ways plants and animals depend on each other. 4 LS 3.c

12. **Predict** You bring a new type of rabbit into a forest ecosystem that has never lived there before. Predict how the rabbit might affect the ecosystem. 4 LS 3.b

13. **Critical Thinking** People cut down an entire forest. Predict how this will affect the animals that live in the area. 4 LS 3.b

⭐ How do living things depend on one another and their environment?

Ecosystem Commercial

Your ecosystem needs your help! Your goal is to design a commercial that describes threats to an ecosystem and tells people how they can help.

What To Do

1. Choose a local ecosystem, such as a wetland, or an ecosystem in some other part of the world, such as a rain forest. Research the possible threats to this ecosystem.

2. Design a commercial. Your commercial can be in the form of a print ad for a newspaper or magazine, a script for a radio ad, or a script for a TV ad. If possible, record your radio or TV ads.

3. Include in your commercial threats to the ecosystem and what steps people should take to improve the problem.

1 Which process *best* describes what happens when plant seeds are carried away from a plant on animal fur or in animal waste? 4 LS 3.c

A seed shelter

B seed distance

C seed collection

D seed dispersal

2 The data table shows four different populations of snails over a three-year period.

Snail Population Each Year			
	Year 1	Year 2	Year 3
Population 1	20	25	28
Population 2	20	23	24
Population 3	20	27	34
Population 4	20	18	16

Which snail population is surviving best in its environment? 4 IE 6.c

A population 1

B population 2

C population 3

D population 4

3 What could happen in an area that has too many predators and not enough prey? 4 LS 3.b

A The animals will learn to adapt.

B More predators will move to the area.

C The predators will not find as much food.

D The predators will help each other.

4 Which process describes what happens when animals help flowers reproduce? 4 LS 3.c

A germination

B pollination

C transportation

D dissemination

5 How do animals use camouflage to survive? 4 LS 3.b

A by standing out from their environment

B by imitating other animals

C by blending in with their environment

D by giving warning calls

6 Which of the following is an example of an abiotic factor? 4 LS 3.a

A worm

B human

C water

D microorganism

7 Carlos made a poster of animals that imitate each other. Which of the following is his? 4 LS 3.b

A bald eagle and golden eagle

B viceroy butterfly and monarch butterfly

C barrel cactus and star cactus

D kit fox and jackrabbit

8 A scientist recorded the change in length of a desert lizard over four years. She recorded her observations in the chart below.

Year	Lizard Length
1	10 cm
2	15 cm
3	17 cm
4	20 cm

Which type of graph should she use to show her data? 4 IE 6.e

A bar graph

B circle graph

C animal graph

D pictograph

9 What might happen if a new organism were introduced to an ecosystem where it had never been before? 4 LS 3.b

A The organism will have no food.

B The organism will not survive at all.

C The organism will affect how other organisms survive.

D There will be no change to the ecosystem.

10 How can an ecosystem *best* be described? 4 LS 3.a

A by its abiotic factors only

B by its biotic factors only

C by its abiotic and biotic factors

D by its climate

Sea Otters

Key to the Kelp Forest

◀ Sea otters dive deep underwater to catch food. Then they float on top of the water to eat.

Sea otters are completely at home in the water. Look how relaxed this one is! Staying warm in the cold ocean can be a challenge, though. Whales, seals, and most other sea mammals have a thick layer of blubber to keep them warm. Sea otters do not have this layer of blubber. But they do have very thick fur to keep them warm—around 700,000 hairs per square inch. That is more hair than you have on your whole head! They also eat a lot of food for energy to stay warm.

Sea otters eat food such as clams, mussels, and their favorite, the purple sea urchin. Sea otters hunt in underwater forests of giant seaweed called kelp. A kelp forest is home to many animals. It is like a tall apartment building with different animals living on every floor.

Every animal in a kelp forest depends on sea otters. Why? On the bottom of the kelp forest, sea urchins eat loose bits of kelp. Sea otters dive down to catch and eat the urchins. All is well if there are enough sea otters around. If not, the number of urchins gets out of balance. The hungry urchins start to gnaw on the growing kelp plants. This causes the plants to break off and float away. As the forest is destroyed, the animals lose their home.

In many places, sea otters are threatened by oil spills, diseases caused by pollution, and other problems. The good news is that a lot of people are working to save them. That's important—not just for the sea otters, but also for the many animals that depend on them!

▲ Sea urchins attach themselves to kelp to eat.

Kelp grows like tall trees in a forest. ▼

 4 LS 3. Living things depend on one another and on their environment for survival.

Careers in Science

Nature Photographer

Picture yourself deep in the woods or far under the ocean. You are ready to capture a special moment on film. To be a nature photographer, you need a keen eye and a strong interest in science. You may face harsh conditions, too—bugs, scorching heat, bone-chilling cold. A nature photographer also needs patience. A single shot of a rare fish might take days or even weeks to get. When you finally capture that perfect moment, it is all worth it.

▲ A nature photographer must know about organisms and the ecosystems where they live.

Forester

Do you love the outdoors? Perhaps you should think about a career as a forester. To become a forester, you need a college degree in forestry science. As a forester, you are the manager of a forest or wilderness area. Your job is to help protect and make the best use of the land. Is it safe for hiking, camping, and hunting? Could part of the land be used for logging or some other industry? These are the types of questions that a forester must face every day.

▲ A forester teaches people about the living things in a forest.

Earth Science

Hot sulfur springs smell like rotten eggs.

Rocks and Minerals

 What are rocks and minerals and where do they come from?

tufa formations, Mono Lake, California

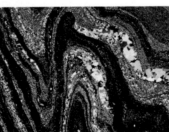
 **4 ES 4.** The properties of rocks and minerals reflect the processes that formed them.

Literature
Magazine
Article

ELA R 4.2.2.
Use appropriate
strategies when
reading for different
purposes (e.g., full
comprehension, location
of information, personal
enjoyment). **ELA W 4.2.1.**
Write narratives.

from *Click*

Rock Secrets

by Betsy James

A rock is never just a rock. A rock is a mystery.

Pick up a rock. Any rock. Does it look as if it has a secret?

Because it does. A big one. As big as a volcano. Or an ocean. Or a ferocious dinosaur. Every rock has a secret story to tell about what the earth was like long ago.

You pick up a rock.

Does every rock have a secret story?

Yes, every single rock—even a tiny pebble from your playground. It won't tell you its story in words. You have to figure it out by looking, feeling, asking, and wondering. But first—Pick up a rock!

Write About It

Response to Literature Every rock has a story to tell about Earth's past. Write a fictional story. A rock collector picks up a rock and it starts to talk, telling its secret story. Make sure your story has a beginning, a middle, and an end.

Minerals: The Building Blocks of Rocks

Look and Wonder

Did you ever wonder what rocks are made of? Why do rocks come in so many different colors, shapes, and textures?

4 ES 4.b. Students know how to identify common rock-forming minerals (including quartz, calcite, feldspar, mica, and hornblende) and ore minerals by using a table of diagnostic properties.

What makes rocks different from each other?

Purpose

Find out ways that rocks are different.

Procedure

1 **Observe** Look at each rock. What color is each rock? How does each rock feel?

2 **Record Data** Write about the properties of each rock in a chart.

3 **Compare** Choose one rock that is more than one color. Use a hand lens to compare the parts that are the same color. How do these parts compare? Are they shiny or dull? Are they rough or smooth?

4 **Compare** Choose another color in the same rock. How do the properties of the parts with this color compare?

Draw Conclusions

5 **Infer** Are the different colored parts of the rock made of the same or different materials? Explain your answer.

6 What makes rocks different from each other?

Explore More

Choose one of the rocks. How could you identify the rock and what it is made of? Now try it.

Materials

- **several different rocks**
- **hand lens**

Step 1

Step 3

 4 IE 6.a. Differentiate observation from inference (interpretation) and know scientists' explanations come partly from what they observe and partly from how they interpret their observations.

Quartz comes in lots of colors, such as rose, white, or purple. It can also be colorless. Quartz is the second most common mineral. ▶

What is a mineral?

Many common substances found on Earth, such as table salt and the graphite in your pencil, are made up of minerals (MIN•uhr•uhlz). **Minerals** are natural, nonliving substances that make up rocks. In fact, you could say that minerals are the building blocks of rocks.

Some rocks, like granite (GRAN•it), are made up of several kinds of minerals. Some of those minerals are shown on these pages. Other rocks, like marble, are often made up of only one mineral. Rocks are different from each other because they are made up of different kinds of minerals.

▲ Calcite is often a white or colorless mineral.

No matter where you go in the world, each type of mineral is made up of the same element or combination of elements. Remember, *elements* are what make up all matter. The mineral graphite is always made up of the element carbon. Table salt is always made up of sodium and chlorine. Each mineral has its own chemical makeup.

Each type of mineral has a certain *crystal* shape. Some crystal shapes are like cubes. Some are like hexagons. A mineral's crystal shape comes from the orderly way in which its atoms are arranged.

Scientists have identified over 3,000 kinds of minerals. Only about 30 of these are common in rocks. Those minerals are called *rock-forming minerals*. Some may even be found in your own backyard!

▲ Hornblende is a mineral that is found in granite. The black specks in granite are often hornblende. Hornblende is not as shiny as mica.

▲ Mica can be peeled easily into thin sheets. Mica is usually black or clear. It can be brown or even purple.

▲ Feldspar is a mineral that makes up about half of Earth's crust. Feldspar is found in several colors.

✔ **Quick Check**

Compare and Contrast Look at the photos of mica and hornblende. How are they alike? How are they different?

Critical Thinking Why do you think some minerals are called *rock-forming minerals*?

How are minerals identified?

Minerals are identified by their many physical properties. One property is color. However, color alone cannot identify minerals. For example, quartz and feldspar can both be white. They can both be a variety of other colors, too. Properties other than color must be used to identify a mineral.

Luster

Luster is a property used to identify minerals. **Luster** describes the way light reflects off the surface of a mineral. Some minerals have a *metallic*, or shiny, luster. Other minerals may be dull. Still others may have a glassy, pearly, or greasy shine to them.

Cleavage

The way a mineral splits is called **cleavage** (KLEE•vij). Cleavage is another property used to identify minerals. Some minerals, like mica (MIGH•kuh), split along a flat surface into thin sheets. Some, like calcite, split along flat surfaces to form a flattened cube-like shape. Still other minerals, like quartz, split apart unevenly.

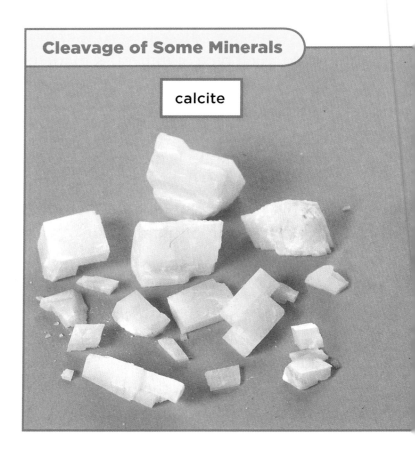

Cleavage of Some Minerals

calcite

▲ Pyrite, often called "fool's gold," has a metallic luster.

mica

quartz

Reading Photos

How would you describe the way each of these minerals splits?

Clue: Look at the shapes of the smaller pieces of each mineral.

Streak

Another way to identify a mineral is to look at its streak. **Streak** is the color of the powder left when a mineral is scratched along a white tile called a *streak plate*. Some minerals leave a streak that is the same color as the mineral itself. Other minerals leave a different streak color. The streak is always the same for a given mineral. For example, calcite can be white or colorless. Its streak is always the same color, though—white.

◀ Hematite leaves a reddish streak as shown on this streak plate.

✔ Quick Check

Compare and Contrast Two minerals are the same color. In what other ways might they be alike? How might they be different?

Critical Thinking Why isn't color alone used to identify minerals?

How can hardness be used to identify minerals?

Hardness is a property that refers to a mineral's ability to scratch another mineral or be scratched by another mineral. The **Mohs' hardness scale** shows the hardness of a few common minerals. There are many more minerals for each level of hardness. Diamond, 10 on the scale, is the hardest mineral. Talc, 1 on the scale, is one of the softest minerals.

Any mineral can be scratched by any mineral with a higher or equal number. For example, quartz can scratch any mineral with a hardness that is less than or equal to 7. Quartz, however, can only be scratched by minerals with a hardness that is greater than 7.

Which mineral do you think is being scratched? How could you find out? ▼

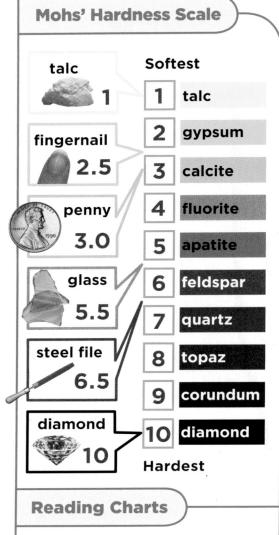

Mohs' Hardness Scale

		Softest
talc	**1**	**1** talc
fingernail	**2.5**	**2** gypsum
penny	**3.0**	**3** calcite
		4 fluorite
		5 apatite
glass	**5.5**	**6** feldspar
		7 quartz
steel file	**6.5**	**8** topaz
		9 corundum
diamond	**10**	**10** diamond
		Hardest

Reading Charts

Which minerals can be scratched by feldspar?

Clue: Look for minerals with a lower number than feldspar on the scale.

You can also tell the hardness of minerals by using some everyday items. Your fingernail can easily scratch gypsum and talc. A penny can scratch calcite, gypsum, and talc. Glass can scratch any mineral with a hardness that is less than 5.5. A steel file can scratch any mineral with a hardness that is less than 6.5. An iron nail can scratch any mineral with a hardness that is less than 4.5.

✔ Quick Check

Compare and Contrast Which mineral on Mohs' hardness scale is harder than all other minerals?

Critical Thinking Why might people want to know the hardness of a mineral?

≡Quick Lab

Identifying Minerals

1 **Observe** Select a mineral sample. Scratch it with your fingernail, a penny, and a file or an iron nail to determine its hardness. Record your observations.

2 **Observe** Use a hand lens to observe the sample's other properties. Record your observations.

3 Draw a line with the mineral across a streak plate. Press hard. Record the streak color.

4 Use the identification table below to name the mineral. Repeat steps 1–4 with other samples.

5 **Draw a Conclusion** Which properties helped you most in identifying the minerals?

Mineral Identification Table					
Mineral	**Hardness**	**Luster**	**Streak**	**Color**	**Other**
pyrite	6–6.5	metallic	greenish-black	brassy yellow	called "fool's gold"
quartz	7	nonmetallic	none	colorless, white, rose, smoky, purple, brown	
mica	2–2.5	nonmetallic	none	dark brown, black, or silver-white	flakes when peeled
feldspar	6	nonmetallic	none	colorless, beige, pink	
calcite	3	nonmetallic	white	colorless, white	bubbles when acid is placed on it

▲ A mineral identification table contains useful information about the properties of minerals.

▲ Toothpaste is made from fluorite.

▲ Gems are used to make jewelry.

Talc is one ingredient of paint. ▼

What are minerals used for?

Minerals are found in many of the things that you see or use every day. Quartz is used to make glass products. Your toothpaste contains fluoride that comes from fluorite. Drywall, used for making walls inside buildings, is made of gypsum. The paint on the walls in your classroom may contain talc or mica. Copper is used to make electrical wires and cooking utensils.

Other useful minerals are *gems*. Gems are valued for their beauty. You may have seen diamonds or rubies in rings or in other jewelry. Diamonds are also used in tools for cutting. Diamonds, rubies, and emeralds are just a few gems that are removed from Earth's crust.

Many of the minerals that we use come from ores. **Ores** are rocks that are mined because they contain useful minerals. Galena (guh•LEE•nuh) is an ore that contains lead. Hematite (HEE•muh•tight) is an ore that contains iron. Bauxite (BAWK•sight) is an ore that contains aluminum.

▲ Quartz is used to make glass products.

This bat is made of aluminum. ▶

✔ *Quick Check*

Compare and Contrast How are ores and gems alike? How are they different?

Critical Thinking Why are diamonds used in tools for cutting?

Summarize the Main Idea

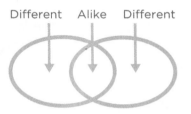

Rocks are different from each other because they are made up of different kinds of **minerals**. (pp. 140–141)

Minerals are identified by their **physical properties** such as color, luster, streak, cleavage, and hardness. (pp. 142–145)

Minerals are **used** to make many everyday products. (p. 146)

Make a FOLDABLES™ Study Guide

Make a three-tab book. Use it to summarize what you learned about minerals.

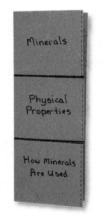

Minerals

Physical Properties

How Minerals Are Used

Think, Talk, and Write

1 **Main Idea** What are rocks made of?

2 **Vocabulary** What are minerals?

3 **Compare and Contrast** How are minerals different from each other? How are they alike?

Different   Alike   Different

4 **Critical Thinking** Silver has a hardness that is about 2. Why isn't silver used to make airplanes?

5 **Test Practice** Which property *best* describes a piece of quartz?

   A the color purple

   B hard

   C soft

   D shiny

 Math Link

Make a Bar Graph
Use the Internet or a field guide to rocks. Choose four minerals. Find their hardness. Make a bar graph to show this information.

Social Studies

Do Research
Research your state mineral. What is it? Where is it found in your state? How did it become your state's mineral? How is this mineral used?

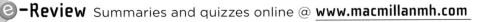

Focus on Inquiry Skills

Measure

You know that there are many kinds of rocks and minerals. Scientists can describe a particular rock by its many properties. Two of the properties that you can use to describe rock samples are mass and length. You **measure** to find a rock's mass and length.

① Learn It

When you **measure**, you find the length, distance, volume, area, mass, or temperature of an object. You can use tools to measure these properties. When you measure, it's a good idea to record the measurements on a chart. That way, you can compare your data.

② Try It

Estimate and **measure** the mass and length of a rock.

▶ Get a rock. Hold it in your hand. Estimate the mass of the rock. Compare the rock to gram masses to help you make a better estimate. Record your estimate in grams in a chart.

▶ Measure the mass of the rock using a balance and gram masses. Place the rock on one side of the balance. Place gram masses one by one on the other side until the two sides are even. Add up the gram masses. This is the mass of the rock. Record the actual mass of the rock.

▶ About how long do you estimate the rock is? Record your estimate in millimeters or centimeters in a chart.

▶ Measure the length of the rock with a metric ruler. Record the actual length.

❸ Apply It

Estimate and **measure** the mass and length of two more rocks. Record this data in a chart like the one shown below.

▶ Look at your data. Did you correctly estimate the mass of each rock? Did you correctly estimate the length of each rock? Which was easier for you to estimate—mass or length?

▶ With practice, you can become better at estimating mass and length. Repeat the activity using different rocks. Record your estimates and actual measurements again in a chart.

▶ Were your estimates closer this time to your actual measurements?

▶ Do you think that you can estimate the mass of a rock before actually picking it up? Try it for several rocks. Then use the balance to measure the actual mass of each rock. What is it about a rock that might cause you to have difficulty estimating its mass before you pick it up?

Rocks	1	2	3
Estimated mass			
Actual mass			
Estimated length			
Actual length			

 4 IE 6.b. Measure and estimate the weight, length, or volume of objects.

Igneous Rocks

Look and Wonder

This amazing landscape made of rock is found in Wyoming. A close look at this rock would show mineral shapes of different sizes and colors. How might this rock have formed? Could the mineral shapes and sizes be a clue?

4 ES 4.a. Students know how to differentiate among igneous, sedimentary, and metamorphic rocks by referring to their properties and methods of formation (the rock cycle).

How does growth rate affect the size of crystals?

Form a Hypothesis

Minerals have different crystal shapes. What affects the size of crystals? Do rocks that cool quickly have minerals with larger or smaller crystals than rocks that cool slowly? Write a hypothesis.

Test Your Hypothesis

1 Measure Place a black paper square on each of two small dishes. Then pour a half teaspoon of salt water onto each paper.

2 Place one plate in a warm place. Place the other in a refrigerator.

3 Predict As the water evaporates, salt crystals will form. Where will water evaporate faster? Crystals will form faster there. Will crystals that form faster be larger or smaller than crystals that form more slowly? Record your prediction.

4 Observe Use a hand lens to compare the dishes after two hours. Repeat 24 hours later.

Draw Conclusions

5 Analyze Data Where did the water evaporate faster? Where were the crystals larger? What is the relationship between rate of growth and size of crystals?

Explore More

Look at two rocks. In which rock did crystals grow more quickly? Explain.

4 IE 6.c. Formulate and justify predictions based on cause-and-effect relationships.

Materials

- **2 pieces of black construction paper**
- **2 small plates**
- **salt water**
- **teaspoon**
- **hand lens**

Step **1**

Step **2**

Main Idea   4 ES 4.a

Different processes that take place on Earth form many different kinds of rocks. Igneous rocks may be formed above the ground or below the ground.

Vocabulary

magma, p. 152

lava, p. 152

igneous rock, p. 152

LOG ON **e-Glossary**
@ www.macmillanmh.com

Reading Skill

Predict

My Prediction	What Happens

How are igneous rocks formed?

Below Earth's crust is a layer of melted rock called **magma**. Like any liquid, magma can flow. It sometimes flows to Earth's surface. Magma that reaches Earth's surface is called **lava**. Magma may reach Earth's surface in a huge explosion. It may also reach the surface slowly and ooze out of cracks in Earth's crust.

Whether above or below Earth's crust, melted rock can cool and harden. When it does, it forms igneous (IG•nee•us) rock. **Igneous rocks** are rocks that form from melted rock. The word *igneous* means "fire-made."

Igneous Rock Formation

Extrusive igneous rocks, such as rhyolite, form when lava cools above Earth's surface. ▶

Intrusive igneous rocks, such as granite, form when magma cools below Earth's surface. ▼

Intrusive Igneous Rocks

Igneous rocks are classified according to the way they are formed. When magma cools and hardens below Earth's surface, an *intrusive* igneous rock is formed. It takes a very long time, sometimes thousands of years, for magma to cool. Because it cools slowly, large mineral crystals are formed. Look at the photo of granite. It has very large crystals.

Extrusive Igneous Rocks

When lava cools and hardens above Earth's surface, an *extrusive* igneous rock is formed. Above Earth's surface, lava cools rather quickly. Sometimes it cools in just a few hours. There is not enough time for large mineral crystals to form. The crystals in this type of igneous rock are usually small. Look at the photo of rhyolite (RIGH•uh•light). The crystals are so small that you cannot see them!

✔ Quick Check

Predict If lava cools in a few hours, what will the size of the crystals be like?

Critical Thinking How can the words *intrusive* and *extrusive* help you remember where these igneous rocks form?
Hint: Look at the beginning letters of each word.

Reading Diagrams

How can you tell from the diagram that magma must be hot?

Clue: Look at the color used to show magma.

LOG ON *Science in Motion* Watch how igneous rocks form @ **www.macmillanmh.com**

▲ The domes of California's Yosemite Valley are made of granite.

What are the properties of some igneous rocks?

The properties of an igneous rock depend upon the way it is formed and the minerals that make it up. Some igneous rocks are hard. Others crumble easily. The size of the mineral crystals within a rock gives a rock its texture. Here are the properties of some igneous rocks.

Properties of Granite

Granite is one of the most common types of igneous rock. It is an intrusive igneous rock, so it has large mineral crystals. Large mineral crystals give granite its coarse texture. It is made up of several minerals. These minerals give granite its variety of colors.

Minerals in Granite

quartz

mica

feldspar

hornblende

Granite is a rock made of several minerals. ▶

Reading Photos

Which minerals make up granite?
Clue: Labels give information.

Properties of Pumice

Pumice (PUM•is) is an extrusive igneous rock. It is sometimes called *lava rock*. The tiny holes in pumice are caused by gases that escape as lava cools. If you pick up a piece of pumice, its weight might surprise you. It is very light. Pumice is often crumbly because of the way it forms.

Properties of Obsidian

Obsidian (uhb•SID•ee•uhn) is another extrusive igneous rock. The lava that forms this rock can cool in just a few hours. Mineral crystals do not have time to form. Because of the way it forms, obsidian is very smooth. It looks like shiny black glass.

✔ Quick Check

Predict You find an igneous rock. It has no visible mineral crystals. Which type of igneous rock is it?

Critical Thinking Why do you think the State Capitol building in Sacramento is made from granite?

≡ *Quick Lab*

Observing Igneous Rocks

1. **Compare** Observe a piece of pumice and a piece of granite. How do the two rocks compare in size and weight?

2. **Predict** Will the rocks sink or float? Explain your answer.

3. **Observe** Place both rocks in water. What happens?

4. **Infer** Use the hand lens to examine each rock. How might the differences in texture have contributed to whether the rocks sink or float?

5. **Infer** One rock cooled slowly inside Earth's crust. The other formed from lava. Which is which? How can you support your inference?

What are some uses of igneous rocks?

The properties of an igneous rock make a difference in how it is used. Granite makes a strong and long-lasting building material because of its hardness. Schools, office buildings, roads, and homes can be made of granite. Gabbro, another type of igneous rock, is often mixed into concrete and used to make sidewalks, bridges, and buildings.

Igneous rocks are also used in products around your home. Soaps or other cleansers in your home may contain pumice. The rough texture of pumice makes it a good substance to scrub off dirt.

✓ Quick Check

Predict Which would make a longer-lasting floor, granite or pumice? Why?

Critical Thinking Do you think that pumice can be used to make buildings? Explain your answer.

The Great Wall of China was made from blocks of granite. This wall was built over 2,000 years ago.

Lesson Review

Summarize the Main Idea

Igneous rocks are formed from magma or lava that cools and hardens. (pp. 152–153)

Where an igneous rock is formed and the minerals that make it up determine its **properties**. (pp. 154–155)

Igneous rocks have many important **uses**. (p. 156)

Make a FOLDABLES™ Study Guide

Make a three-tab book. Use it to summarize what you read about igneous rocks.

Igneous Rocks:

Properties:

Uses:

Think, Talk, and Write

1 **Main Idea** How are igneous rocks formed?

2 **Vocabulary** What is lava? Write about it.

3 **Predict** A volcano sends lava high into the air. What kind of igneous rock will form? Explain.

My Prediction	What Happens

4 **Critical Thinking** How can you tell if an igneous rock has cooled slowly or quickly?

5 **Test Practice** Which sentence describes how an intrusive igneous rock forms?

- **A** Magma cools and hardens.
- **B** Sediments settle in layers.
- **C** Granite settles in layers.
- **D** An igneous rock splits in half.

Writing Link

Write a Paragraph
Research an igneous rock. Write a paragraph that tells about the uses of this rock.

Math Link

Use Numbers
Some rocks near Earth's crust are about three billion years old. How do you write three billion as a numeral?

▲ **Sisir is a geologist.**

MEET
Sisir Mondal

Every year, for about a month, Sisir Mondal travels across the globe to places like India and South Africa. Sisir travels to those places to study rocks.

In the field, Sisir studies large layers of igneous rock. Sisir collects rock samples. He studies them closely to figure out their textures and what kinds of minerals the rocks contain. Based on his observations, he makes a geologic map of the area.

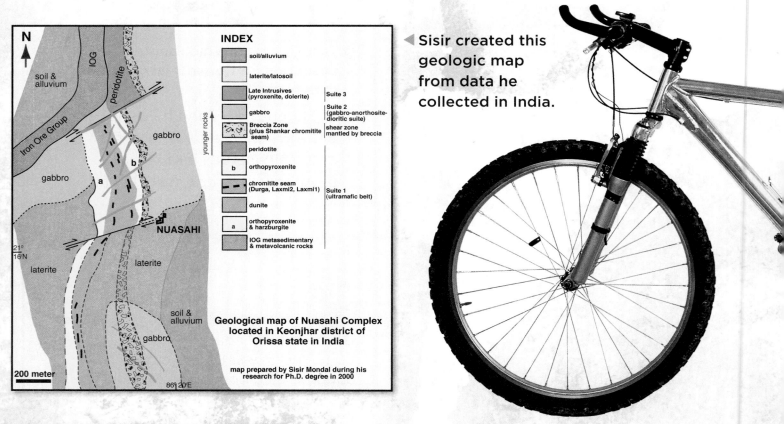

◄ **Sisir created this geologic map from data he collected in India.**

INDEX

soil/alluvium	
laterite/latosoil	
Late Intrusives (pyroxenite, dolerite)	Suite 3
gabbro	Suite 2 (gabbro-anorthosite-dioritic suite)
Breccia Zone (plus Shankar chromitite seam)	shear zone mantled by breccia
peridotite	
b orthopyroxenite	
chromitite seam (Durga, Laxmi2, Laxmi1)	Suite 1 (ultramafic belt)
dunite	
a orthopyroxenite & harzburgite	
IOG metasedimentary & metavolcanic rocks	

younger rocks

N

soil & alluvium

IOG

Peridotite

Iron Ore Group

gabbro

gabbro

b

a

gabbro

NUASAHI

21° 16'N

laterite

laterite

soil & alluvium

gabbro

200 meter

86°20'E

Geological map of Nuasahi Complex located in Keonjhar district of Orissa state in India

map prepared by Sisir Mondal during his research for Ph.D. degree in 2000

AMERICAN MUSEUM OF NATURAL HISTORY

ELA R 4.2.1. Identify structural patterns found in informational text (e.g., compare and contrast, cause and effect, sequential or chronological order, proposition and support) to strengthen comprehension.

Meet a Scientist

Back in the museum, Sisir takes a much closer look at the rock samples he collected. He uses microscopes and other tools to see what stories the rocks tell. Sisir wants to know why certain minerals are found in the rocks. He's particularly interested in finding rocks that contain metallic elements like chromium and platinum. Why are those metals important? People use them every day. Chromium is used to make many things, including steel. Platinum is a precious metal, used in everything from jewelry to catalytic converters in cars.

▲ Sisir is looking for rock samples.

◀ **Chromium is used to make bicycle frames.**

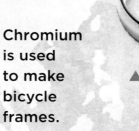

▲ **These rings are made of platinum.**

Compare and contrast

▶ **explains how things are alike**

▶ **explains how things are different**

▶ **uses compare words, such as *like* and *both*, and contrast words, such as *unlike* and *but***

 Write About It

Compare and Contrast Read the article again. How is the work Sisir does in the field similar to the work he does in the lab? How is it different? Make a Venn diagram to organize your ideas. Then use your diagram to write an essay.

 e-Journal Write about it online @ **www.macmillanmh.com**

159
EXTEND

Sedimentary Rocks

Look and Wonder

Here is a fossil of an animal that lived long ago. How did it become part of the rock around it?

4 ES 4.a. Students know how to differentiate among igneous, sedimentary, and metamorphic rocks by referring to their properties and methods of formation (the rock cycle).

Explore

What properties can help you infer how some rocks were formed?

Make a Prediction

Can the properties of rocks give you clues about how they were formed? Write a prediction.

Test Your Prediction

1. **Observe** Use a hand lens to observe the properties of each rock. Which rocks are made of smaller particles? Record your observations.

2. **Communicate** List the properties of each rock sample in a chart.

Draw Conclusions

3. **Infer** Which rocks may have formed from sand or gravel? What properties help you infer this?

4. **Infer** Shale and limestone are rocks that are found on the bottom of the ocean. Which of the rock samples might be shale or limestone? What evidence supports your answer?

5. **Communicate** Share your conclusions with your classmates. Did you form similar conclusions?

Explore More

How can an animal become part of a rock? Make a plan to find out.

4 IE 6.a. Differentiate observation from inference (interpretation) and know scientists' explanations come partly from what they observe and partly from how they interpret their observations.

Materials

- **four different rock samples**
- **hand lens**

Step 1

Step 2

Properties of Rock Samples
Rock 1
Rock 2
Rock 3
Rock 4

Main Idea 4 ES 4.a

Most sedimentary rocks form when sediments settle in layers. Over a long period of time, the layers change to rock.

Vocabulary

sediment, p. 162

sedimentary rock, p. 162

fossil, p. 164

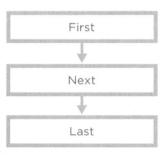
LOG ON e-Glossary
@ www.macmillanmh.com

Reading Skill

Sequence

```
┌─────────────┐
│    First    │
└─────────────┘
       ↓
┌─────────────┐
│    Next     │
└─────────────┘
       ↓
┌─────────────┐
│    Last     │
└─────────────┘
```

How are sedimentary rocks formed?

Rocks like the ones you see below are formed by tiny particles called **sediments**. Some sediments are tiny particles of rocks and minerals. Other sediments are bits of plants, bones, shells, or other animal materials. **Sedimentary** (sed•uh•MEN•tuh•ree) **rocks** are rocks that form from sediments that become pressed together in layers. What makes sediments turn into rock?

The colors of these rock layers are a result of different types of sediments that formed the rock millions of years ago. ▼

Layers Form

Sediments can be picked up and carried away by water, wind, and ice. Most often they are carried away by moving water such as in rivers and streams. Eventually the sediments are dropped off in a new place. Over long periods of time, new layers of sediments are carried and dropped on top of older layers. The weight of the top layers squeezes out the water and air from the lower layers. It also presses together the sediments on the bottom. Dissolved minerals cement the sediments together to form sedimentary rock.

Layers of Sediments

A
B
C
D

Reading Diagrams

Which is the youngest layer of sediment?

Clue: The layers form from bottom to top.

✔ Quick Check

Sequence What is the sequence of how most sedimentary rocks are formed?

Critical Thinking Why do most sedimentary rocks form above Earth's surface?

What are the properties of some sedimentary rocks?

Like igneous rocks, a sedimentary rock's properties result from the way the rock was formed and the materials it was made from. Some sedimentary rocks are soft. Others are hard. Many sedimentary rocks have distinct layers. Other sedimentary rocks may not show any layers. Here are the properties of some common sedimentary rocks.

Properties of Limestone

Limestone is one kind of sedimentary rock. It is usually white. It forms on the bottoms of oceans from the remains of once-living things. Limestone often contains shells or bones from animals. It can even contain the remains of plants. The remains of animals or plants from long ago are called **fossils**.

Properties of Sandstone

Can you guess what kind of sediment sandstone is made from? Its name should give you a clue. Sandstone is made when bits of sand become cemented together. It is made mostly of quartz. Sandstone that formed in water may have layers that look like ripples.

▲ Often the cementing material, iron oxide, stains sandstone red.

Fossils in Rocks

Reading Photos

Where do you think this rock was formed?

Clue: Think about where this animal lived.

Properties of Conglomerate

Conglomerate (kuhn•GLOM•uhr•it) is formed from larger rocks. It may be made up of rounded pebbles, stones, or even boulders once carried by fast-flowing waters.

The word *conglomerate* comes from a Latin word that means "lumped together." Rocks become mixed with sand and are bound together by natural cement. Because they are made of a collection of other rocks, conglomerates are coarse and chunky.

▲ Unlike many sedimentary rocks, conglomerates may not show distinct layers.

✔ Quick Check

Sequence How does a conglomerate form?

Critical Thinking What is the same about all sedimentary rocks?

≡Quick Lab

A Model Sandstone Rock

1. **Observe** Scratch a piece of sandstone with a penny. Record what happens.

2. Put glue into a container. Mix water with the glue until it becomes runny.

3. **Make a Model** Fill a small, clean, empty milk carton halfway with sand. Slowly pour the glue mixture onto the sand until the sand is soaked. Stir the glue and sand together. Let the carton sit for a few days.

4. **Compare** Carefully peel away the milk carton from the hardened model rock. Scratch the model rock with a penny. What happens? How are the model and the actual rock alike? How are they different?

What are some uses of sedimentary rocks?

Many sedimentary rocks are useful. For example, limestone is used to make chalk. Shale is used to make bricks, china, and pottery. When shale is combined with limestone, it is used to make cement.

Bituminous (bigh•TEW•muh•nuhs) coal, or soft coal, formed over millions of years when dead plants were buried in ancient swamps and forests. When we burn coal, the energy stored in those ancient plants gives us energy today.

Some sedimentary rocks help us to piece together Earth's history. Fossils in sedimentary rocks can show us what the living things of the past looked like.

▲ Chalk is made of limestone.

▼ Shale is sometimes used for making pottery.

▲ We use bituminous coal as a source of energy.

✔ Quick Check

Sequence Suppose fossils are found in upper layers of sedimentary rocks. Some are found in lower layers. Which fossils are probably older?

Critical Thinking Do you think that we will always have coal to use for energy? Explain your answer.

Lesson Review

Summarize the Main Idea

Sedimentary rocks are often formed by layers of sediments.
(pp. 162–163)

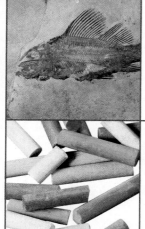
The **properties** of sedimentary rocks depend on the minerals they are made up of and the way they are formed. (pp. 164–165)

Sedimentary rocks have many **uses**.
(p. 166)

Make a FOLDABLES™ Study Guide

Make a three-tab book. Use it to summarize what you learned about sedimentary rocks.

Sedimentary Rocks:

Properties:

Uses:

Think, Talk, and Write

1. **Main Idea** Explain how long it takes for a sedimentary rock to form.

2. **Vocabulary** What are sediments?

3. **Sequence** How do sedimentary rocks form? Explain what happens first, next, and last.

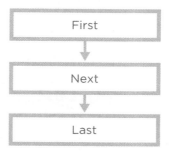

First
Next
Last

4. **Critical Thinking** You have an unknown rock sample. How can you convince your friend that the rock is sedimentary?

5. **Test Practice** Which rock is an example of a sedimentary rock?

   A gabbro
   B pumice
   C limestone
   D obsidian

Writing Link

Writing That Compares
Research two kinds of sedimentary rock. Use the Internet or a field guide to rocks and minerals. Write how the rocks are alike. Write how the rocks are different.

Math Link

Solve a Problem
The length of an animal's footprint is sometimes about one-quarter the length of its hind leg. A fossil footprint of a Tyrannosaurus is about $4\frac{1}{2}$ feet. What was the length of its hind leg?

Be a Scientist

sedimentary rock samples

hand lens

colored pencils

Inquiry Structured

What are the features of sedimentary rocks?

Form a Hypothesis

Sedimentary rock can form when sand, rocks, fossils, shell fragments and other items are pressed together. What are the basic characteristics of sedimentary rock? Write your hypothesis in the form, *"A rock is sedimentary if . . ."*

Test Your Hypothesis

1. **Observe** Use a hand lens to study the sedimentary rock samples.

2. **Communicate** Draw a detailed picture of each rock. Under each picture, record the color, texture, and special features of each rock.

3. **Infer** What do you think the rocks are made from? What clues helped you determine this?

Draw Conclusions

4. **Compare** What similarities did you see in your samples?

5. **Infer** What if you were given a smooth, black rock? How would you determine if it is a sedimentary rock?

Step 1

Step 2

Inquiry Guided

How are sedimentary rocks formed?

Form a Hypothesis

How can a sedimentary rock form? Write a hypothesis.

Test Your Hypothesis

Make a plan to model how a sedimentary rock forms. Write out the steps you will follow. Record your results and observations.

Draw Conclusions

Compare the sedimentary rock of your group to the rock of another group. What are some similar features between the two models?

Inquiry Open

What else would you like to learn about sedimentary rocks? For example, how is limestone formed? Design an investigation to answer your question. Your investigation must be written so that another group can complete the investigation by following your instructions.

Remember to follow the steps of the scientific process.

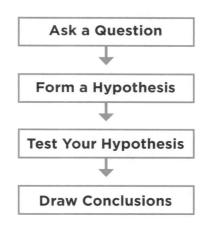

Ask a Question

↓

Form a Hypothesis

↓

Test Your Hypothesis

↓

Draw Conclusions

Materials

modeling clay

paper plate

plastic knife

construction paper

pebbles

shells

 4 IE 6.f. Follow a set of written instructions for a scientific investigation.

Metamorphic Rocks

Look and Wonder

This rock is different from the rocks you have learned about. Are there any clues in this rock that tell you how it may have formed?

4 ES 4.a. Students know how to differentiate among igneous, sedimentary, and metamorphic rocks by referring to their properties and methods of formation (the rock cycle).

How can you interpret clues in rocks?

Materials

- **three rock samples**
- **hand lens**

Purpose

Find out how clues in rocks can help you classify them.

Procedure

1 **Observe** View each rock with a hand lens. Record each rock's properties in a chart like the one shown below.

Sample	Color	Texture	Layers	Crystals
A				
B				
C				

2 **Classify** Recall what you learned about rocks so far. Based on the properties you recorded, which rock is igneous and which rock is sedimentary?

3 **Analyze Data** Which properties of the third rock are different from the others?

Draw Conclusions

4 **Draw Conclusions** What can you interpret from a rock's properties?

Explore More

How might the third rock have formed? What properties provide clues?

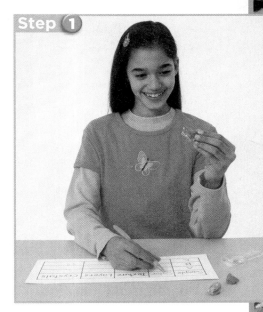

Step 1

 4 IE 6.a. Differentiate observation from inference (interpretation) and know scientists' explanations come partly from what they observe and partly from how they interpret their observations.

Main Idea 4 ES 4.a

Extreme heat and pressure can cause any kind of rock to change to a metamorphic rock. The rock cycle shows how rocks are constantly changing.

Vocabulary

pressure, p. 172

metamorphic rock, p. 172

geologist, p. 178

rock cycle, p. 180

LOG ON ℮-Glossary
@ www.macmillanmh.com

Reading Skill

Summarize

Reading Diagrams

Why do you think metamorphic rocks are formed on the bottom layers, beneath Earth's surface?

Clue: Observe what is at the bottom layers of rock.

How are metamorphic rocks formed?

Think about the rock under your feet. Layers of rock sit on top of layers of rock. This causes a force called **pressure** (PRESH•uhr) to build deep in Earth. This pressure squeezes rocks together.

Temperatures under Earth's surface can be very high. What happens to rocks under so much heat and pressure? Their physical properties change. The mineral makeup of the rocks may change, too. Rocks formed from other rocks by extreme heat and pressure deep inside Earth are called **metamorphic** (met•uh•MAWR•fik) **rocks**. They can be formed from igneous, sedimentary, or even from other metamorphic rocks.

Metamorphic Rock Formation

pressure

metamorphic rock

magma

Rocks That Are Made Over

One type of metamorphic rock is called gneiss (NIGHS). The colorful bands in gneiss are formed when the igneous rock, granite, is heated under great pressure.

Shale is a soft sedimentary rock. With heat and pressure, shale can change into slate. Slate has a different mineral makeup than shale. Some of its physical properties are different, too. Slate is much harder than shale, for example, but both break apart easily into layers.

The chart below shows some metamorphic rocks with the rocks they formed from.

✔ *Quick Check*

Summarize How is metamorphic rock formed?

Critical Thinking Why can you think of a metamorphic rock as a rock that has been made over?

BEFORE
Original Rock

AFTER
Metamorphic Rock

granite (igneous rock) → gneiss

limestone (sedimentary rock) → marble

sandstone (sedimentary rock) → quartzite

slate (metamorphic rock) → schist

What are the properties of some metamorphic rocks?

Just like igneous and sedimentary rocks, metamorphic rocks have different physical properties. They have different properties because they are each made from different minerals. The amount of heat and pressure a metamorphic rock undergoes also determines its properties.

Properties of Gneiss

In some metamorphic rocks, such as gneiss, minerals get rearranged and pressed into thin layers. The layers are called *bands*. The bands can be straight across. They can also be wavy.

The crystals in gneiss are large and easily seen. This gives gneiss its coarse texture. It feels rough.

Properties of Quartzite

Quartzite is a metamorphic rock without layers. It looks a lot like sandstone from far away. It has a similar color and is made of small mineral crystals. It has a medium texture.

▲ Quartzite is very hard and can have a glassy appearance.

▲ This sample of gneiss shows distinct bands, or layers.

Marble is usually white, but may be found in other colors too.

Properties of Marble

Marble is another metamorphic rock without layers. The crystals in marble can vary in size. Where crystal size is small, marble has a fine texture. Where crystal size is large, marble has a coarse texture.

Properties of Slate

Slate is another metamorphic rock whose minerals settle into layers. The crystals in slate are very small. They are packed together and are not easily seen. The small crystals give slate its fine texture. It feels smooth.

◀ Slate has very thin, flat layers.

✔ Quick Check

Summarize Why do metamorphic rocks have different properties?

Critical Thinking Two metamorphic rocks contain the same exact mineral content. How can they be classified as two different rocks?

▲ The shingles on this roof are made of slate.

What are some uses of metamorphic rock?

You see examples of metamorphic rock all around you. Metamorphic rocks are used in buildings, sidewalks, statues, jewelry, and many other items.

Slate is used to make tiles for walkways. Because slate is waterproof, it is also used for roofs.

Marble, which forms from limestone, is used for buildings and for statues. That's because marble does not break apart in layers when you carve it.

A rock called *lapis lazuli* (LAP•is LAZ•uh•lee) is another type of metamorphic rock formed from limestone. The rock is used to make jewelry and other objects.

◄ This guardian lion in Bangkok is made of marble.

These items are made of lapis lazuli.

Quartzite is used in glassmaking and ceramics. Tile floors, stone walls, and swimming pools may also be made from quartzite.

Many metamorphic rocks are ground up into small chunks. The chunks are often used in the gravel you see in driveways and on the side of the road.

Another metamorphic rock is called anthracite (AN•thruh•sight) coal. Coal is mined from Earth and burned as fuel. Most coal is used in its softer, sedimentary rock form, bituminous coal. However, anthracite coal is found deeper in Earth's layers. Because of the intense pressure on it, anthracite coal is a much harder coal than its sedimentary form. It burns cleaner and longer than soft coal.

▲ Quartzite is used to make glass.

✔ Quick Check

Summarize Tell some uses of metamorphic rock.

Critical Thinking Do you think that metamorphic rocks are more useful than sedimentary or igneous rocks? Explain your answer.

This rock wall is made of slate. ▼

How can you be a rock detective?

Identifying rocks is the work of scientists called **geologists** (jee•AHL•uh•jists). A geologist studies Earth's history by examining rocks. A geologist's work is much like detective work. Suppose someone handed you an unknown rock. Like a geologist, you would use the rock's physical properties to classify it. Texture, crystal shape and size, and layers are just some of the clues that a good rock detective uses to identify a rock.

Sedimentary Rocks

Rocks that contain fossils of once-living things are most likely sedimentary. Most sedimentary rocks have layers. If you can easily break apart a rock like mudstone or clay, it is most likely sedimentary rock.

Fossils are found in sedimentary rocks, such as shale, sandstone, or limestone. ▼

Igneous Rocks

The texture of a rock is also a clue to its identity. When you touch a rock, does it have a smooth, glassy texture? Then you might be looking at an igneous rock. Many of the minerals in igneous rock are also shiny and twinkle when held in the light. Igneous rocks are also hard and show no layering.

▲ Obsidian is black and sometimes has brown streaks. It has a glassy texture.

▲ This is what gneiss crystals look like under a special microscope.

Metamorphic Rocks

Colored bands in a rock are clues to identifying metamorphic rock. Many of these rocks have mineral crystals that line up in the same direction. Certain minerals are only found in metamorphic rocks. For example, if you find a rock that has talc or graphite in it, you can be sure it is metamorphic. Even though metamorphic rocks are formed under intense heat and pressure, some of the minerals they contain may be soft.

✔ Quick Check

Summarize Which properties help to identify a rock?

Critical Thinking Do you think that you could find a fossil in a metamorphic rock? Explain.

What is the rock cycle?

You learned how the three kinds of rocks form. Did you know that, over time, all rocks can change from one kind to another? The cycle by which rocks change from one form to another is called the **rock cycle**.

Quick Check

Summarize What is the rock cycle?

Critical Thinking Do you think the rock cycle can happen quickly? Explain your answer.

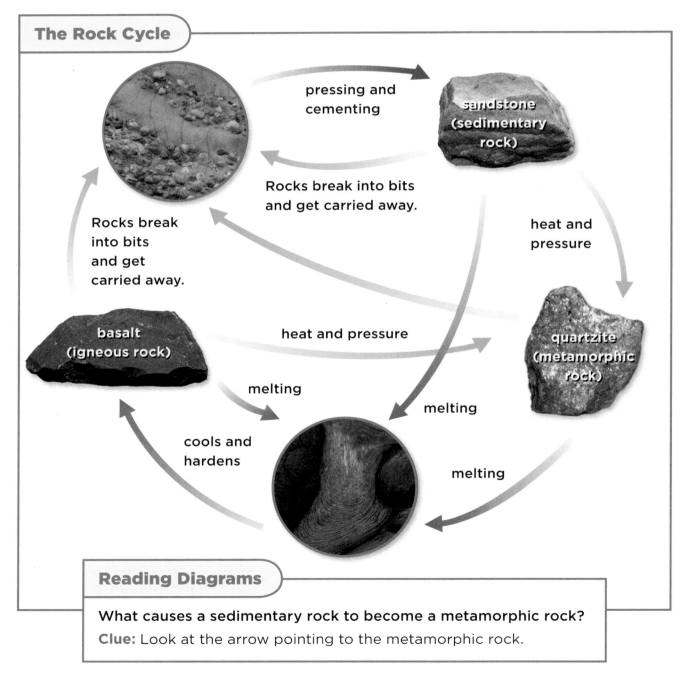

The Rock Cycle

pressing and cementing

sandstone (sedimentary rock)

Rocks break into bits and get carried away.

Rocks break into bits and get carried away.

heat and pressure

heat and pressure

basalt (igneous rock)

melting

quartzite (metamorphic rock)

melting

cools and hardens

melting

Reading Diagrams

What causes a sedimentary rock to become a metamorphic rock?

Clue: Look at the arrow pointing to the metamorphic rock.

Lesson Review

Summarize the Main Idea

Metamorphic rocks form deep inside Earth from great heat and pressure. (pp. 172–173)

Metamorphic rocks are identified by their **properties** and minerals. (pp. 174–179)

The **rock cycle** is a never-ending cycle by which rocks change from one type to another. (p. 180)

Make a FOLDABLES Study Guide

Make a three-tab book. Use it to summarize what you read about metamorphic rocks.

Think, Talk, and Write

1. **Main Idea** Does a rock stay the same forever? Explain your answer.

2. **Vocabulary** What are metamorphic rocks?

3. **Summarize** How can you tell a sedimentary rock apart from a metamorphic rock?

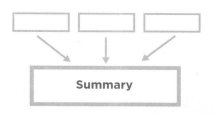

Summary

4. **Critical Thinking** How is the rock cycle a lot like recycling?

5. **Test Practice** Which phrase describes how a metamorphic rock changes into another kind of metamorphic rock?

    A sediments form

    B minerals dissolve

    C heat and pressure change the rock

    D magma cools

Writing Link

Write a Story
Write a story about how you, a rock detective, identify a rock no one else recognizes. Tell how you would go about classifying the rock. Make up a name for the new rock.

Art Link

Make a Poster
Cut out pictures that show different ways we use rocks. Organize the pictures on a poster. Then, share your poster with the class.

Marble Memorials

Each of these memorials honors a past American president. Both are made of marble from different parts of the United States.

Now here are two differences. Unlike the statue of Lincoln, made of marble, the statue of Jefferson is made of bronze, a metal. The Lincoln statue is 120 tons, but the Jefferson statue is only five tons.

A good description

▶ uses details to create a picture for the reader

▶ includes words that describe

▶ can use details to compare things

▲ Lincoln Memorial

▲ Jefferson Memorial

 Write About It

Descriptive Writing Compare two things made from rocks. Use words that tell about likenesses, such as *both*, *like*, *and*, and *too*. Use words that tell about differences, such as *but* and *unlike*.

 **e-Journal** Write about it online @ **www.macmillanmh.com**

ELA W 4.1.3. Use traditional structures for conveying information (e.g., chronological order, cause and effect, similarity and difference, posing and answering a question).

It Is Hard to Be a Rock

A rock collector has a collection of 100 metamorphic rocks. The table shows the number of each type of rock she has.

Fractions and decimals

▶ **To find a fraction, use the total number of rocks as the denominator. Use the number of rock samples for a particular rock as the numerator.**

Example: The fraction of rocks that are quartzite is $\frac{10}{100}$, or $\frac{1}{10}$. So, $\frac{1}{10}$ of the rocks are quartzite.

▶ **To find a decimal, divide the numerator by the denominator: $\frac{10}{100} = 0.10$**

Rock Collection of 100 Samples			
	Number in Collection	**Fraction**	**Decimal**
marble	5	$\frac{5}{100} = \frac{1}{20}$	0.05
slate	5	?	?
schist	50	?	?
quartzite	10	$\frac{10}{100} = \frac{1}{10}$	0.10
gneiss	25	?	?
anthracite	4	?	?
soapstone	1	?	?

 Solve It

Fill in the missing fractions and decimals from the chart.

 MA NS 4.1.6. Write tenths and hundredths in decimal and fraction notations and know the fraction and decimal equivalents for halves and fourths (e.g., $\frac{1}{2} = 0.5$ or .50; $\frac{7}{4} = 1\frac{3}{4} = 1.75$).

Summarize the Main Ideas

All rocks are made up of minerals. Minerals are identified by physical properties. (pp. 138–147)

Igneous rocks form when melted rock cools and hardens above or below the ground. (pp. 150–157)

Most sedimentary rocks form when sediments settle in layers. Over time, the layers change to rock. (pp. 160–167)

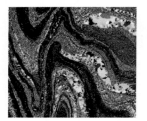

Extreme heat and pressure can form metamorphic rocks. The rock cycle shows how rocks change. (pp. 170–181)

Make a FOLDABLES™ Study Guide

Tape your lesson study guides to a piece of paper as shown. Use your study guide to review what you have learned in this chapter.

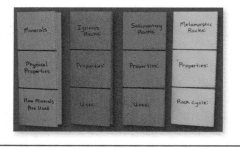

Fill each blank with the best word from the list.

lava, p. 152   minerals, p.140

luster, p. 142   ore, p. 146

magma, p. 152   rock cycle, p. 180

metamorphic   sedimentary
rock, p. 172   rock, p. 162

1. Igneous rock that cools above the Earth's surface comes from _____. 4 ES 4.a

2. The process by which one kind of rock changes to another is called the _____. 4 ES 4.a

3. Quartz and feldspar are examples of _____. 4 ES 4.b

4. Melted rock below Earth's surface is called _____. 4 ES 4.a

5. Hematite, mined for its iron, is an _____. 4 ES 4.b

6. Tiny particles of rocks pressed together in layers form _____. 4 ES 4.a

7. The property that tells how a mineral reflects light is _____. 4 ES 4.b

8. A rock that forms from another kind of rock is called a _____. 4 ES 4.a

 e-Review Summaries and quizzes online @ **www.macmillanmh.com**

Answer each of the following in complete sentences.

9. Compare and Contrast Compare granite, an igneous rock, with sandstone, a sedimentary rock. How are they different? 4 ES 4.a

granite   sandstone

10. Measure How can you measure the hardness of a mineral? 4 ES 4.b

11. Critical Thinking The Moon has inactive volcanoes but no wind or running water. What kinds of rocks might you expect to find on the Moon? Explain your answer. 4 ES 4.a

12. Descriptive Writing Shale is a sedimentary rock that turns to slate, a metamorphic rock. Describe the changes that take place when shale is turned into slate. 4 ES 4.a

★ What are rocks and minerals and where do they come from?

CHAPTER 3

Be a Rock Detective

Your goal is to use the information you have learned in this chapter to become a good rock detective.

What to Do

1. Go on a rock hunt. Gather a few rocks. Look around your schoolyard, a nearby park, or around your home.

2. Use what you have learned about rocks to classify them as igneous, sedimentary, or metamorphic. For each rock, make a list of the properties that you used to classify it.

Analyze Your Results

See what kind of a rock detective you really are. Look in a field guide to rocks and minerals and try to locate the rocks you found.

• Did you classify your rocks correctly?

• Were you able to determine the names of any of the rocks you found? If so, write the names of the rocks at the top of your lists.

1 What kind of rock forms when sand is pressed together in layers? 4 ES 4.a

A metamorphic rock

B igneous rock

C sedimentary rock

D cleavage

2 What are all rocks made of? 4 ES 4.b

A sand and mud from rivers, lakes, and streams

B magma or lava

C nonliving substances called minerals

D colored pebbles

3 Which physical properties are *most* helpful to identify minerals? 4 ES 4.b

A size, ability to float

B luster, streak

C weight, color

D crystal shape, width

4 Which kind of rock forms when extreme heat and pressure cause a rock to change form? 4 ES 4.a

A metamorphic rock

B igneous rock

C sedimentary rock

D cleavage

5 Which mineral is softest? 4 ES 4.b

Moh's Hardness Scale	
Mineral	**Hardness**
gypsum	2
calcite	3
quartz	7
diamond	10

A diamond

B gypsum

C quartz

D calcite

6 A rock is soft and has layers. The rock is *most* likely 4 ES 4.a

A sedimentary rock.

B igneous rock.

C metamorphic rock.

D granite.

7 Use the mineral identification table on page 145 to answer this question.

A certain mineral has a hardness of 2 and is nonmetallic. It flakes when peeled. The unidentified mineral is *most* likely 4 ES 4.b

A pyrite.

B granite.

C calcite.

D mica.

8 A student predicts sedimentary rocks will absorb water. To test his prediction, he conducts the following experiment.

He finds the mass of three samples of rock. He puts each rock in a plastic cup filled with water for 24 hours. He then takes each rock out and finds the mass of each rock again. His results are below:

Sedimentary Rocks		
Rock sample	Before placed in water	After placed in water
1	12 grams	14 grams
2	17 grams	22 grams
3	16 grams	18 grams

What did he observe to know that his prediction was correct? 4 IE 6.d

A The mass of each rock was the same after being in water.

B The rocks changed color after being in water.

C The mass of each rock was smaller after being in water.

D The mass of each rock was greater after being in water.

9 **Which kind of rock forms when magma cools and hardens?** 4 ES 4.a

A metamorphic rock

B igneous rock

C sedimentary rock

D cleavage

10 A student had three metamorphic rocks. Each was about the same size but a different color. She placed the gray rock on a balance and recorded its mass. Then she found the mass of the white rock and the black rock. She recorded their masses as well. To be sure that she measured correctly, she found the mass of each rock two more times. The mass of each rock is shown for each trial in the chart below.

Rocks			
Trial	Gray rock	White rock	Black rock
1	11 grams	6 grams	8 grams
2	11 grams	6 grams	8 grams
3	11 grams	6 grams	8 grams

Based on her data, she may conclude that 4 IE 6.b

A the gray rock has less mass than the black rock.

B the white rock has more mass than the black or gray rocks.

C rocks of different colors have the same mass.

D the white rock has the least mass.

Slow Changes on Earth

⭐ **What causes Earth's surface to change slowly?**

Bridal Veil Falls, Yosemite National Park, California

 4 ES 5. Waves, wind, water, and ice shape and reshape Earth's land surface.

Literature
Poem

ELA R 4.3.5.
Define figurative
language (e.g., simile,
metaphor, hyperbole,
personification) and
identify its use in literary
works. **ELA W 4.2.4.**
Write summaries that
contain the main ideas of
the reading selection and
the most significant details.

Sierra Mountains

SIERRA

BY DIANE SIEBERT

I am the mountain.
From the sea
Come constant winds to conquer me—
Pacific winds that touch my face
And bring the storms whose clouds embrace
My rugged shoulders, strong and wide;
And in their path, I cannot hide.

And though I have the strength of youth,
I sense each change and know the truth:
By wind and weather, day by day,
I will, in time, be worn away;
For mountains live, and mountains die.
As ages pass, so, too, will I.

 Write About It

Response to Literature

Diane Siebert uses personification to describe how rock is slowly worn away. How does rock change? How did making the mountain seem human make you feel? Write a summary. Use your own words to explain what this poem is about.

Weathering

Look and Wonder

These rocks are part of Buttermilk Boulders near Bishop, California. There are big rocks, little rocks, snow, and ice. How did the little rocks get there? What broke the bigger rocks into smaller ones?

 4 ES 5.b. Students know natural processes, including freezing and thawing and the growth of roots, cause rocks to break down into smaller pieces.

How can freezing water change rock?

Make a Prediction

What do you predict happens to rocks when water freezes in the cracks of rocks?

Test Your Prediction

1. **Make a Model** Fill the plastic bottle all the way to the top with water. Put the cap on tightly. Wrap a cloth or dish towel around the bottle. This is a model of water in a crack in a rock.

2. Place your model in a freezer and leave it overnight.

3. **Predict** What will happen to the water and the bottle?

4. **Observe** Unwrap the bottle. What happened to the water and the bottle?

Draw Conclusions

5. **Analyze Data** Did your observations match your prediction?

6. **Infer** What caused the bottle to change?

7. **Infer** What do you think happens when water freezes inside a crack in a rock?

Explore More

Experiment Repeat the activity. This time, use real rocks with small cracks in them.

Materials

- **small plastic bottle**
- **water**
- **cloth or dish towel**

Step 1

Step 2

4 IE 6.c. Formulate and justify predictions based on cause-and-effect relationships.

What is weathering?

You are hiking across the desert in Arches National Park in Utah. You round a bend and see a big window in the middle of a rock. It was once a huge, solid rock. What caused the rock to change?

Rocks are constantly changing. Freezing and thawing, plants, wind, and pressure can cause rocks to break into smaller pieces. The breaking down of rocks is called **weathering** (WETH•uhr•ing).

Physical weathering happens when such things as wind and rain break rocks down. Physical weathering causes rocks to simply change size and shape. The chemicals they are made of do not change. Here are some things that cause physical weathering.

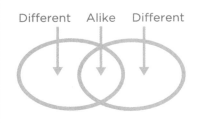

North Window Arch in Arches National Park, Utah, was formed by physical weathering.

Freezing and Thawing

Water from rain or melted snow enters small cracks in rocks. If the water freezes, it *expands*, or takes up more space. This causes cracks to widen. Later the water may *thaw*, or melt. Over time, repeated freezing and thawing breaks rocks apart.

Plants

Did you ever trip on a sidewalk that had been cracked by a tree's roots? A plant's roots can force their way through small cracks in rock. As the roots grow larger, they cause the cracks to widen and the rocks to break apart.

Exfoliation

Some buried rocks, like granite, are changed when heavy layers of rock wear away. The outer layers of the once-buried granite expand more than the layers below. This causes the outer layers of rock to peel off like the layers of an onion. This kind of physical weathering is called *exfoliation* (eks•foh•lee•AY•shuhn).

Abrasion

Winds can also change rock. Winds that carry bits of sand can break down the softer parts of rocks. The sharp edges of sand wear away rock. This wearing away of rock by blowing sand is called *wind abrasion* (uh•BRAY•zhuhn).

▲ These roots will eventually split the rock apart.

▲ The dome of rock in Half Dome is an example of weathering by exfoliation.

✔ Quick Check

Compare and Contrast What do all kinds of physical weathering have in common?

Critical Thinking Why wouldn't rocks in most hot deserts be weathered by freezing and thawing?

What are some other causes of weathering?

Have you ever observed a worn stone statue? What do you think caused it to weather? Chances are the changes were caused by chemical weathering. A rock can break down when minerals in the rock are changed chemically. When these changes happen, **chemical weathering** takes place. Oxygen, acids, and carbon dioxide can react with the minerals in rock and cause chemical weathering.

Oxygen

Have you ever seen an iron chain become rusty over time? This happens when oxygen in air dissolves in water. It then reacts with iron to form rust. Rocks with iron can rust and break down, too.

Weathered Limestone

▲ This limestone cave is part of Carlsbad Caverns in New Mexico. It is the result of chemical weathering that has been taking place for millions of years.

Acids

Most of the water in rivers and in soil contains acids. Decaying plants put acids in soil. Water soaking into the soil dissolves these acids. When dissolved acid comes into contact with rock, the acid reacts with the rock's minerals. The rock changes chemically. After a long time, the rock changes shape and breaks down.

◀ Hematite contains iron. Things with iron can rust and break down when the iron mixes with oxygen.

Carbon Dioxide

Carbon dioxide, a gas in air, combines with rainwater. When this happens, *carbonic acid* forms. This weak acid can react with minerals in some rocks. Carbonic acid caused the limestone cave shown above to form.

Carbonic acid also weathers rocks in soil. Decaying plant and animal matter puts carbon dioxide into the soil. Rainwater enters soil and combines with the carbon dioxide.

Quick Lab

Chemical Weathering

1 Place a piece of chalk in each of two jars. Pour one cup of water over one piece of chalk. Pour one cup of soda over the second piece of chalk. Soda contains carbonic acid.

2 Place the jars on a shelf for a few days.

3 **Observe** What changes do you see?

4 **Draw Conclusions** What does acid do to rock?

✓ Quick Check

Compare and Contrast What is the same about all kinds of chemical weathering?

Critical Thinking Where do you think the acid in acid rain comes from?

How is soil formed?

If you look at soil with a hand lens, you will find that it contains many things. Soil mostly consists of bits of weathered rock, minerals, and humus (HYEW•muhs). *Humus* is decayed plant or animal material. Soil also contains water, air, and bacteria. It can take thousands of years for weathering to break down rocks to form soil.

Over time, layers of soil called **horizons** (huh•RIGH•zuhns) form. Each horizon has its own properties.

Soil horizons are different from place to place. That's because the rocks and humus that make up soil are different from place to place. In some places, the horizons might look like the ones below.

✔ Quick Check

Compare and Contrast What is different about Horizons A, B, and C?

Critical Thinking In which horizon layer would you expect to find the most humus? Why?

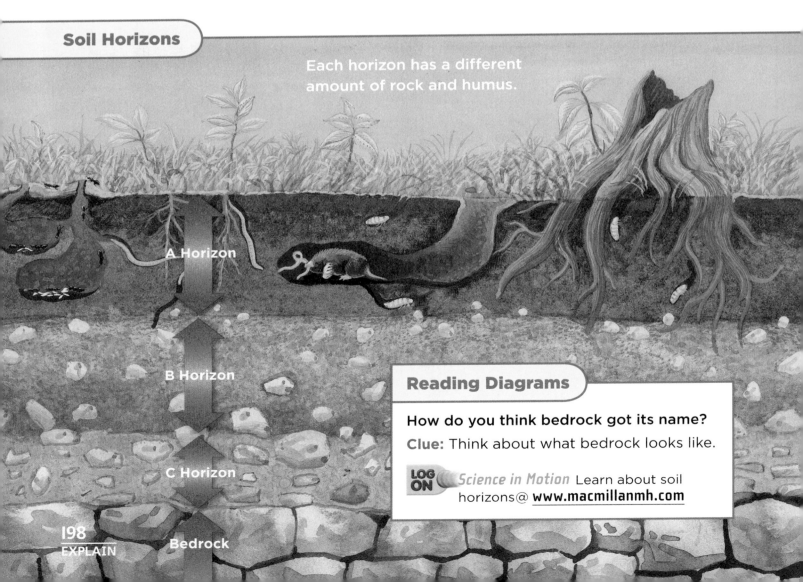

Soil Horizons

Each horizon has a different amount of rock and humus.

A Horizon

B Horizon

C Horizon

Bedrock

Reading Diagrams

How do you think bedrock got its name?

Clue: Think about what bedrock looks like.

LOG ON *Science in Motion* Learn about soil horizons@ **www.macmillanmh.com**

Lesson Review

Summarize the Main Idea

Physical weathering causes Earth's rocks to break apart into smaller pieces. (pp. 194–195)

Chemical weathering also causes rocks to break down into smaller pieces. (pp. 196–197)

Soil has weathered rock, minerals, humus, air, water, and bacteria in it. (p. 198)

Make a FOLDABLES™ Study Guide

Make a three-tab book. Use it to summarize what you learned about weathering.

Weathering

Physical Weathering

Chemical Weathering

Soil

Think, Talk, and Write

1 **Main Idea** What are four causes of weathering?

2 **Vocabulary** What is weathering?

3 **Compare and Contrast** How are physical and chemical weathering alike? How are they different?

Different   Alike   Different

4 **Critical Thinking** Natural resources are materials that are found on Earth. Why is soil an important natural resource?

5 **Test Practice** What causes soil types to be different from place to place? Choose the best answer.

  A their color

  B the size of the rocks

  C the amount of oxygen in the air

  D the kinds of rocks and humus

Writing Link

Make a Poster
Look in your neighborhood or by your school for rocks. Which rocks show signs of physical weathering? Which rocks show signs of chemical weathering? Make a poster with captions to show how the rocks are similar, yet different.

Math Link

Solve a Problem
It can take about 700 years for 2 cm of soil to form. About how long would it take a layer of topsoil 24 cm thick to form?

Communicate

You just read that physical weathering changes rocks. How do scientists figure out things like that? They do experiments, record their observations, and analyze the results. Then scientists **communicate** their experiments and findings to others. They may do this by writing, or by making oral presentations.

① Learn It

Talking, writing, and drawing are just some ways to **communicate**. Scientists talk, write, and draw to communicate their procedures for and results from an experiment. It's important to write your procedure and record data when you do an experiment. That way, others can follow your directions to see if they get the same results.

2 Try It

Follow the directions below to see if rocks carried in water weather over time. **Communicate** your results with words and pictures as you go along.

▶ Measure a piece of marble, quartz, sandstone, and talc each across its widest part. Record that data and a description of each rock in a chart like this one.

Rock	Measurements/ Descriptions at Start	Measurements/ Descriptions at End
Marble		
Quartz		
Sandstone		
Talc		

▶ Place the rocks in a plastic jar. Add just enough water in the jar to cover the rocks. Screw the lid on tightly.

▶ Shake the jar hard. Continue shaking the jar for one minute. Stop and rest your arm, then shake the jar again. Do this until you shake the jar for a total of five minutes.

▶ Remove the rocks. Measure the width of each rock again. Record this data in your chart.

▶ Communicate which rock showed the most weathering. Tell which rock showed the least. Use information from your chart for reference.

3 Apply It

What do you predict would happen if you put the same rocks back in the jar and shook it for five more minutes? For ten more minutes? Write the steps for your experiment. Then trade your steps with a partner. Can your partner follow your instructions? Can you follow your partner's instructions? **Communicate** your results. Did the class get similar results?

 4 IE 6.f. Follow a set of written instructions for a scientific investigation.

Erosion and Deposition

Look and Wonder

The Mississippi River is the second longest river in the United States. Its name means "great river." Parts of the river look brown. In fact one of the river's nicknames is "Muddy Mississippi." How do you think the river gets this way?

4 ES 5.a. Students know some changes in the earth are due to slow processes, such as erosion, and some changes are due to rapid processes, such as landslides, volcanic eruptions, and earthquakes. • **4 ES 5.c.** Students know moving water erodes landforms, reshaping the land by taking it away from some places and depositing it as pebbles, sand, silt, and mud in other places (weathering, transport, and deposition).

How can sediments enter rivers?

Purpose
Find out what sediments can do when they enter a river.

Procedure

1. **Make a Model** Mix soil, sand, and pebbles together. Place a mound of the soil mixture at one end of the pan. Press the mixture lightly. This mixture is the "land."

2. Prop up the pan on two or three books.

3. Pour a little clean water at the bottom of the pan where there is no soil. This water is the "river."

4. **Experiment** Use a watering can to pour "rainwater" over the "land."

5. **Communicate** What do you observe in the water at the bottom of the pan? Where did it come from?

Draw Conclusions

6. **Infer** How can sediments enter a river?

7. **Infer** What can sediments do to a river?

8. **Predict** What happens to sediments after they enter a river?

Explore More

Experiment Can wind add sediments to a river? Design an experiment to find out.

 4 IE 6.f. Follow a set of written instructions for a scientific investigation.

Materials

Soil

- large, deep aluminum pan
- potting soil
- sand
- pebbles
- 2 or 3 books
- water
- watering can

Step 1

Step 4

Main Idea 4 ES 5.a
4 ES 5.c

The movement of weathered rock from one place to another is called erosion. As wind and water move rock from one place to another, the shape of the land changes.

Vocabulary

erosion, p. 204

deposition, p. 205

LOG ON e-Glossary
@ www.macmillanmh.com

Reading Skill

Cause and Effect

Cause	→	Effect
	→	
	→	
	→	
	→	

What causes erosion?

You learned that weathering breaks down rocks. But what then happens to weathered rocks? Have you ever watched a river flow? You may have seen sediments and small rocks being carried along in the flowing water. These sediments and small rocks are weathered rock. The transport of weathered rock is called **erosion** (i•ROH•zhuhn). Weathering and erosion work together to change and shape the land.

Flowing Water

Flowing water is the biggest cause of erosion. Rainwater carries sediments into streams and rivers. The moving water then flows downhill and carries the sediments along. Eventually, the sediments are dropped off in a new place.

Waves also cause erosion. First, waves break rocks apart. The waves then carry the rocks and sand to a new place.

Waves transport sand, rocks, and shells and deposit them in new places. ▼

This is a satellite photograph of the Mississippi River. Sediments are deposited at the mouth of the river where it flows into the Gulf of Mexico. ▶

Wind

Wind picks up very small pieces of rock, sand, and soil. It then carries them to other places. This is erosion by wind. At the same time, wind weathers the rock by abrasion.

Dropping Off Sediments

Bits of rock, sand, and soil are picked up and transported by wind or water. Then they are dropped off. The dropping off of weathered rock is called **deposition** (dep•uh•ZISH•uhn). Rivers and streams deposit sediments along their banks, or sides. Many of the finer sediments reach the mouths, or ends, of rivers. There they are deposited in huge amounts. Winds, too, can pick up sand and soil and deposit them many miles away.

✔ *Quick Check*

Cause and Effect What are two causes of erosion?

Critical Thinking How do weathering and erosion work together?

◀ Wind and water work together to change this rock in Colorado Springs, Colorado.

The Dust Bowl

Northeast

Midwest

West

Southeast

Dust Bowl

Southwest

Reading Maps

Which areas were affected by the Dust Bowl?

Clue: Labels give information.

What affects erosion?

Some soils and rocks erode faster than others. For example, sandy soil is blown or washed away more easily than hard-packed clay. The size of sediments also affects erosion. Pieces of sand, for example, can be blown or washed away more easily than pebbles. The strength of wind and water also affects the rate of erosion. Floods, heavy rains, and strong winds cause erosion to occur quickly. Plants also affect how quickly soil erodes.

Extreme Erosion

During the 1920s, the farmers in some states farmed many acres of land. At first, harvests were plentiful. After only a few years the soil became overused. Then in 1930 a drought began. There was little rain for nearly ten years. Crops would not grow. The soil became bare and was exposed to strong winds. Without plants to hold the soil in place, the dry soil began to blow away. This event became known as the Dust Bowl.

Many farmers lost their farms during the dust storms of the 1930s.

Terrible dust storms took place. Thick, black clouds of dust swirled about for many miles. People called the dust storms "black blizzards." Dry soil blew everywhere. It got into the cracks of houses. It piled up in closets and on dishes. Up to 30 cm (12 in.) of soil were lost in some places.

Effects of the Dust Bowl

The results of the Dust Bowl were devastating. Many animals died because there were no plants for them to eat. Thousands of farmers had to leave their homes. They were forced to move west in search of a new life.

Quick Lab

Erosion Rate

1. **Make a Model** Place clay soil and sandy soil side by side in an aluminum pan. Prop the end of the pan on a pile of two or three books.

2. **Experiment** Use a watering can to slowly pour water over the soil at the propped-up end. Pour water in a back and forth motion over both soils.

3. **Observe** What happens to each soil?

4. **Draw Conclusions** Which soil has a faster rate of erosion?

Clay Soil

Sandy Soil

✔ Quick Check

Cause and Effect What caused the Dust Bowl?

Critical Thinking Which might erode the sides of a stream faster—a flood or a drought? Explain.

How can soil erosion be slowed?

The Dust Bowl taught people that it was important to *conserve* soil. Conserving soil means using methods to save it and slow erosion. Today farmers use methods to slow erosion. They plant trees between fields to slow wind erosion. They also plant crops in strips. One strip has plants to hold the soil. The next strip is planted with a food crop. Then the next year the strips are changed. This method of farming is called *strip farming*.

Another method, *contour plowing*, is used on land that slopes. Farmers plow their fields across a slope, rather than up and down. The shape of the plowed land prevents soil from eroding.

▲ Strip farming and contour plowing help to keep soil from eroding.

✔ Quick Check

Cause and Effect If farmers use contour plowing, what will happen?

Critical Thinking Could the Dust Bowl happen again? Explain.

A Living Fence

Reading Photos

How can trees slow the effects of wind on soil erosion?

Clue: Observe how the trees have been planted.

Lesson Review

Summarize the Main Idea

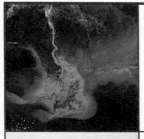 **Erosion** and **deposition** happen when sediments move from one place on Earth's surface to another. (pp. 204–205)

 Erosion is affected by soil type, sediment size, and wind and water strength. (pp. 206–207)

 There are methods farmers can use to conserve soil. (p. 208)

Make a FOLDABLES™ Study Guide

Make a trifold book. Use it to summarize what you learned about erosion and deposition.

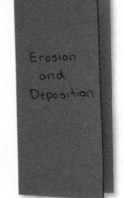

Erosion and Deposition

Think, Talk, and Write

1 **Main Idea** What do wind and water do to land?

2 **Vocabulary** What is deposition?

3 **Cause and Effect** What are some causes of erosion? What are some effects?

Cause	→	Effect
	→	
	→	
	→	
	→	

4 **Critical Thinking** How is erosion different from deposition?

5 **Test Practice** Which one of the following causes erosion?
  A soil
  B sunlight
  C waves
  D cracks in rocks

 Writing Link

Write a Story
Suppose you are a grain of sand in a stream. Write a story about traveling to the beach from the mountains.

 Social Studies

California's Central Valley
Find out about farming in California's Central Valley. How do farmers deal with erosion there? Write a report of your findings.

Be a Scientist

shallow pan

potting soil

gravel

pebbles

**plastic cup
with water**

**spray bottle
with water**

Inquiry Structured

What is erosion and deposition?

Form a Hypothesis

What happens when water erosion occurs by a stream? Write your hypothesis in the form, *"If erosion occurs near a stream, then . . ."*

Test Your Hypothesis

1. **Measure** Put 2 cm of potting soil in a shallow pan.

2. **Make a Model** Press gravel and pebbles down into the soil to make a stream bed. Mold the soil, gravel, and pebbles so they are higher on the sides than on the bottom.

Step 2

3. Use a plastic cup to gently pour water into the stream. Let the water soak in. Add more water until a stream forms.

Step 3

4. **Make a Model** Use a spray bottle to simulate rain. Spray the soil along the edge of the stream bed at one end of your stream. Continue spraying until the soil is soaked and the bank of the stream begins to erode. Record your observations.

Step 4

Draw Conclusions

5 **Infer** What was modeled in Step 4?

6 **Communicate** What happened to the soil as it entered the stream?

Inquiry Guided

How does soil get deposited?

Form a Hypothesis

What types of materials cause the most deposition to happen in a river? Answer the question in the form, *"Deposition occurs most with . . ."*

Test Your Hypothesis

Design an experiment to investigate how items in a river can cause deposition to occur. Write out the steps you will follow. Record your results and observations.

Draw Conclusions

Did your test support your hypothesis? Why or why not? Share your results with your classmates. Which materials caused the most deposition in your classmates' experiments?

Inquiry Open

What else would you like to learn about soil erosion and deposition? For example, what types of plants can decrease soil erosion during heavy rain? Design an investigation to answer your question. Your investigation must be organized to test only one variable, or one item being changed. Your investigation must be written so that another group can complete the investigation by following your instructions.

Remember to follow the steps of the scientific process.

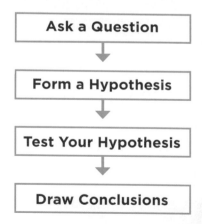

Ask a Question

Form a Hypothesis

Test Your Hypothesis

Draw Conclusions

 4 IE 6.f. Follow a set of written instructions for a scientific investigation.

Lesson 3

Landforms: Changing Over Time

Look and Wonder

Valleys, cliffs, beaches, and rocks are constantly changing. What forces could have formed this valley near Yosemite, in central California?

4 ES 5.a. Students know some changes in the earth are due to slow processes, such as erosion, and some changes are due to rapid processes, such as landslides, volcanic eruptions, and earthquakes. • **4 ES 5.c.** Students know moving water erodes landforms, reshaping the land by taking it away from some places and depositing it as pebbles, sand, silt, and mud in other places (weathering, transport, and deposition).

How does running water shape the land?

Make a Prediction

What can happen to a mountain when water moves over it? Write a prediction.

Test Your Prediction

1 **Make a Model** Place a pile of soil in the pan. Pour a small amount of water in the soil and mix it. Form a mountain by gently pressing the soil into a mound.

2 **Observe** Fill the watering can with water. Slowly pour water in a steady stream over the mountain. What happens?

Draw Conclusions

3 **Communicate** Did your results match your prediction? What happened when you poured water over your model?

4 **Draw Conclusions** What would happen to the soil if you continued to pour water over it?

5 **Infer** What can water do to the land on Earth?

Explore More

Experiment What might moving ice do to a mountain? Design an experiment to find out.

4 IE 6.a. Differentiate observation from inference (interpretation) and know scientists' explanations come partly from what they observe and partly from how they interpret their observations.

Materials

- **soil**
- **aluminum pan**
- **watering can**
- **water**

Step **1**

Step **2**

► Main Idea
4 ES 5.a
4 ES 5.c

Earth's surface is always changing. It is shaped and reshaped by water, waves, wind, and ice. Changes that occur to land can take place slowly or quickly.

► Vocabulary

landform, p. 214

canyon, p. 215

valley, p. 216

delta, p. 217

sand dune, p. 221

glacier, p. 222

LOG ON ⓔ-Glossary
@ www.macmillanmh.com

► Reading Skill

Summarize

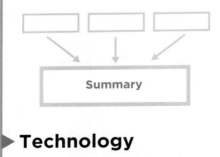

Summary

► Technology

SCIENCE QUEST ◉ Explore how landforms change over time on Science Island.

This canyon in Utah is called Dead Horse Point. ▶

What is a landform?

If you traveled by airplane across North America, you might see huge mountains. You might see deep valleys and winding rivers. In areas farther north, you might see huge sheets of ice. You might see desert areas farther south with unusually shaped rocks jutting up from the land. You might see beaches along shorelines. You might even see huge, vast, flat stretches of land without any hills or mountains. These are called *plains*. Hills, valleys, mountains, and plains are just some of the natural features on Earth's surface. Natural features on Earth's surface are called **landforms**.

Canyon Formation

Fast Changes, Slow Changes

Some landforms change in a short period of time—sometimes hours. A mudslide quickly changes a hillside, for example. You will learn about some fast changes to land in the next chapter. Most landforms, however, change over very long periods of time. The landform below took millions of years to form. Swiftly running water carved out the land under the Colorado River. It then carried away the broken rocks and sediments. The riverbed became deeper and deeper. The river eventually carved a canyon.

A **canyon** is a deep, narrow valley with steep sides. Canyons often have rivers at the bottom.

In this lesson, you will learn how running water, waves, wind, and ice change land. Changes to land are due to weathering, erosion, and deposition.

✓ Quick Check

Summarize How do canyons form?

Critical Thinking Why does a canyon take a long time to form?

Reading Photos

How do you know that this canyon is still forming?

Clue: Look at the bottom of the canyon.

High in the mountains melting snow and rainwater flow downhill.

Mountain streams form valleys.

How can running water change land?

Rainfall that does not soak into the ground flows downhill. As it flows, the water forms a channel. The water flows into streams and rivers. It flows from the tops of mountains to the sea. Running water changes the land along the sides and bottoms of streams and rivers. Here is one example of how running water can change land.

Down from the Mountains

High in the mountains rain falls and snow melts. The water begins its journey downhill. The water forms small streams. As small streams of water come together, they form small rivers. As the rivers journey downhill, they cut away land along their sides and carry away sediments. This cutting away of the land forms a **valley**. In high mountains, the rivers cut deep valleys shaped like the letter V.

Rivers Curve

As water continues to move downhill off a mountain, the land becomes flatter. Here the river runs a bit slower. It becomes wider. The river erodes land on one side and deposits sediments along the other side. This causes the river to develop curves. Older rivers form very broad, looping curves. Over time the curves of the river change.

Into the Ocean

Rivers may empty into other rivers. A river may eventually empty into the ocean. Here the river runs even more slowly. It drops sediments that have been carried for miles at the mouth of the river. The sediments form an area of land called a **delta**.

✔ *Quick Check*

Summarize Tell why rivers form curves.

Critical Thinking Why do you think delta soils are fertile?

Sediments are deposited at the mouth of the river. These sediments form an area of land called a delta.

The land flattens and water begins to flow in curves, cutting along riverbanks.

Wave action will eventually erode this cliff in Cabo San Lucas, Mexico. ▶

◀ Rocky coastlines, like this one, are worn away by wave action.

How can waves change land?

Did you ever feel the power of ocean waves? The force of waves can change a beach. Waves can pick up tons of sand. The sand can be deposited somewhere else. The size of a beach may shrink in one place, but grow in another. During a storm, powerful winds cause very large waves. The waves can wash away much of a beach in just a few hours!

Changing Rocky Cliffs

Over time the powerful force of waves can change rocky cliffs. Waves pound a cliff. The constant action of waves breaks large chunks of rock off the bottom of the cliff. The chunks fall. Waves then grind these rock chunks into smaller rocks. As the bottom part of the cliff erodes, it hollows out the base of the cliff. When the top part of the cliff is no longer supported, it collapses and falls. Then waves break the large chunks of rock into smaller pieces. The smaller rocks are washed away. Ever so slowly, the rocky cliffs become smaller and smaller.

Barrier Islands

Barrier islands are long, narrow strips of land formed by deposits of sand. They run parallel to a coast. The islands form a barrier between the coast and the ocean. Barrier islands protect coastlines from erosion. Most eastern states of the United States have barrier islands.

Barrier islands are constantly reshaped by waves. Waves both remove and deposit sediments on the side of the island that faces the open ocean. Waters on the side that faces the coast change the island, too. Those waters bring sand to the island. On barrier islands, the side facing the coast gets built up while the other side erodes.

✔ Quick Check

Summarize Tell how waves change cliffs.

Critical Thinking What might happen to a coast if barrier islands erode away?

▼ Barrier islands protect the coast of Long Island in New York.

ocean

bay

coast

barrier island

How does wind change land?

Wind can act like a sandblaster. Wind carrying sand and bits of rock scratches the surface of rocks like sandpaper. This causes small bits of rock to break off. Then the wind picks up the new bits and carries them away. The erosion of rocks by wind takes many, many years.

Rock Sculptures

In many dry areas like the American Southwest, wind erosion sculpts rocks. Swirling sand carried by wind attacks cracks in rocks. It attacks the softer spots of rock, too. This is especially true of sandstone. Heavy rains also wash away loose rock pieces. The result is unusual rock formations. Eventually every part of a rock will be eroded by wind and water.

▲ Winds constantly change the shape of sand dunes, such as these in Death Valley, California.

This pedestal rock is found in Bisti Badlands Wilderness Area in New Mexico. ▼

Disappearing Rocks

Reading Photos

Where is this rock more sculpted? Why?

Clue: Think about where sand and water travel.

How Sand Dunes Form

1. Wear safety goggles. Pour a 2-cm layer of sand in the tray. Place a pebble in the tray.

2. **Observe** Gently blow through a straw at the sand. Blow in the direction of the pebble. What happens?

⚠ **Be Careful.**

3. **Infer** How does this activity show how some sand dunes are formed?

Sand Dunes

Have you ever been to a beach and tumbled down tall hills of sand? How did the hills get there? Wind did it! Winds can blow sand into hills called **sand dunes**. Sand dunes are formed by particles of sand that are picked up by wind. As dry sand blows, objects such as rocks or grasses block it. The movement of the sand particles is slowed by the object. A sand dune begins to take shape.

There are different kinds of sand dunes. Each kind has a different shape. Some are shaped like crescent moons. Others, called "sword" dunes, are long, wavy ridges. Another kind of sand dune is called a "star" dune.

✔ Quick Check

Summarize How is land shaped by wind?

Critical Thinking Why do you think sand dunes have different shapes?

▲ Hubbard Glacier in Alaska is 122 kilometers (76 miles) long.

▲ A glacier leaves a *U*-shaped valley behind, like the one shown below in White River National Forest, Colorado. ▼

How can ice change land?

On colder parts of Earth, large, thick sheets of ice called **glaciers** (GLAY•shuhrz) slowly creep over the land. Millions of years ago, glaciers covered much of Earth.

Glaciers are formed in cold areas where more snow falls than can melt. The thick snow slowly changes into ice. The bottom becomes fluid-like. It begins to flow downhill. The ice at the bottom and sides of a glacier freezes onto rocks. As the glacier continues to move, it tears the rocks right from the ground. The glacier tears rocks from the sides of a valley as well. Sometimes rocks the size of a house are torn up and moved. A glacier widens, deepens, and straightens a valley into a *U* shape.

✔ Quick Check

Summarize How can a glacier change the land?

Critical Thinking Why do you think the valleys formed by glaciers are in the shape of a *U*?

Lesson Review

Summarize the Main Idea

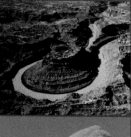

Erosion and weathering are processes that usually change **landforms** slowly. (pp. 214–215)

Water, waves, and wind weather and erode Earth's surface. (pp. 216–221)

Glaciers shape the land as they move over it. (p. 222)

Make a **FOLDABLES**™ Study Guide

Make a layered-look book. Use it to summarize what you learned about changing landforms.

Think, Talk, and Write

1 **Main Idea** Does Earth's surface stay the same? Explain your answer.

2 **Vocabulary** What is a glacier?

3 **Summarize** How does a sand dune form?

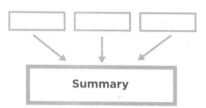

Summary

4 **Critical Thinking** Compare the way a glacier changes Earth's surface to the way water running down a mountain changes Earth's surface.

5 **Test Practice** Which change to Earth's surface can happen quickly?

   A a canyon forms

   B a valley forms

   C a beach erodes

   D a glacier forms

Writing Link

Expository Writing
Research the effects of floods and sediments on the Sacramento Delta area of California. Write a report about your findings.

Math Link

Use Numbers
Each year the Mississippi River dumps 516 million tons of eroded materials into the sea. Three hundred forty million tons of this are fine sediments. How many tons of eroded materials are *not* fine sediments? Write the number.

Land Over Time

Mountains seem like mighty giants. But are they? Weathering can break down even the mightiest mountain. Let's see how.

Wind carries seeds. Some seeds may land on patches of soil on rock and sprout. The roots find small cracks in the rock. The roots grow larger. At the same time, rains fill the cracks. When it gets cold, the water freezes. As a result, the ice expands and widens the cracks more. Eventually, the roots get thicker. The cracks widen more until some pieces of the rock break off. In time, these smaller pieces of rock will become smaller yet. Over millions of years, weathering will break the mountain down.

Expository writing

▶ presents the main idea in a topic sentence and supports it with facts and details

▶ tells only the important information

▶ draws a conclusion based on the information presented

Greetings from California

Write About It

Expository Writing Write a paragraph in which you summarize "Land Over Time." In your own words, tell the main idea. Write the most important details.

 e-Journal Write about it online @ **www.macmillanmh.com**

ELA W 4.2.4. Write summaries that contain the main ideas of the reading selection and the most significant details.

Mt. McKinley   Mt. Whitney   Mt. Shasta   Wheeler Peak

Disappearing Mountains

This table shows the heights of some mountain peaks in the United States.

Heights of Mountain Peaks			
Mountain Peak	State	Height (meters)	Height (feet)
Mt. McKinley	Alaska	6,194	20,320
Mt. Whitney	California	4,417	14,491
Mt. Shasta	California	4,317	14,162
Wheeler Peak	Nevada	3,982	13,065

Mountains erode by small amounts each year. Suppose Mt. McKinley erodes 2 feet each year. How many years would it take for the mountain to be 20,300 feet?

 Solve It

If the erosion rate is 1 meter each year, what will be the height of:

1. Mt. Shasta in 20 years?
2. Mt. Whitney in 15 years?
3. Wheeler Peak in 80 years?

Problem Solving

► To find the number of years, you can skip count backward by 2 from 20,320 ft. to 20,300 ft.:

20,320   20,318   20,316
20,314   20,312   20,310
20,308   20,306   20,304
20,302   20,300

It would take 10 years.

► Another way is to find the number of feet lost. Then you can divide the difference of feet by 2.

20,320 − 20,300 = 20 ft., and 20 ÷ 2 = 10.

It would take 10 years.

 MA NS 4.3.1. Demonstrate an understanding of, and the ability to use, standard algorithms for the addition and subtraction of multidigit numbers.

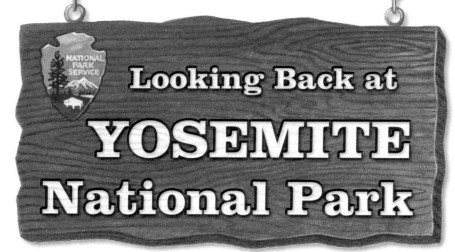

Looking Back at **YOSEMITE National Park**

Yosemite Valley once looked very different than it does now. How can geologists find out how it has changed? They can read the rocks to investigate how Yosemite Valley got to look the way it does today.

AMERICAN MUSEUM OF NATURAL HISTORY

ELA R 4.2.1 Identify structural patterns found in informational text (e.g., compare and contrast, cause and effect, sequential or chronological order, proposition and support) to strengthen comprehension.

In 1906, President Theodore Roosevelt made Yosemite Valley and its surrounding forests a national park. Now each year millions of people visit Yosemite National Park to explore and learn about its geological clues for themselves.

▲ President Roosevelt and John Muir at Glacier Point in Yosemite, California

500 million years ago

A sea covers the area that is now Yosemite. Sediments slowly build up on the ocean floor, growing thousands of feet high. The lower layers become rock.

90 million years ago

Underground, magma rises and cools into a huge block of granite.

10–5 million years ago

The Sierra Nevada is formed as the block of granite is pushed upwards. The Merced River carves Yosemite Valley into a canyon.

3–1 million years ago

An ice age brings glaciers that fill the V-shaped valley. They widen it, deepen it, and carve it into a U-shaped valley.

10,000 years ago

The last glacier finally melts. Lake Yosemite is formed when rocks dam the valley. Creeks plunge off cliffs, creating waterfalls.

Write About It

Summarize Write a few sentences that tell about the history of Yosemite National Park from long ago to the present. Use a summary chart to help organize your writing.

LOG ON e-Journal Write about it online @ www.macmillanmh.com

A summary

▶ states the main ideas

▶ includes the most important details

▶ uses your own words

Summarize the Main Ideas

Certain natural processes cause rocks to break down into smaller pieces. These smaller pieces help to form Earth's different soils. (pp. 192–199)

The movement of weathered rock from one place to another changes the shape of the land. (pp. 202–209)

Earth's surface is shaped and reshaped by running water, waves, wind, and ice. (pp. 212–223)

Make a **FOLDABLES**™ Study Guide

Tape your lesson study guides to a piece of paper as shown. Use your study guide to review what you have learned in this chapter.

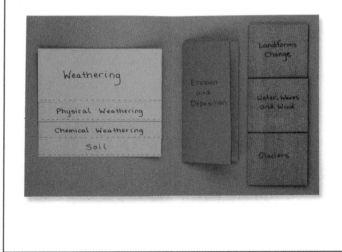

Fill each blank with the best word from the list.

canyon, p. 215   **glacier**, p. 222

chemical weathering, p. 196   **landform**, p. 214

deposition, p. 205   **physical weathering**, p. 194

erosion, p. 204   **sand dune**, p. 221

1. A U-shaped valley is formed by a _____. 4 ES 5.c

2. Sediments are dropped along a river's banks by _____. 4 ES 5.c

3. A limestone cave is formed by _____. 4 ES 5.b

4. Wind forms a _____. 4 ES 5.c

5. The breaking down of rock in which its chemical makeup does not change is called _____. 4 ES 5.b

6. A valley is a kind of _____. 4 ES 5.c

7. A fast-running river can carve out a deep _____. 4 ES 5.c

8. The transport of weathered material is called _____. 4 ES 5.a

LOG ON ℮-Review Summaries and quizzes online @ **www.macmillanmh.com**

Answer each of the following in complete sentences.

9. Summarize Describe the events that result in a river that curves back and forth. 4 ES 5.c

10. Communicate Design a poster that explains different ways to slow erosion. 4 ES 5.a

11. Critical Thinking Imagine you are climbing a mountain. You discover a fossil of a fish. Explain how this can happen. 4 ES 5.a

12. Explanatory Writing Explain what caused the Dust Bowl to happen. 4 ES 5.a

 What causes Earth's surface to change slowly?

CHAPTER 4

Land Features

fjord   rift valley   wadi   sea stack

gorge   butte   limestone cave

What to Do

1. Choose one of the land features from the list above. Find out how weathering and erosion formed it.

2. Make a poster of the land feature you chose. Draw and label it. You might include an illustration from a magazine or a photo that you find on the Internet.

3. Write a definition of the land feature. Also include information about how weathering and erosion formed this land feature. Be sure to identify the cause or causes of erosion as wind, running water, waves, or ice.

4. Share your poster with the class. What do all of the land features have in common?

Limestone Cave

A limestone cave forms as a result of chemical weathering.

1 A large rock breaks into smaller pieces through a process called 4 ES 5.b

 A erosion.

 B sedimentation.

 C freezing and thawing.

 D weathering.

2 Which one of the following is usually a slow process? 4 ES 5.a

 A beach erosion by a storm

 B a volcanic eruption

 C weathering by freezing and thawing

 D a landslide

3 The sediments along the side of this stream are an example of 4 ES 5.c

 A deposition.

 B transport.

 C erosion.

 D weathering.

4 A student conducted multiple trials on different types of soils to see which type erodes fastest. The soils were in pans each propped up at the same angle. She slowly poured water from a watering can over the soil. She continued pouring until all of the soil had eroded away. Then she averaged and recorded her findings in the chart below. 4 IE 6.d

Soils	
Soil Description	**Time to Erode**
sandy soil	20 seconds
topsoil	40 seconds
clay soil	1 minute

Which one of the following statements *best* describes her results?

 A Clay soil will erode the fastest.

 B Sandy soil will erode the fastest.

 C Topsoil will erode the slowest.

 D Sandy soil will erode the slowest.

5 A student completed an experiment only once. The results did not turn out as she predicted. What should she do next? 4 IE 6.d

 A Do the experiment again.

 B Change her prediction to fit the results.

 C Throw her data table away.

 D Decide it was a good experiment.

6 Which one of the following is an example of chemical weathering? 4 ES 5.b

   A bits of sand striking rock surfaces

   B freezing and thawing of rocks

   C carbonic acid reacting with minerals in rock

   D roots growing in the cracks of rocks

7 Which one of the following is the biggest cause of erosion? 4 ES 5.a

   A landslides

   B flowing water

   C wind

   D weathering

8 What is the usual order by which a landform is changed? 4 ES 5.c

   A deposition, erosion, weathering

   B weathering, deposition, erosion

   C erosion, deposition, weathering

   D weathering, erosion, deposition

9 What happens during physical weathering? Choose the *best* answer. 4 ES 5.b

   A It snows.

   B Rain freezes in the cracks of rocks.

   C The size and shape of rocks are changed.

   D The roots of plants widen cracks in rocks.

10 Each of the following statements about physical and chemical weathering is true EXCEPT 4 ES 5.b

   A humus forms.

   B rocks get smaller.

   C mountains get smaller.

   D soil forms.

11 Which landform is the result of deposition? 4 ES 5.c

   A a delta

   B a canyon

   C a valley

   D a plain

Fast Changes on Earth

⭐ What causes Earth's surface to change quickly?

 **4 ES 5.** Waves, wind, water, and ice shape and reshape Earth's land surface.

233

ELA R 4.2.6. Distinguish between cause and effect and between fact and opinion in expository text. **ELA W 4.2.4.** Write summaries that contain the main ideas of the reading selection and the most significant details.

homes in the Los Angeles, California area damaged by mudslides

California's Weather Woes

When it rains, it pours! From February 17 to 23, Southern California got more rain than it could absorb. The rain broke local records in Los Angeles, where rainfall totaled 9.14 inches. That's only six inches less than the city usually gets in an entire year!

Though the sun finally came out, the damage from the supersize storm will be long-lasting. Cleanup is both expensive and exhausting. Firefighters worked overtime responding to calls for help. Nine people died in weather-related accidents.

Mudslides on hills caused some houses to collapse. Many people were forced to leave their homes.

 Write About It

Response to Literature This article tells how during one week in February, California got very heavy rains. Write a summary of the article. Start by telling the main idea. Then include the effects of the heavy rains.

 e-Journal Write about it online @ **www.macmillanmh.com**

Landslides

Look and Wonder

This is Highway 1 in Big Sur, California. Look at the mountains and the rocks on the beach. How did the rocks get there?

4 ES 5.a. Students know some changes in the earth are due to slow processes, such as erosion, and some changes are due to rapid processes, such as landslides, volcanic eruptions, and earthquakes.

How does gravity affect materials on Earth?

Make a Prediction

Predict what gravity will do to rocks and soil on a hill.

Test Your Prediction

1. Stir equal amounts of sand, gravel, and soil in the pan. Pat the mixture into a flat layer.

2. **Predict** What will happen when you raise one end of the pan? Record your prediction.

3. **Observe** Raise one end of the pan 4 cm at a time. Observe what happens. Make a data table to record your results.

* **deep aluminum baking pan**
* **measuring cup**
* **sand**
* **gravel**
* **potting soil**
* **metric ruler**

Height of Pan	Observations
4 cm	
8 cm	

Step 1

Draw Conclusions

4. **Draw Conclusions** What caused the materials in the pan to change?

Explore More

Experiment What might happen if you poured water on the soil mixture as you raised the pan? How might this affect the results? Try it.

 4 IE 6.d. Conduct multiple trials to test a prediction and draw conclusions about the relationships between predictions and results.

Step 3

► Main Idea   4 ES 5.a

Some changes to Earth's surface take place quickly. Gravity and fast-flowing water can cause rapid changes on Earth.

► Vocabulary

gravity, p. 238

landslide, p. 238

flood, p. 240

mudslide, p. 241

LOG ON **e-Glossary**

@ www.macmillanmh.com

► Reading Skill

Cause and Effect

Cause	→	Effect
	→	
	→	
	→	
	→	

► Technology

SCIENCE QUEST Explore changing landforms on Science Island.

How do landslides change the land quickly?

Did you ever see a pile of rocks in a fallen rock zone? How did the rocks get there? Part of the answer is a force called gravity. **Gravity** is a pulling force that acts on all objects.

In many places, Earth's surface is angled, or sloped. Gravity pulls materials like weathered rocks and soil from a high place to a low place. This happens all the time. The downhill movement of loose rock and soil can happen slowly. This might be only one or two centimeters a year. When a large amount of loose rock and soil moves rapidly, a **landslide** occurs.

This landslide in California was caused by the Loma Prieta earthquake in 1989.

La Conchita Landslide

Over 35 homes were damaged in the La Conchita landslide in January of 2005.

Reading Photos

How can a landslide cause property damage?
Clue: Look at the bottom of this mountain.

Causes of Landslides

Sometimes a landslide is caused by things that quickly shift the land, such as an earthquake. Fires, volcanic eruptions, and storms can also cause landslides. Building in sloped areas and clearing the land can cause landslides, too.

Landslides can even occur due to the freezing and thawing of rocks. When water freezes in the cracks of rocks, it can split them apart. The pieces of rock can become loose and quickly slide down a slope. No matter what causes a landslide, gravity plays the main role.

Effects of Landslides

A landslide can move millions of kilograms of soil and rock. It can carry trees, homes, and cars with it. A landslide can cause property damage. In California, landslides often occur along the coast and in the mountains.

✔ Quick Check

Cause and Effect What is one cause of a landslide?

Critical Thinking Why can landslides happen on sloped areas anywhere in the United States?

Reading Photos

Why did flooding along the Mississippi River cause billions of dollars in damage in the early 1990s?

Clue: Look at what these photos show you about flooding.

How do floods change the land quickly?

You learned how moving water changes land slowly to form a canyon. Moving water can also cause land to change quickly. Heavy rains bring lots of water. Often the water does not soak into the ground quickly enough. The ground may not be able to hold any more water. When this happens, water runs on top of the land. It may flow into streams and rivers. The sides of a stream or river may overflow, causing a **flood**. In cities, water drains may not be able to carry water away fast enough. The drains overflow and the streets become flooded.

Effects of Floods

Homes, cars, and buildings can be damaged by floodwaters. Floods carry mud into homes and streets. When the floodwaters go down, the mud is left behind.

Floodwaters erode soil quickly. Some floodwaters are so strong they may wash away soil that supports bridges and roads, causing them to collapse. Floodwaters can also wash away anything in their path, including trees, animals, and cars.

Floods and Mudslides

Heavy rains can soak the land on a slope. The land may change into a river of mud and rock. This is called a **mudslide**. Large amounts of soil and other materials are left behind by a mudslide. This means water from a flood may not be able to drain properly. The damage caused by flooding may be made worse by the materials left behind by the mudslide.

This car in San Bernardino was buried by a mudslide on December 25, 2003. ▼

≡*Quick Lab*

Flooding the Land

1. Pile an equal amount of soil and rocks in one corner of a pan to form a steep slope. Place small twigs in the soil to represent trees.

2. Use the watering can to quickly pour water over all parts of the pan. This models rain.

3. **Observe** When did it begin to flood?

4. **Observe** What happens to the rocks, soil, and "trees"?

✔ *Quick Check*

Cause and Effect What damage can a flood cause?

Critical Thinking How is a mudslide different from a landslide?

What are some safety tips for landslides and floods?

Landslides and floods happen in all parts of the United States. There is not much that can be done to prevent a landslide or flood. There are things that people can do to stay safe when they are likely to happen.

FLOOD AREA

On the Lookout for Landslides

- During heavy rains, listen to local news reports for possible landslide warnings.
- Be aware of signs of a possible landslide. These include small slides and new cracks in foundations of buildings. They also include tilting trees and telephone poles. Listen for unusual sounds like cracking trees.
- If you are near a landslide, move away from its path. If you can't, curl up into a tight ball. This will help to protect your head.

On the Lookout for Floods

- During heavy rains, listen to local weather reports for possible flood warnings.
- Know the meanings of terms used in weather reports. A flood watch means that flooding is possible. A flood warning means that a flood is occurring or will occur soon.
- If there is a flood watch for your area, be ready to leave right away. If there is a warning for your area, move to higher ground.
- If caught in a flood, do not walk in moving water. If you must walk, walk where the water is not moving.

FALLING ROCKS

✓ *Quick Check*

Cause and Effect What is the effect of being prepared for a flood or a landslide?

Critical Thinking You are on high ground in an area that has flooded. Rescue teams are on their way. Should you stay or leave? Why?

Lesson Review

Summarize the Main Idea

Landslides change the shape of a hill or mountain rapidly. (pp. 238–239)

Floods and **mudslides** change the land quickly and may cause damage to property. (pp. 240–241)

FLOOD AREA

You can **protect yourself** from landslides, mudslides, and floods by being prepared. (p. 242)

Make a **FOLDABLES**™ Study Guide

Make a three-tab book. Use it to summarize what you learned about landslides, floods, and mudslides.

Landslides

Floods and Mudslides

Protect Yourself

Think, Talk, and Write

1. **Main Idea** What two things are responsible for causing the fast changes on Earth that you learned about in this lesson?

2. **Vocabulary** What is a landslide?

3. **Cause and Effect** What is the effect of landslides, floods, and mudslides on land?

Cause → Effect
→
→
→
→

4. **Critical Thinking** Why wouldn't it be a good idea to drive a car onto a flooded road?

5. **Test Practice** Which one of the following can cause a landslide to happen?

   A an earthquake
   B a river or stream
   C wind
   D a bridge

Writing Link

Persuasive Writing
Do you think people should be allowed to build homes in places where landslides or floods are likely to happen? Write about it. Include facts to back up your opinion.

Health Link

Make a Poster
Do research online to find out more about how to prepare for and stay safe during landslides and floods. Make a poster that shows what you found.

Experiment

You just read that soil, rocks, and trees slide down a hill or mountain rapidly during a landslide. Scientists learn a lot about landslides by doing **experiments** and drawing conclusions from the results.

① Learn It

When you **experiment**, you make and follow a procedure to test a hypothesis. It's important to record what you observe while you experiment. That information can help you draw a conclusion about whether your hypothesis is supported. It is also important to try your procedure several times. That way, you know if your results are true.

② Try It

Do you think that anything can be done to lessen damage from landslides on hilly landscapes? Write your idea in the form of a hypothesis. Then **experiment** and test your hypothesis by following the procedure below.

Procedure

① Spread soil in the bottom of a long, planter box. Push rocks, twig-trees, and small, wooden blocks (houses) into the soil. Sprinkle the soil with water until it is damp.

② Cover a table with a plastic tablecloth. Set the box on it and prop up one end of the box with two or three large books. Place a cookie tray under the other end of the box.

3 Predict what would happen to the soil in a heavy rainstorm. Record your prediction in a chart like this.

Step	Predictions	What I Observed
Step 3: rainstorm on unprotected landscape		
Step 5: wall near top		
Step 6: barrier near bottom		

4 Use a watering can to pour water at the high end of the box. Record what happens.

5 Repeat the activity. This time, bury a block in the soil near the top of the box to make a wall.

6 Repeat the activity. This time, stick a piece of wood as wide as the box into the soil near the low end of the box to make a fence, or barrier.

Draw Conclusions

▶ Based on the results of your experiment, can anything be done to prevent or lessen damage caused by landslides? Explain your answer.

▶ Was your hypothesis supported or not? Explain.

3 Apply It

What do you hypothesize would happen if the wooden barrier were near the top of the hill? If there was one barrier at the top and one at the bottom? If every house had a wooden fence around it? Design an **experiment** to test one of those ideas, or one of your own. Remember to write your hypothesis and predictions, record your observations, and draw conclusions from your observations.

4 IE 6.d. Conduct multiple trials to test a prediction and draw conclusions about the relationships between predictions and results.

Lesson 2
Earthquakes

Look and Wonder

In 1989, the third game of the World Series was about to begin. Suddenly, in the San Francisco Bay area, bridges and buildings began to shake. Some buildings collapsed. What caused the earth to move?

 **4 ES 5.a.** Students know some changes in the earth are due to slow processes, such as erosion, and some changes are due to rapid processes, such as landslides, volcanic eruptions, and earthquakes.

246
ENGAGE

What happens when the ground moves?

Purpose

When the ground moves, land can change. Find out what kinds of changes can happen.

Procedure

1 **Make a Model** Place the books side by side. Make sure there is a tiny space between them. Build a house from sugar cubes across the books.

2 **Experiment** With a pencil, tap the edge of one book gently. What happens? Tap the edge of one book with more force. Record your observations.

3 **Experiment** Move the books in opposite directions. Record your observations.

Draw Conclusions

4 **Compare** How does the damage caused by moving the books in opposite directions compare to the damage caused by tapping?

5 **Infer** What do you think happens when Earth's surface moves?

Explore More

What could happen to a mountain if the surface below it began to move? Model it.

4 IE 6.a. Differentiate observation from inference (interpretation) and know scientists' explanations come partly from what they observe and partly from how they interpret their observations.

Materials

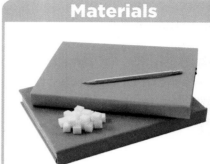

- **2 identical books**
- **sugar cubes**
- **pencil**

Step **1**

Step **2**

Main Idea 4 ES 5.a

Earth's outer layer, the crust, is made up of large slabs of rock called plates. The sudden movement of these plates causes changes to occur on Earth's surface.

Vocabulary

crust, p. 248

plates, p. 248

fault, p. 249

earthquake, p. 249

tsunami, p. 252

LOG ON ⊜-Glossary
@ www.macmillanmh.com

Reading Skill

Cause and Effect

Cause	→	Effect
	→	
	→	
	→	
	→	

What are earthquakes?

You know that Earth's surface is always changing. Most changes occur very slowly over long periods of time. However, some changes can occur very quickly. For example, the sudden shifting of Earth's crust during the 1989 World Series changed Earth's surface in just 15 seconds. The **crust** is Earth's outermost layer. What causes the crust to shift or move? The answer is found in the way that Earth's crust is put together.

Earth's Moving Crust

Earth is made up of layers. The crust is the thinnest layer. It is made up of gigantic slabs of rock, called **plates**. The map on the next page shows that the plates fit together like the pieces of a puzzle. The plates are always moving.

Route 14 near Sylmar, California was heavily damaged as the result of an earthquake on January 17, 1994. ▼

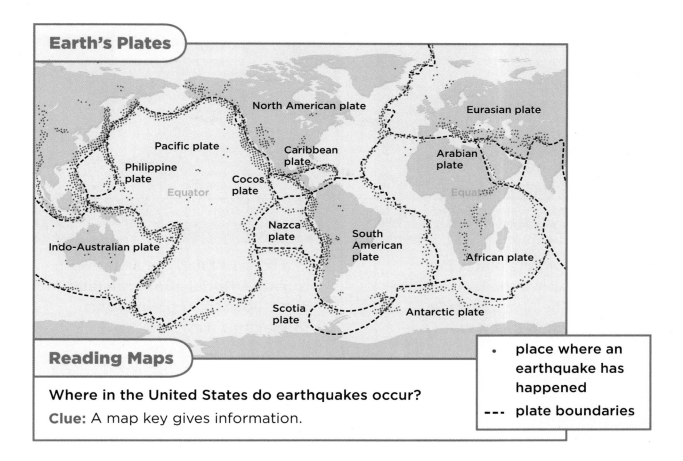

Earth's Plates

North American plate

Eurasian plate

Pacific plate

Caribbean plate

Arabian plate

Philippine plate

Cocos plate

Equator

Equator

Nazca plate

Indo-Australian plate

South American plate

African plate

Scotia plate

Antarctic plate

Reading Maps

Where in the United States do earthquakes occur?

Clue: A map key gives information.

- • place where an earthquake has happened
- --- plate boundaries

There are breaks or cracks in Earth's crust where the plates come together. These cracks are called **faults**. Some places Earth's plates slide slowly past each other along a fault. Some places the plates push together or move under or over each other. At other places, the plates move apart. When plates move, earthquakes may occur. **Earthquakes** are movements in Earth's crust that are caused by a sudden shift of Earth's plates. Earthquakes are not the only changes that happen when plates move. Mountains and volcanoes form as plates move, too.

Where Earthquakes Happen

Not all places on Earth have earthquakes. As the red dots show on the map above, most earthquakes happen near the edges of Earth's plates. There is an area around the Pacific Ocean where some of Earth's plates meet. It is here that most earthquakes happen.

✔ Quick Check

Cause and Effect What can happen when plates move?

Critical Thinking How is where earthquakes happen related to Earth's plates?

Normal Fault

Reverse Fault

▲ In a *normal fault*, the plates pull apart. Rocks above the fault surface move down. The Sierra Nevada mountains formed this way.

▲ In a *reverse fault*, the plates push together. Rocks above the fault move upward. The Himalayas formed this way.

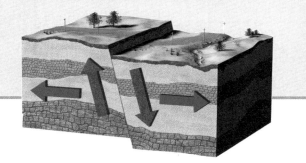

What causes an earthquake?

Most earthquakes happen where Earth's plates meet. The plates are always moving. Sometimes they move slowly, only a few centimeters a year. The slow movement along faults is called *creep*. In places where the faults are creeping, large earthquakes do not usually occur.

At other times, however, the motion is sudden. The energy released by the sudden motion of plates shakes the crust. It can set a large earthquake in motion.

Three Types of Faults

Earth's plates move in different directions. This causes different kinds of faults to form. The different faults are shown on these pages.

Along their edges, some plates pull apart. When this happens, rocks above the fault move down. Along other edges, some plates push together. This causes rocks above the fault to move upward. Finally, some plates slide past each other. In this type of fault, the rocks do not move up or down, they just slide.

250
EXPLAIN

Strike-Slip Fault

▲ In a *strike-slip fault,* rocks slide past each other in different directions. The San Andreas Fault is an example of this.

An Earthquake's Vibrations

During an earthquake the ground may vibrate, or shake. It may seem to roll. Sometimes the ground will split open. The vibrations of an earthquake are strongest where the earthquake first begins—below the ground. The vibrations move through Earth's crust in all directions. Did you ever drop a pebble in water? Did you see how the ripples of water moved? The vibrations of an earthquake move in a similar way. As the vibrations travel away from the center of the earthquake, they weaken. Even so, the vibrations may be felt for hundreds of kilometers!

Quick Lab

Types of Faults

1. **Observe** Study the diagrams on these pages.

2. **Make a Model** Use blocks to show the movement of rock in each kind of fault.

3. **Infer** Which type of fault might cause a mountain to be built up?

✓ Quick Check

Cause and Effect What causes an earthquake to happen?

Critical Thinking An earthquake's vibrations weaken as they move away from its center. Why do you think this happens?

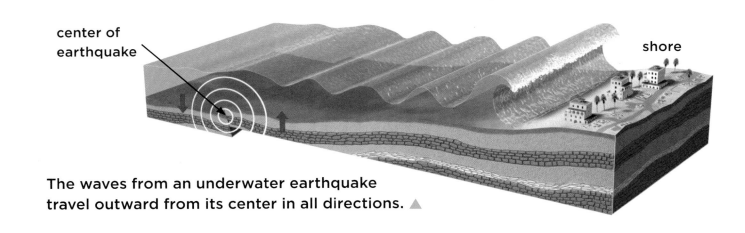

center of earthquake

shore

The waves from an underwater earthquake travel outward from its center in all directions. ▲

What is a tsunami?

Did you ever watch ocean waves? The waves rise and fall along the shore. Sometimes a giant ocean wave, called a **tsunami** (sew•NAH•mee), occurs. Tsunamis are usually caused by earthquakes on the ocean floor. Only a few are caused by underwater landslides and volcanoes.

The force of an earthquake on the ocean floor can cause a large wave to form. In the middle of the ocean, a tsunami may pass under a ship without being noticed. That is because the wave may not be very high. As the wave moves closer to the shore, it drags along the ocean floor. This slows the wave down. Soon the wave gets higher.

Tsunami Aftermath

before

after

Reading Photos

What changes did a tsunami cause here?

Clue: Look at the "after" photo. Compare it with the "before" photo.

▲ At least 283,000 people lost their lives in the tsunami of December 2004. Most of those people were from Sumatra.

Effects of Tsunamis

A tsunami can cause a great deal of damage when it reaches land. Sometimes a tsunami is one huge wall of water. At other times, it may be a series of smaller waves. Tsunami waves can travel at great speeds—up to 960 kilometers (600 miles) per hour. That is as fast as some jet planes. Tall or not, one wave or more, tsunamis can wash away shores and damage property. They can also harm people and animals.

In December of 2004, a large earthquake took place in the Indian Ocean. It happened off the western coast of Sumatra. Waves on Sumatra were up to 30 meters (100 feet) high.

Two hours after the earthquake, a tsunami struck Sri Lanka 1,200 kilometers (750 miles) away. Waves there were about 9 meters (30 feet) high. Seven hours after the earthquake, large waves reached Port Elizabeth, South Africa. That is more than 8,000 kilometers (5,000 miles) away from where the earthquake happened.

✔ Quick Check

Cause and Effect What causes a tsunami?

Critical Thinking When might an earthquake that occurs on land cause a tsunami to occur?

What are some safety tips for earthquakes and tsunamis?

You live in an area where earthquakes can happen. If you live on the coast, a tsunami could happen, too. Here are some things that people can do to stay safe where earthquakes and tsunamis are likely to happen.

Earthquake Safety

- Place large, heavy, or breakable objects on lower shelves. Bolt down heavy appliances.
- Locate safe spots in your house. This might be under a sturdy table or against an inside wall.
- Hold family earthquake drills. Find a safe spot, then drop, cover, and hold on. Stay away from glass and things that could fall on you. Arrange a meeting place outside your home.

- If outside during a quake, move quickly to an open space. Avoid buildings, power lines, trees, or things that may fall on you.
- If you are in a car, the driver should stop driving. Never stop under a tree or under a bridge. Stay in the car.
- If you are trapped under debris, don't move or kick. Cover your mouth.

Tsunami Safety

- If you live near the coast and you hear of an earthquake, listen to local news reports for possible tsunami warnings.

- If there is a tsunami warning for your area, move to high ground right away. Do not stay to gather your things.

✔ Quick Check

Cause and Effect An earthquake strikes. You are inside your home. What might happen if you do not take cover?

Critical Thinking How might a tsunami warning system help people stay safe during a tsunami?

TSUNAMI HAZARD ZONE

IN CASE OF EARTHQUAKE, GO TO HIGH GROUND OR INLAND

Lesson Review

Summarize the Main Idea

Earth's crust is made up of plates. **Earthquakes** occur when plates move suddenly along a fault. (pp. 248–251)

A **tsunami** is a giant wave usually caused by an earthquake on the ocean floor. (pp. 252–253)

You can **protect yourself** during earthquakes and tsunamis by being prepared. (p. 254)

Make a FOLDABLES Study Guide

Make a three-tab book. Use it to summarize what you learned about earthquakes and tsunamis.

Think, Talk, and Write

1. **Main Idea** Is Earth's crust always moving? Explain your answer.

2. **Vocabulary** What is an earthquake?

3. **Cause and Effect** A tsunami occurs. What are some of its effects?

Cause	→	Effect
	→	
	→	
	→	
	→	

4. **Critical Thinking** Why is it important to study earthquakes?

5. **Test Practice** You are in your home. You feel an earthquake. What should you do?

   A Pack your things quickly.
   B Move to a safe place.
   C Get in your car and drive away.
   D Stand under a tree.

Writing Link

Make a Dictionary
Find out the definitions of terms related to earthquakes. Make a dictionary of such terms as *focus, aftershock, epicenter, seismic waves,* and *magnitude.*

Social Studies Link

Draw a Map
Draw a map of California. Label some of its major cities. Find out about the San Andreas Fault. Show its location on your map. Label it.

Be a Scientist

Materials

long, deep aluminum pan

wax paper

sand

container of water

Inquiry Structured

What affects the size of a tsunami?

Form a Hypothesis

Earthquakes can happen on the ocean floor. How can the strength of an earthquake affect the size of a tsunami? Write your hypothesis in the form, *"If an earthquake is very strong, then . . ."*

Test Your Hypothesis

1. **Make a Model** Cut a piece of wax paper to cover all but a small portion of the bottom of the pan. Place the wax paper in the pan so that 10 cm of the paper hangs over the end of the pan.

Step 1

2. **Make a Model** Pour sand into the pan to cover the wax paper. This will model the "ocean floor." Add a mound of sand to the end of the pan not covered with wax paper. This will represent the "shore" in your model.

Step 2

3. Slowly add water to the pan. Add just enough water to cover the "ocean floor." Do not cover the "shore" with water.

Step 3

④ **Experiment** Hold the 10-cm end of wax paper with two hands. Gently move the wax paper up and down to model a weak earthquake. Do not pull on the wax paper. What do you observe?

⑤ **Use Variables** Repeat Step 4, but increase the speed you use to move the wax paper up and down. This models a stronger earthquake. What do you observe?

Draw Conclusions

⑥ **Infer** Based on your experiment, how do you think the strength of an earthquake affects the size of a tsunami?

Step ④

Inquiry Guided

What affects the strength of a tsunami?

Form a Hypothesis

Does the distance from where the earthquake starts on the ocean floor make any difference in the strength of the waves on land? Answer the question in the form, *"If the distance from where the earthquake begins increases, then the waves will . . ."*

Test Your Hypothesis

Design a plan to test your hypothesis. Write out the materials you need and the steps you will follow. Record your results and observations.

Draw Conclusions

Did your test support your hypothesis? Why or why not?

Inquiry Open

What else would you like to know about tsunamis? For example, how do warning systems work to warn coastal towns of an incoming tsunami? Design an investigation to answer your question.

Remember to follow the steps of the scientific process.

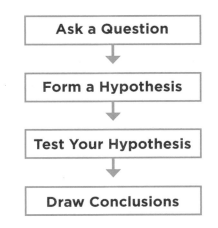

Ask a Question
↓
Form a Hypothesis
↓
Test Your Hypothesis
↓
Draw Conclusions

---

4 IE 6.d. Conduct multiple trials to test a prediction and draw conclusions about the relationships between predictions and results.

Remembering an Earthquake

Sometimes nature can be very violent. I was reminded of this one early Sunday morning in my home in San Francisco. This is what happened.

First, a deep rumbling sound woke me. I heard things starting to rattle. "It must be an earthquake!" I thought. I knew I had to get out of the house.

Next, I found my way through the early dawn light. Mom and Dad had woken up, too. We made our way to the backyard.

Then, the ground began to shake and roll. The earthquake lasted only a minute, but it had seemed much longer. Finally, the shaking stopped. I knew that life would go back to normal soon.

A personal narrative

▶ tells a story from personal experience

▶ expresses the writer's feelings, using the "I" point of view

▶ tells where and when the event happened

▶ uses details that appeal to the reader's senses

▶ uses time-order words, such as *first, next, then*, and *finally,* to tell the sequence of events

 Write About It

Narrative Writing Write a personal narrative about an event that you experienced. What happened? What did you do? How did you feel? Why do you still remember the experience? Use the "I" point of view. Include time-order words to show the order of events.

LOG ON ℮-Journal Write about it online @ **www.macmillanmh.com**

 ELA W 4.2.1. Write narratives: a. Relate ideas, observations, or recollections of an event or experience. b. Provide a context to enable the reader to imagine the world of the event or experience. c. Use concrete sensory details. d. Provide insight into why the selected event or experience is memorable.

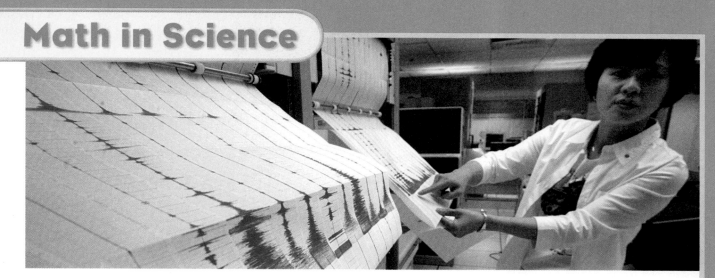

▲ An earthquake being tracked in Taipei, Taiwan on June 6, 2003 measured 6.3 on the Richter scale.

Shake, Rattle, and Roll

In 1935, Charles Richter devised a scale to compare the energy released by earthquakes. The Richter scale rates earthquakes from 1 to 10. Earthquakes less than 2.5 are not usually felt. Earthquakes greater than 8.0 cause a lot of destruction. This chart shows the strengths of some California earthquakes from 1994 to 2005.

Comparing Decimals

First, line up the decimal points. Compare the values of each digit starting at the left. Find the first place where the digits are different. Compare these digits.

6.0 Parkfield
↓
6.7 Northridge

6.0 < 6.7

The earthquake at Northridge, CA was stronger than the earthquake at Parkfield, CA.

 Solve It

1. Compare the strengths of the earthquakes in Truckee, CA and Crescent, CA. Use < or >.
2. Order the Richter scale readings in the chart from weakest to strongest.

Date	Place	Richter Scale
1/17/94	Northridge	6.7
9/28/04	Parkfield	6.0
6/14/05	Crescent City	7.2
6/26/05	Truckee	4.8

MA NS 4.1.2. Order and compare whole numbers and decimals to two decimal places.

Volcanoes

Look and Wonder

On May 18, 1980, Mount St. Helens interrupted the quiet morning. This once-quiet volcano became active. Are there other volcanoes on Earth? Where are they found?

4 ES 5.a. Students know some changes in the earth are due to slow processes, such as erosion, and some changes are due to rapid processes, such as landslides, volcanic eruptions, and earthquakes.

Where are Earth's volcanoes?

Materials

- **tracing paper**

Purpose

Find out where volcanoes usually form.

Procedure

1. Place tracing paper over the map below. Trace the continents and the triangles (volcanoes).

2. **Observe** Turn to page 249. Place your tracing on top of the map. Where do most volcanoes occur?

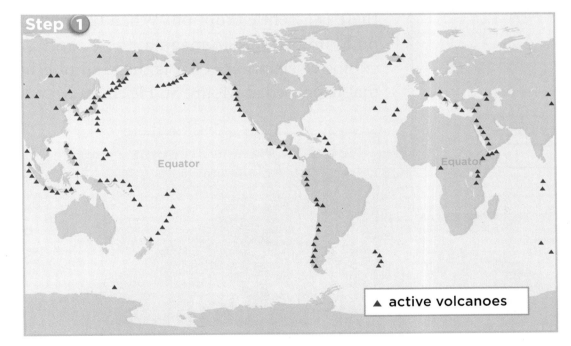

Step 1

Equator

Equator

▲ active volcanoes

Draw Conclusions

3. **Infer** What is the relationship between the location of plates and volcanoes?

Explore More

Do more volcanoes occur on land or in water? How could you find out?

4 IE 6.f. Follow a set of written instructions for a scientific investigation.

Main Idea 4 ES 5.a

Sudden changes to Earth's surface can be caused by volcanoes.

Vocabulary

volcano, p. 262

hot spot, p. 264

crater, p. 266

LOG ON e-Glossary
@ www.macmillanmh.com

Reading Skill

Sequence

First
↓
Next
↓
Last

What is a volcano?

A **volcano** is a mountain that builds up around an opening in Earth's crust. Sometimes melted rock, gases, and pieces of rock are forced out of a volcano. This is called an *eruption*. A volcanic eruption can cause land to change suddenly.

Did you ever shake a can of soda and then open it? The gases inside the soda explode in a spray. When some volcanoes erupt, something similar happens. Gases trapped in *magma*, or melted rock, come to the surface. The gases begin to escape. When gas escapes easily, there is a gentle eruption. When trapped gases build up pressure in magma, there can be an explosive eruption. That is the kind of eruption that happened at Mount St. Helens in May 1980.

Mount St. Helens Changes

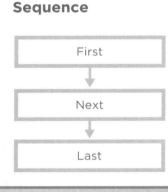

before

Reading Photos

How did Mount St. Helens change after the eruption in 1980?

Clue: Compare the "after" photo with the "before" photo.

after

Volcano Formation

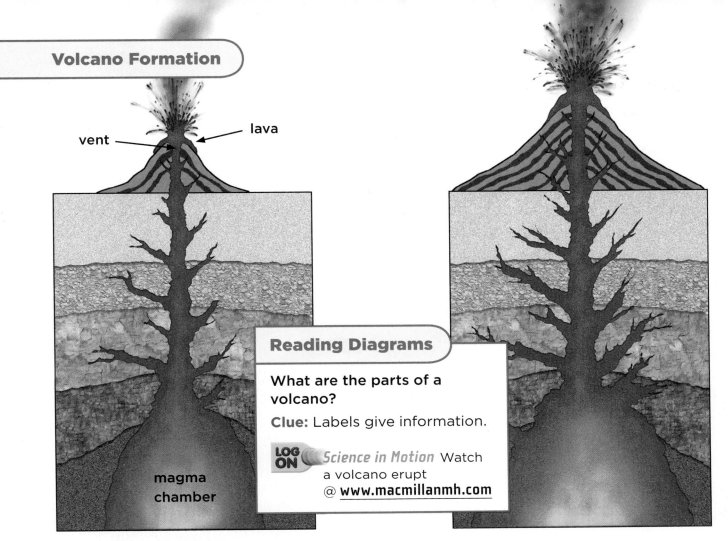

vent — lava

magma chamber

Reading Diagrams

What are the parts of a volcano?

Clue: Labels give information.

LOG ON *Science in Motion* Watch a volcano erupt @ **www.macmillanmh.com**

▲ A volcanic mountain forms when ash and lava build up around the vent.

Rising Magma

You know that magma is found deep below Earth's surface. Magma can rise up through a central opening in a volcano. This opening is called a *vent*. Once magma reaches Earth's surface it is called *lava*. Lava can ooze from the volcano slowly. At other times it leaves the volcano in an explosion. When lava flows over Earth, it cools and hardens. Over time it causes a mountain to form. Mount St. Helens is a volcano formed by the lava flows and ash deposits that built up around it.

✔ Quick Check

Sequence Describe the steps of a volcano forming.

Critical Thinking How is volcano formation different from erosion and weathering? Hint: Think about what each process does to the land.

263
EXPLAIN

Where do volcanoes form?

Most volcanoes occur along faults. Why do volcanoes occur there?

Where Earth's plates move together, one plate can be pushed beneath another. The plate moving down melts and is changed to magma. Like heated air or water, magma rises. It rises up through Earth's crust to form volcanoes.

Volcanoes also form where Earth's plates move apart. They form along the edges of the spreading plates. These are called *rift volcanoes*. Most rift volcanoes form along the ocean floor.

Hot Spots

Sometimes volcanoes form where plates do not meet. An example is the Hawaiian Islands. These volcanic islands formed in the middle of a plate. How? Geologists think that a plate may move over a hot spot. A **hot spot** is a place where magma partially melts through Earth's crust. As a plate moves over a hot spot, magma rises, forming a volcano.

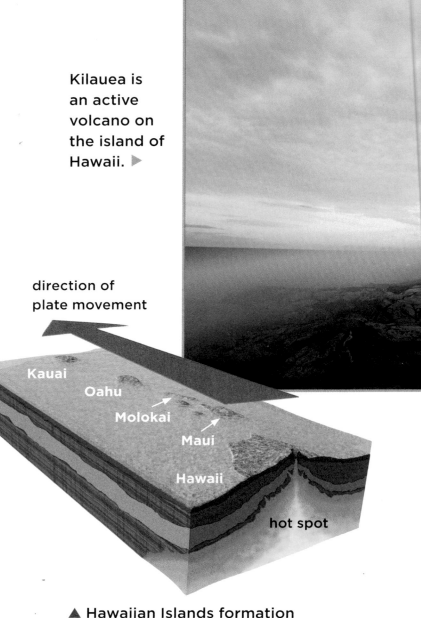

Kilauea is an active volcano on the island of Hawaii. ▶

direction of plate movement

Kauai
Oahu
Molokai
Maui
Hawaii

hot spot

▲ Hawaiian Islands formation

Surtsey is a volcanic island near Iceland. It rose out of the sea in 1963. The island is still forming. ▶

Look at the map of the Hawaiian Islands. They are a chain of islands. As the plate moved over the hot spot, each island was formed. Hawaii is the youngest island. It is still forming over the hot spot. It is an *active volcano*. This means that the volcano is still erupting. The island of Kauai is the oldest island. It passed over the hot spot a long time ago. It is a *dormant volcano*. This means that the volcano no longer erupts.

✔ Quick Check

Sequence How did the Hawaiian Islands form? Explain the sequence.

Critical Thinking Could another Hawaiian island ever form? If so, where would it form?

Model Hawaiian Islands Formation

1. **Make a Model** Use several coins of different sizes to represent each of the Hawaiian Islands shown on page 264. Line up the "islands" next to a sheet of wax paper. The wax paper represents a plate.

2. Draw a 2-cm red spot on butcher paper to represent a hot spot.

3. Place the wax paper on top of the butcher paper. Place the first "island" on the wax paper over the hot spot. Slide the "plate" to your left about 5 cm away from the "hot spot." Stop.

4. Repeat for each of the other "islands." Stop when the last island is over the hot spot.

5. **Infer** Which islands are dormant volcanoes? Are there any active volcanoes? Explain.

6. **Predict** What will eventually happen to the last island?

What are some kinds of volcanoes?

Not all volcanoes are the same. They have different shapes. A volcano's shape depends on the kind of lava that erupts from it. The diagrams on these pages show some kinds of volcanoes.

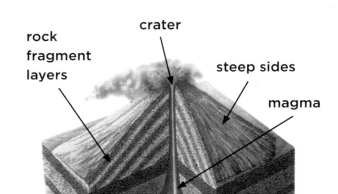

rock fragment layers

crater

steep sides

magma

Cinder-Cone Volcano

A *cinder-cone volcano* is shaped like a cone. It has steep sides. The magma in this kind of volcano is thick. A lot of gas is trapped in the magma. Because the magma is thick, it can become clogged in the volcano. Pressure builds up from gases in the magma. The gases finally explode out of the magma. Lava bursts into the air. It falls in pieces around the vent. A cup-like shape forms around the vent of a volcano. This is called a **crater**.

This cinder-cone volcano is found in Lassen Volcanic National Park in northeastern California. ▼

Shield Volcano

A *shield volcano* has sides that are wide and flat. It is formed by layers of lava that build up over time. The lava flows gently out in all directions. The lava may flow from one or more openings. The Hawaiian Islands are an example of shield volcanoes.

Composite Volcano

A *composite volcano* is made up of layers of lava and ash. It forms during periods of quiet eruptions and explosive eruptions. The eruptions seem to take turns. An eruption may be explosive one time. Then it may have a quiet period in which lava flows gently. Over time the layers build up to form a cone shape. This kind of volcano is usually symmetric. That means the shape on one side of the cone matches the shape on the other side.

▲ Mauna Loa, a shield volcano, is the world's largest volcano.

 Quick Check

Sequence What sequence might a composite volcano follow as it forms?

Critical Thinking Look at the photo on page 262. What kind of volcano was Mount St. Helens before its 1980 eruption?

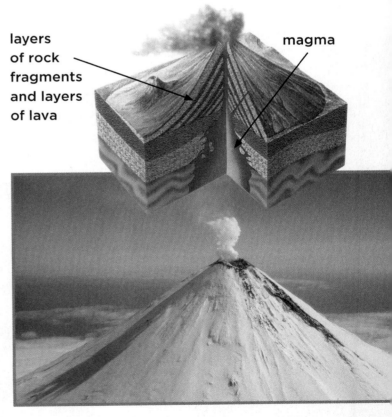

▲ Shishaldin is a composite volcano in the Aleutian Islands.

How can you be safe around volcanoes?

In the past, scientists did not always know when a volcano was going to erupt. Today special equipment helps scientists to predict eruptions. People cannot prevent eruptions. However, there are things people can do to stay safe where volcanoes are still active.

Volcano Safety

- Stay away from active volcano sites and lava flows.
- Have a pair of goggles and a breathing mask available for each member of your family in your emergency supply kit.
- If your town has a warning system, follow all instructions.
- Leave the area immediately, if told to do so. Wear long-sleeved shirts and long pants.
- If you are indoors near an erupting volcano, close all windows and doors. Make sure your pets are inside.
- If you are caught outdoors, find the nearest shelter and stay inside.

✓ Quick Check

Sequence What might be the very first thing to do if a volcanic eruption were predicted for your area?

Critical Thinking Why is it important to use safety goggles and a breathing mask if you are in the area during an eruption?

Summarize the Main Idea

Magma makes its way to Earth's surface in a **volcano**. Volcanoes form along Earth's moving plates and at hot spots.
(pp. 262–265)

Some **kinds of volcanoes** are cinder-cone, shield, and composite.
(pp. 266–267)

You can **protect yourself** during an erupting volcano by being prepared.
(p. 268)

Make a FOLDABLES™ Study Guide

Make a three-tab book. Use it to summarize what you learned about volcanoes.

Think, Talk, and Write

1 **Main Idea** What are some sudden changes to Earth that are caused by volcanic eruptions?

2 **Vocabulary** What is a volcano?

3 **Sequence** What is the last thing that happens in the life of a volcano?

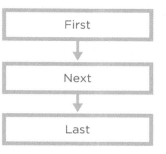

First

Next

Last

4 **Critical Thinking** Why is it important to study volcanoes?

5 **Test Practice** An eruption is predicted in a certain area. People there should do all of the following things EXCEPT

  A Take a drive to see the volcano.

  B Listen to a local radio station.

  C Make preparations to leave.

  D Make sure there are goggles and a breathing mask for each person in their family.

Math Link

Solve a Problem
Mount St. Helens was 2,950 m tall before the eruption of 1980. Today it is 2,532 m tall. How much of the mountain was lost during the eruption?

Art Link

Make a Flip Book
Draw pictures on index cards of a volcano forming. Put the cards in order so that when flipped, the drawings show how a volcano forms.

Meet Ro Kinzler

Ro Kinzler is fascinated by volcanoes and volcanic rocks, and she'd go just about anywhere to find out more about them. She is a scientist at the American Museum of Natural History.

Ro travels to the Cascades in Northern California to collect lava samples from active volcanoes like Mount Shasta and Medicine Lake. She wants to study how magma moves through Earth. Back in the lab, Ro does experiments to heat and squeeze the lava samples she collected to find out how they were formed deep in Earth.

▲ Ro's favorite place to collect lava samples is Kilauea volcano in Hawaii.

AMERICAN MUSEUM OF NATURAL HISTORY

ELA R 4.2.1. Identify structural patterns found in informational text (e.g., compare and contrast, cause and effect, sequential or chronological order, proposition and support) to strengthen comprehension.

You don't just find volcanoes on land. There are lots of them on the ocean floor. Ro and other scientists have gone to the bottom of the ocean to study them in special underwater vehicles called submersibles. The scientists visited the Mid-Atlantic Ridge, part of the longest volcano chain in the world. Ro is one of the few people to have ever seen it. She peered out the portholes of the submersible Alvin with other scientists to make careful observations of the rock formations. They used these to create geologic maps of the ocean floor.

Alvin is a submersible specially made to dive to great depths. ▶

Write About It

Cause and Effect Read the article with a partner. Fill out a cause-and-effect chart to record why Ro visits volcanoes and collects lava samples. Tell what happens as a result of her work.

LOG ON e-Journal Write about it online @ www.macmillanmh.com

Cause and Effect

▶ The *cause* answers the question "Why did something happen?"

▶ The effect answers the question "What happened as a result?"

Summarize the Main Ideas

Some changes to Earth's surface take place very quickly. Gravity and fast-flowing water cause some rapid changes. (pp. 236–243)

The sudden movement of Earth's plates can cause sudden changes to occur on Earth's surface. (pp. 246–255)

Sudden changes to Earth's surface caused by volcanoes. (pp. 260–269)

Make a **FOLDABLES**™ Study Guide

Tape your lesson study guides to a piece of paper as shown. Use your study guide to review what you have learned in this chapter.

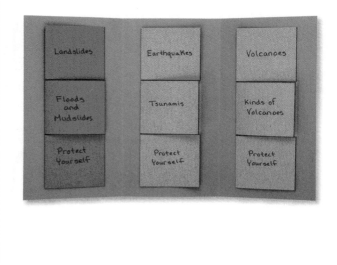

Fill each blank with the best word from the list.

crater, p. 266   mudslide, p. 241

earthquake, p. 249   plates, p. 248

fault, p. 249   tsunami, p. 252

landslide, p. 238   volcano, p. 262

1. An underwater earthquake can cause a _____. 4 ES 5.a

2. Dry soil and rocks fall suddenly down a slope during a _____. 4 ES 5.a

3. A crack in Earth's crust where two moving plates meet is a _____. 4 ES 5.a

4. A sudden shifting of Earth's crust is an _____. 4 ES 5.a

5. Heavy rains on a slope can cause a _____. 4 ES 5.a

6. A mountain that builds up around an opening in Earth's crust is called a _____. 4 ES 5.a

7. The cupped shape at the top of a volcano is a _____. 4 ES 5.a

8. Earth's crust is made of huge moving slabs of rock called _____. 4 ES 5.a

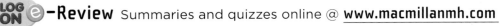

Answer each of the following in complete sentences.

9. **Cause and Effect** Why do earthquakes happen more in California than in other places in the United States? 4 ES 5.a

10. **Experiment** Do earthquakes occur more often during one time of the year? For example, are there more earthquakes during the winter or summer? How could you go about designing a plan to answer this question? 4 IE 6.d

11. **Critical Thinking** A volcano with thick magma is more likely to have an explosive eruption than one with thin magma. Explain why you think this is so. 4 ES 5.a

12. **Persuasive Writing** A land developer wants to build homes at the base of a large mountain in an area that is known for earthquakes and flooding. Write a letter to the town board explaining why you think homes should not be allowed to be built there. 4 ES 5.a

 What causes Earth's surface to change quickly?

CHAPTER 5

A Public Safety Announcement

Your goal is to prepare a safety announcement about earthquakes.

- Research information about earthquake safety. You may find information online, such as at government sites. You might also contact national and local organizations that specialize in disaster relief.

- Your research should focus on one of these areas: What to Do Before an Earthquake, What to Do During an Earthquake, and What to Do After an Earthquake.

- Prepare a 3–5 minute oral presentation. You may want to include photos, drawings, or posters.

- After the oral reports, develop a final public safety announcement. It should contain information gathered by the whole class and include all three areas of earthquake safety.

1 A small dam in the Sacramento River basin is normally 10 feet high. The graph below shows the high-water marks in the basin for several years.

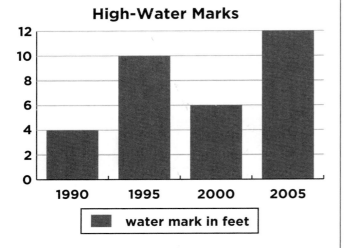

High-Water Marks

water mark in feet

In which year would there have been flooding? 4 IE 6.e

A 1990

B 1995

C 2000

D 2005

2 Vibrations caused by an earthquake are felt in the 4 ES 5.a

A fault.

B mountains.

C crust.

D "Ring of Fire."

3 Over time, which of the following can form over a hot spot? 4 ES 5.a

A an isthmus

B a peninsula

C an island

D a continent

4 The following table shows the number of hours lava flowed from a volcano for four days.

Day	Crater	South Vent	East Vent
1	6 hours	4 hours	3 hours
2	6 hours	6 hours	5 hours
3	10 hours	16 hours	5 hours
4	15 hours	16 hours	16 hours
5	?	?	?

If the pattern of the eruption continues for another day, what sort of data would you expect on the fifth day? 4 IE 6.d

A Lava will no longer flow from the crater.

B Lava will no longer flow through either vent.

C Lava will flow for fewer hours.

D Lava will flow for the same number of hours or more.

5 Which of the following cause rapid changes in Earth's surface? 4 ES 5.a

A erosion, thawing, fires

B landslides, volcanoes, earthquakes

C floods, weathering, deposition

D storms, wind, freezing

6 Which type of rock will be changed most by a flood? 4 ES 5.a

A small sedimentary rocks

B small rocks with many minerals

C small metamorphic rocks

D small igneous rocks

7 A scientist collected data on earthquakes in the United States over four years. She recorded her data in a chart.

Earthquakes in the United States	
Strength	**Number of Earthquakes**
great	0
major	1
strong	2
moderate	32
light	245
minor	800

Which of the following inferences could she make from the data? 4 IE 6.a

A A minor earthquake is likely to happen somewhere in the United States every year.

B A major earthquake is likely to happen somewhere in the United States every year.

C A moderate earthquake is not likely to happen somewhere in the United States.

D A light earthquake can never happen in the United States.

8 What happens when Earth's plates move toward each other slowly, over thousands of years? 4 ES 5.a

A Faults are formed.

B Earthquakes occur.

C Volcanoes are formed.

D Mountains are formed.

9 Breaks in Earth's crust experience slow movement called 4 ES 5.a

A a strike-slip fault.

B creep.

C a reverse fault.

D a normal fault.

10 An earthquake is usually caused by a 4 ES 5.a

A slab of rock called a plate.

B fault.

C sudden shift of Earth's plates.

D slow movement of Earth's plates.

11 Each of the following statements about volcanoes is true, EXCEPT 4 ES 5.a

A volcanoes have different shapes.

B volcanoes may erupt gently or explosively.

C volcanoes can change the land suddenly.

D volcanoes always form where plates meet.

LICHEN:

Life on the Rocks

Here's a little story for you about how lichen (LIGH-kuhn) came to be. Fungus was down on his luck, just barely getting by and always a little hungry. One day he met Alga. They took a likin' to each other and decided to be friends. Now they never go anywhere alone.

Well, maybe it didn't happen exactly like that, but that little story may help you remember what lichen is. Actually, lichen is not one thing but two. It is a team effort. Half the team is an alga. Algae (AL-jee) are tiny green protists. They use sunlight to make their own food. The other

▼ **This gray reindeer lichen grows in clumps on the ground.**

team member is a fungus. Fungi (FUN-jigh) are living things that often grow and feed on dead things. They help to break down dead things and recycle them. Mushrooms are one type of fungus.

Some lichen are crusty and flat and grow on a rock's surface. Others are leafy and often grow on tree bark. Still other lichens are thick branching ones, such as reindeer moss, that grow in clumps on the ground.

In a lichen, each partner helps out the other. The alga makes food for both of them. The fungus provides a "house" that protects the alga from drying out in sunlight. Lichens are able to live in places where few other living things can. Lichens, for example, are often the first things to grow on bare rock.

The lichen forms a crust on the rock. It grows very slowly and begins to break down the rock. Acids it gives off form tiny cracks in the rock. Water fills the tiny cracks and, when the water freezes, causes the cracks to widen. Over time, blowing bits of soil get caught in the lichen. Plant seeds may take root. After many years, the rock is covered with soil and plants. This all starts with fungi and algae!

▲ This leafy-type lichen grows on tree bark.

▲ This flat, crusty lichen grows on bare rock.

 4 ES 5. Waves, wind, water, and ice shape and reshape Earth's land surface.

277

Careers in Science

Surveying Technician

How can you find out exactly where your land ends and your neighbor's begins? You need a survey technician! Survey technicians create maps and locate boundaries of the land. They use special instruments to calculate distances. To join a surveying crew, you will probably need a 1- or 2-year degree in surveying technology. You will also need a steady hand, strong math skills, and a lot of knowledge about computers. Computers are being used more and more in surveying.

▲ Special instruments are used to measure land.

Geologist

If your interest is rocks, or if you are just curious about planet Earth, you may want to become a geologist. Geologists learn about Earth's layers of rocks. They use that knowledge in many ways. Some geologists, for example, work for large industries locating gold, oil, or minerals. Other geologists study earthquakes and volcanoes. Still other geologists try to figure out how Earth has changed over time, and how it might change in the future. To be a geologist, you will need a college degree. Most geologists go to school for several years after college, too. So if you want to be a real rock hound, you had better hit the books!

▲ This geologist wears a special thermal suit while collecting lava samples.

LOG ON **e-Careers** More careers online @ **www.macmillanmh.com**

Physical Science

Aurora Borealis is another name for Northern Lights.

Electricity

How do we use electricity?

4 PS 1. Electricity and magnetism are related effects that have many useful applications in everyday life.

Literature
Poem

ELA R 4.3.2. Identify the main events of the plot, their causes, and the influence of each event on future actions. ELA W 4.2.3. Write information reports.

BENJAMIN FRANKLIN

Ben Franklin made a pretty kite
   and flew it in the air
To call upon a thunderstorm
   that happened to be there,
And all our humming dynamos
   and our electric light
Go back to what Ben Franklin found,
   the day he flew his kite.

*An excerpt from a poem
by Rosemary and
Stephen Vincent Benét*

Huge dynamos like these produce electricity for your home.

Write About It

Response to Literature This poem shows how Ben Franklin made an incredible discovery. Do research online to find out more about Ben Franklin and electricity. Then write a report. Include facts and details from more than one source.

LOG ON **e-Journal** Write about it online @ **www.macmillanmh.com**

Static Electricity

Look and Wonder

Lightning bolts flash through the sky. You rub a balloon against your clothing and it sticks to a wall. What do lightning bolts and rubbed balloons have in common?

 4 PS 1.e. Students know electrically charged objects attract or repel each other.

How do rubbed balloons interact?

Make a Prediction

How do balloons rubbed with wool or plastic wrap interact?

Test Your Prediction

1. Inflate two balloons. Then tie a piece of string to the end of each balloon.

2. Rub a wool cloth 20 times against one of the balloons. Rub the other balloon 20 times with plastic wrap.

3. **Experiment** Holding the strings, bring the balloons near each other. Observe what happens. Record the result.

4. **Predict** What would happen if you rubbed both balloons with the wool and held them near each other?

5. **Experiment** Test your prediction. Record the result.

Draw Conclusions

6. How do balloons interact when rubbed with wool or plastic wrap?

Explore More

What do you think would happen if you rubbed both balloons with plastic wrap? What would happen if you held one of the rubbed balloons near other objects? Plan a test and try it.

4 IE 6.c. Formulate and justify predictions based on cause-and-effect relationships.

Materials

- **2 balloons**
- **2 pieces of string, 25 cm each**
- **wool cloth**
- **plastic wrap**

Step 2

Step 3

Main Idea 4 PS 1.e

Some particles of matter have a negative or positive charge. Opposite charges attract each other. Like charges repel each other.

Vocabulary

electrical charge, p. 286

static electricity, p. 288

discharge, p. 290

conductor, p. 292

insulator, p. 292

LOG ON e-Glossary
@ www.macmillanmh.com

Reading Skill

Main Idea

Main Idea	Details

What is electrical charge?

Have you ever seen lightning flash during a storm? Have you watched a baseball game under the bright ballpark lights? If so, then you have seen electricity in action. Electricity powers lights, ovens, and computers. Electricity makes your clothes stick together when you take them out of the clothes dryer.

Just what is electricity? That's not so easy to answer. There are different kinds of electricity, but all electricity is the result of electrical charges. To understand electrical charge, you have to start with matter. Everything around you is made of matter. This book is made of matter. You are made of matter. Like color and hardness, **electrical charge** is a property of matter.

Charged particles in the girl's hair are attracted to the charged balloon. ▶

Positive and Negative Charges

There are two types of electrical charges. These charges are called positive and negative. You cannot see or feel electrical charge the way you can see color or feel hardness. However, you can observe how charges interact with each other. A positive charge and a negative charge *attract*, or pull, each other. Positive charges *repel*, or push away, each other. Negative charges repel each other, too.

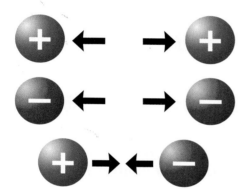

▲ Two positive (+) charges repel each other. So do negative (-) charges. Opposite charges attract each other.

Charges Add Up

All matter is made up of tiny particles. Some of these particles are positively charged. Others are negatively charged. Most matter has the same number of positive charges as negative charges. The positive and negative charges cancel each other out. This means that the matter is *neutral* (NEW•truhl)—it has no overall electrical charge.

▲ Over 2,500 years ago, Greeks discovered that amber rubbed with fur attracted feathers. In fact, the word *electricity* comes from the ancient Greek word for amber.

When two objects touch, charged particles can move from one object to the other. Negative charges move more easily than positive charges. Some objects, such as wool, are likely to give up negative charges. Other objects, such as plastic wrap, are likely to accept negative charges.

✔ Quick Check

Main Idea How do negative charges interact? How do a negative charge and a positive charge interact?

Critical Thinking How would two neutral balloons interact?

What is static electricity?

Suppose you rub a balloon with a wool cloth. Negative charges would move from the wool to the balloon. This would produce a buildup of negative charges in the balloon. A *buildup* means that it has more of one kind of charge than the other. The buildup gives the balloon an overall negative charge. The wool would be left with a buildup of positive charges. The buildup of electrical charges on an object is called **static electricity**.

You know that charged particles can move between objects when the objects touch. Even more charged particles can move when objects rub against each other. Rubbing objects together causes them to touch in more places. Rubbing produces a larger buildup of charge.

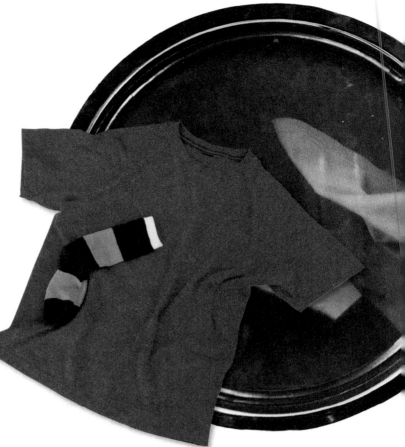

▲ Negative charges move between clothes in a dryer. A positively charged sock will stick to a negatively charged shirt.

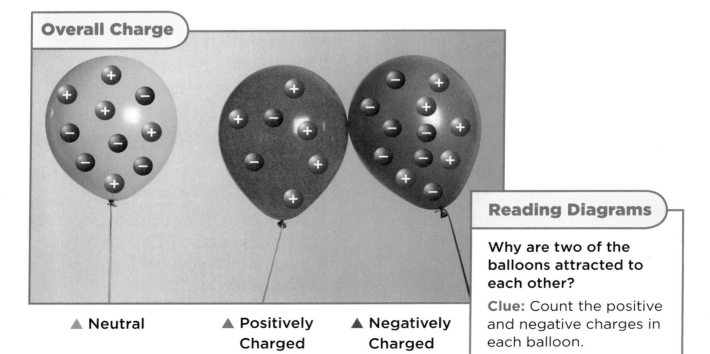

Overall Charge

▲ Neutral   ▲ Positively Charged   ▲ Negatively Charged

Reading Diagrams

Why are two of the balloons attracted to each other?

Clue: Count the positive and negative charges in each balloon.

Charged particles moving from one object to another produce a buildup of electrical charge. Charged particles moving inside an object can also produce a buildup of charge.

When you hold a negatively charged balloon near a wall, it repels the negative charges in the wall. It also attracts the positive charges in the wall. This pull makes the balloon "stick" to the wall.

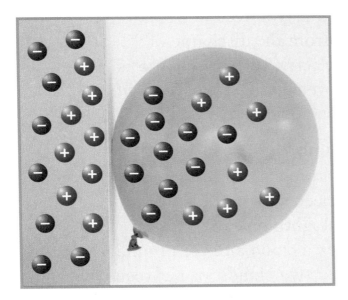

▲ The charges in the balloon cause charges in the wall to move. The balloon is then attracted to the wall.

✔ Quick Check

Main Idea What causes static electricity?

Critical Thinking Why do dog and cat hairs stick to your clothes?

≡ Quick Lab

Producing Static Electricity

1 Tear a piece of tissue paper into small pieces.

2 Give a comb a negative charge by running it through your hair about ten times.

3 **Observe** Hold the comb near the tissue paper. What happens?

4 **Experiment** Repeat steps 2 and 3, running the comb through your hair 20 times, then 30 times.

5 **Draw Conclusions** What difference did you notice when you combed your hair more than ten times? Why does this happen?

▲ Charges build up inside a plasma ball. The spark you see is an electrical discharge.

What is an electrical discharge?

It is a dry winter day. You shuffle across a carpet and touch a doorknob. Zap! You get an electrical shock.

When you walk across a carpet, electrical charges from the carpet build up on your body. You become negatively charged. When you touch a metal doorknob, the negative charges move from your body into the doorknob. You receive a small shock from the discharge of static electricity. A **discharge** is the movement of static electricity from one object to another.

Lightning

Lightning is the discharge of static electricity inside a storm cloud. Lightning can occur between a cloud and the ground, between two clouds, or between two oppositely charged parts of one cloud.

◀ The shock you get from a metal doorknob is a discharge of static electricity.

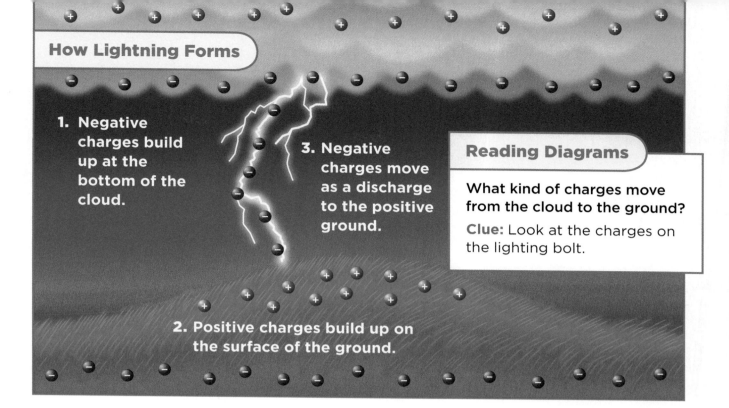

How Lightning Forms

1. Negative charges build up at the bottom of the cloud.

2. Positive charges build up on the surface of the ground.

3. Negative charges move as a discharge to the positive ground.

Reading Diagrams

What kind of charges move from the cloud to the ground?

Clue: Look at the charges on the lighting bolt.

Storms are full of wind and moisture. Water droplets in the clouds bump and rub against one another. Some droplets become positively charged and move to the top of the cloud. Others become negatively charged and gather at the bottom of the cloud.

These negative charges repel and attract charges in the ground below. The negative charges in the cloud push down on the negative charges in the ground. Positive charges then cover the top of the ground. Suddenly, negative charges streak down to the positively charged ground. As the negative charges move through the air, they make the spark that you see as lightning.

Lightning Safety

1. Find shelter inside a building, car, or truck.

2. If you are far from any shelter, then go to the lowest point and crouch down. Lightning often hits the tallest object in an area.

3. If you are in the water, then get out. Lightning often strikes swimming pools, lakes, and other bodies of water.

✔ *Quick Check*

Main Idea What causes an electrical discharge?

Critical Thinking Why does the top of the ground have a positive charge during a storm?

▲ Electrical wires are made of metal covered by an insulator like rubber or plastic.

What are conductors and insulators?

You know that you can get a shock from a metal doorknob. If you touch the wooden door first, you can avoid that surprising shock. Why?

The metal is a conductor. **Conductors** are materials that let charges flow through them easily. Charges race quickly from your body into the doorknob. You feel the fast discharge as a shock. Metals such as copper and silver are good conductors. Even you can be a conductor. That is why you can get a shock when another person touches you.

Wood is an insulator. **Insulators** are materials that do not let charges flow through them easily. When you touch the wooden door, charges move slowly onto the surface of the door. Because this discharge is slow, you don't feel it. Rubber, plastic, and glass are also good insulators.

✔ Quick Check

Main Idea What is the difference between a conductor and an insulator?

Critical Thinking How do insulating gloves protect electricians?

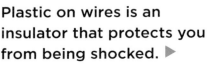

Plastic on wires is an insulator that protects you from being shocked. ▶

Lesson Review

Summarize the Main Idea

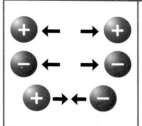 **Electrical charges** can be negative or positive. Opposite charges attract each other. Like charges repel each other. (pp. 286–287)

Static electricity is a buildup of electrical charges. A discharge is a movement of static electricity. (pp. 288–291)

Electrical charges pass easily through **conductors** but not through **insulators**. (p. 292)

Make a FOLDABLES™ Study Guide

Make a three-tab book. Use it to summarize what you learned.

Think, Talk, and Write

1. **Main Idea** How do electrical charges interact?

2. **Vocabulary** What is an electrical discharge?

3. **Main Idea** What is lightning? How does it form?

Main Idea	Details

4. **Critical Thinking** If you are outside during a thunderstorm, you should not touch metal objects such as a flagpole or metal fence. Explain why.

5. **Test Practice** Which is a good electrical conductor?

   A copper

   B rubber

   C glass

   D wood

 Math Link

Rounding Charges

Tesla coils produce huge amounts of static electricity. Suppose that a Tesla coil has a buildup of 6,819,212 negative charges. Round this number to the nearest hundred. The nearest ten thousand. The nearest million.

 Social Studies Link

Learn About Ancient Science

Thales of Miletus and Democritus were ancient Greek philosophers. Use a library or the Internet to research them and their scientific theories.

Analyze Data

You discovered that static electricity can cause objects to attract each other. How can you make that attraction stronger? Do some objects produce static electricity more easily than others? You can **analyze data** from experiments to help you answer questions like these.

① Learn It

When people do experiments, they collect information called data. Data might be how many ducks hatched in a pond or at what temperature something melts. When you **analyze data**, you use information that has been gathered to answer questions or solve problems. It is usually easier to analyze the data if it has been organized and placed on a chart or a graph. In that way you can quickly see differences in the data.

② Try It

You know that scientists **analyze data**. They may make a chart of the data. This helps them to organize the information and analyze the results of the experiment. You can do it, too.

Kind of Material	Number of Rubs	Pieces of Cereal
Wool	1	8
Wool	2	20
Wool	3	34
Paper towel	1	16
Paper towel	2	32
Paper towel	3	46

▶ Look at the chart. It shows how many pieces of cereal were picked up by a balloon rubbed with two different materials—wool and a paper towel.

▶ Analyze the data to help you answer these questions: How did the amount of cereal change with the number of rubbings? Which material created the most powerful static attraction?

❸ Apply It

Charts and graphs not only help you **analyze** your **data**. They also help you share that data with other people. Use the data from the chart to make a bar graph. Put the data in order from fewest rubbings to most rubbings. Use the data to answer these questions: about how many pieces of cereal would be picked up if the balloon were rubbed with wool four times? With the paper towel four times?

 **4 IE 6.e.** Construct and interpret graphs from measurements.

Electric Circuits

Look and Wonder

You flip a switch on the wall, and the room lights up. Have you ever wondered how a lamp or a flashlight works? How does electricity travel to the bulb?

4 PS 1.a. Students know how to design and build simple series and parallel circuits by using components such as wires, batteries, and bulbs.

What makes a bulb light?

Make a Prediction

How can you connect a battery, a wire, and a light bulb to make the bulb light up?

Test Your Prediction

1. **Experiment** Work with your group to try to light the bulb using the materials.

2. **Communicate** Draw each setup. Record your results.

3. **Compare** When your light bulb is lit, compare your setup to those of other groups. Which made the bulb light? How are the setups the same?

Draw Conclusions

4. How many setups could you find that made the bulb light? Compare with your classmates. Did they find other setups that worked?

5. Look at the setups that lit the bulb. What do you think is necessary to make a bulb light up?

Explore More

Experiment How could you light two bulbs using only one battery? Can you think of more than one way?

 4 IE 6.c. Formulate and justify predictions based on cause-and-effect relationships. •**4 IE 6.d.** Conduct multiple trials to test a prediction and draw conclusions about the relationships between predictions and results.

Materials

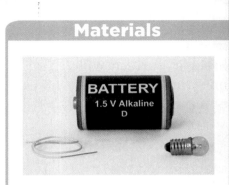

BATTERY
1.5 V Alkaline
D

- **D cell battery**
- **20-cm-long insulated wire**
- **light bulb**

Step 1

Step 2

Does not work.

Read and Learn

Main Idea 4 PS 1.a

Electric current is a flow of electrical charges. Electric current will only flow through a complete circuit.

Vocabulary

electric current, p. 298

circuit, p. 299

series circuit, p. 300

parallel circuit, p. 302

voltage, p. 304

resistance, p. 304

LOG ON e-Glossary
@ www.macmillanmh.com

Reading Skill

Cause and Effect

Cause → Effect
→
→
→
→

Technology

SCIENCE QUEST Explore electricity on Science Island.

▲ Electric current provides the power that lights up Los Angeles at night.

What is electric current?

You learned that electrical charges can build up as static electricity and be discharged. Electrical charges can also be made to flow continuously through materials. A flow of electrical charges is known as an **electric current**. An electric current is different from static electricity, in which charges build up and stay in one place. Electric current keeps charges moving, like water flowing in a river or stream.

◄ When you plug a device into an outlet, the device becomes a part of a circuit.

Circuits

To make an electric current, you need a path to carry the current. The path along which electric current flows is called a **circuit** (SUR•kit). A simple circuit has three basic parts. It has a power source, such as a battery. This powers a load, such as a lamp or a computer. Connectors, such as wires, carry electrical charges between the power source and the load.

Many circuits have a switch. A *switch* turns electric current on and off. The lights in your classroom are controlled by a switch.

Open and Closed Circuits

To keep charges moving, the circuit cannot have any breaks. A complete, unbroken circuit is called a *closed circuit*. If the circuit has any breaks or openings, it is called an *open circuit*. Electric current cannot flow in an open circuit.

When a light bulb burns out, it makes an open circuit. This happens because a wire inside the bulb breaks in two. The circuit no longer has a complete path, so electric current cannot flow through it.

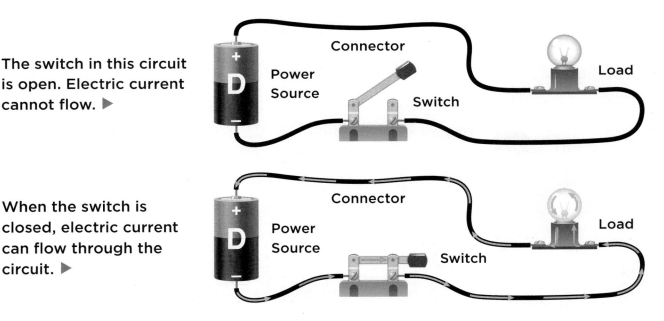

The switch in this circuit is open. Electric current cannot flow. ▶

When the switch is closed, electric current can flow through the circuit. ▶

✔ Quick Check

Cause and Effect You connect the ends of a wire to the terminals of a battery. What will happen?

Critical Thinking Electric current travels from a power source to a lamp through one wire and prong. What is the other prong and wire used for?

What is a series circuit?

Picture a one-way circular road. All the cars on this road travel in the same direction in a line. This is how a series circuit works. In a **series circuit**, all the electrical charges flow in the same direction along a single path.

The parts of a series circuit are connected in one loop. The electric current moves along one path. The current moves from the power source through the wires to one load. It then moves through another load. Finally, the current returns through a wire to the power source.

The photo below shows a series circuit. You could add another battery and a wire to the circuit. Then the batteries would also be connected in series. A circuit is a series circuit as long as all of the parts are connected one after another.

Series Circuit

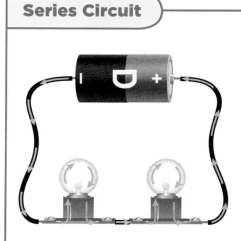

In a series circuit, the parts are connected like links in a chain. The electric current passes through each part one at a time.

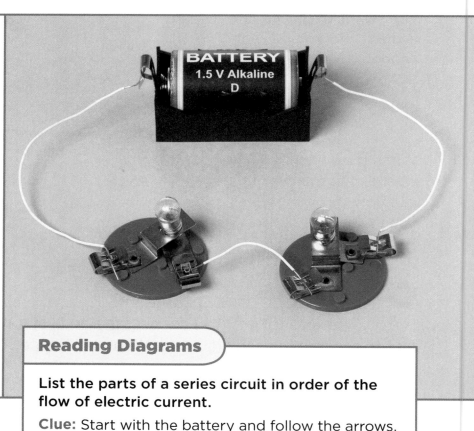

Reading Diagrams

List the parts of a series circuit in order of the flow of electric current.

Clue: Start with the battery and follow the arrows.

If any part of a series circuit is removed or broken, the circuit is open. None of the parts will work because current cannot flow in an open circuit.

 Quick Check

Cause and Effect One bulb in a series circuit burns out. Will current flow in the circuit?

Critical Thinking A string of small lights are a series circuit. If the first light in the string burns out, what happens to the others? What if the last light burns out?

≡Quick Lab

Make a Series Circuit

1 Screw two light bulbs into sockets.

2 Use a wire to connect one socket to a battery's positive terminal.

3 Use another wire to connect the second socket to the first socket.

4 **Observe** Use a third wire to connect the second socket to the battery's negative terminal. What happens?

5 **Experiment** What happens if you remove one of the light bulbs?

⚠ **Be Careful.** The light bulbs may become hot.

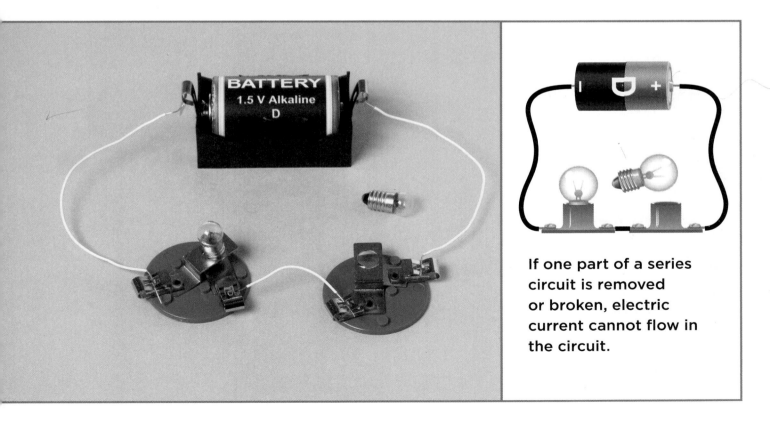

If one part of a series circuit is removed or broken, electric current cannot flow in the circuit.

What is a parallel circuit?

A series circuit is like a circular road on which all the cars follow the same path. A parallel circuit is like a group of roads which all lead to the same place but along different paths.

A **parallel circuit** is a circuit in which the electric current flows through more than one path. These different paths are often called *branches*. The branches of a parallel circuit divide the electric current between them. Some of the electric current flows through one branch, some flows through another branch.

The photo below shows a parallel circuit. Suppose that you connected two light bulbs on the bottom branch of the circuit. That branch would then be connected like a series circuit. Your circuit is no longer just a parallel circuit. It is a combination of a series and a parallel circuit. Many circuits in electrical devices, even the circuits in your home, are combination circuits.

Parallel Circuit

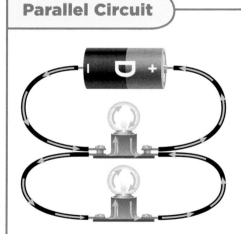

In a parallel circuit, each part, or branch, has its own path for electric current. The electric current passes through all of them at the same time.

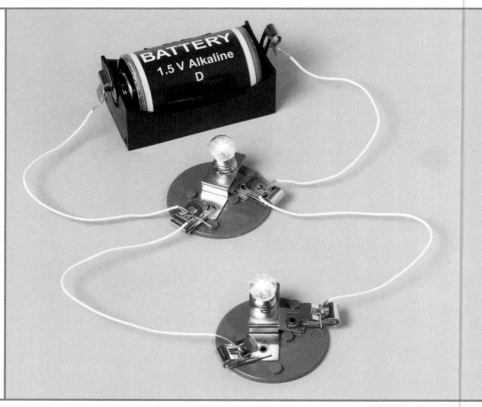

If any branch of a parallel circuit is removed or breaks, current will still flow through the other branches. If a light bulb on one branch burns out, the light bulbs on other branches will still glow.

✓ Quick Check

Cause and Effect A parallel circuit has two light bulbs. One of the bulbs burns out. What happens to the other bulb?

Critical Thinking If a light bulb in your home burns out, what happens to the other lights? Are the lights part of a series or a parallel circuit?

BATTERY
1.5 V Alkaline D

If one branch of a parallel circuit is removed or broken, current will still flow in other branches.

Reading Diagrams

Does current flow through the socket without a bulb?

Clue: Look at the arrows along the wires.

What affects electric current?

The amount of electric current that can flow through a circuit depends on voltage (VOHL•tij) and resistance.

Voltage

Voltage is the strength of a power source. A power source with more voltage can produce more electric current. Voltage is measured in units called volts. A D-cell battery has 1.5 volts. Most wall outlets, which get power from a power plant, have 120 volts.

Resistance

Resistance is the ability of a substance to oppose or slow down electric current. Increasing the resistance of a circuit decreases the flow of electrical charges through it. Resistance allows electrical energy to be changed into other forms of energy, such as light and heat.

Copper wires are good conductors. They have very little resistance, so they can carry a great deal of electric current. Rubber is an insulator that has a large amount of resistance. It is difficult to make any electric current flow through rubber.

▲ The burner has a lot of resistance. The resistance causes the stove top to heat up and glow.

Short Circuits

A path with almost no resistance is sometimes called a *short circuit*. A short circuit can stop the rest of the circuit from operating properly. It can also be dangerous. In a short circuit, the wire heats up and may cause a fire.

✓ Quick Check

Cause and Effect If you add light bulbs to a series circuit, the circuit has a higher resistance. What happens to the electric current in the circuit?

Critical Thinking If you decrease the resistance of a circuit, what will happen to current in the circuit?

Summarize the Main Idea

A flow of electrical charges is known as **electric current**. Current only flows through closed circuits. (pp. 298–299)

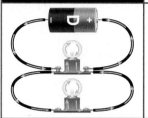

Series circuits have one path for electric current. **Parallel circuits** have many paths. (pp. 300–303)

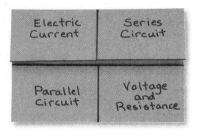

The amount of current that flows through a circuit depends on **voltage** and **resistance**. (p. 304)

Make a FOLDABLES Study Guide

Make a four-door book. Use it to summarize what you learned.

Electric Current	Series Circuit
Parallel Circuit	Voltage and Resistance

Think, Talk, and Write

1 Main Idea What is required for a circuit to work?

2 Vocabulary Compare a series circuit to a parallel circuit. How are they different? What parts are the same?

3 Cause and Effect How does changing the voltage of a power source affect the electric current flowing in a circuit?

Cause → Effect
→
→
→
→

4 Critical Thinking Suppose you try to turn on a lamp and it doesn't work. Name a few things that could cause the lamp not to work.

5 Test Practice Electric current cannot flow through

  A a closed circuit
  B an open circuit
  C a series circuit
  D a parallel circuit

Math Link

Distance and Speed
In a certain circuit, a charged particle moves two millimeters every minute. How far does the particle move in an hour? A day?

Art Link

Draw a Circuit
Make a drawing of a circuit. Label the different parts of your circuit. Is yours a series circuit, a parallel circuit, or a combination of both?

Be a Scientist

D cell battery

battery holder

3 light bulbs

3 bulb sockets

4 pieces of wire

Inquiry Structured

How do many loads affect electric current in a circuit?

Form a Hypothesis

You can compare the amount of electric current in circuits by observing light bulbs. A very bright bulb has more current than a dim bulb. How does connecting bulbs in a series circuit affect electric current in the circuit? Write your hypothesis in the form *"If you add light bulbs to a circuit, then . . ."*

Test Your Hypothesis

1. Insert the battery into the battery holder. Screw the light bulbs into the bulb sockets.

2. Use two wires to connect the battery holder to the bulb socket.

3. **Observe** Look at the light bulb. Does it shine brightly or is it dim?

4. **Experiment** Disconnect a wire from one side of the light bulb. Make a series circuit by connecting another socket and light bulb with a piece of wire.

5. **Observe** Are the two bulbs brighter or dimmer than the bulbs in the first circuit?

6. **Experiment** Add the third bulb and socket to the series circuit. How bright are the light bulbs now?

Step 2

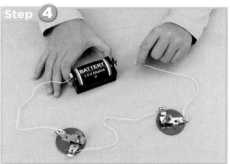

Step 4

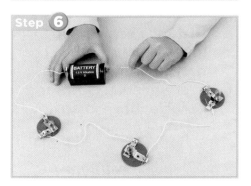

Step 6

Draw Conclusions

7 How did adding bulbs to the circuit change the brightness of the bulbs?

8 **Infer** How did adding bulbs change the amount of current in the circuit?

9 Adding bulbs increases the amount of resistance in a circuit. Write a new hypothesis. *"If you increase the resistance in a circuit, then . . ."*

Inquiry Guided

How do many power sources affect electric current in a circuit?

Form a Hypothesis

Have you ever noticed that different devices use different numbers of batteries? A remote control might use two batteries. A stereo might use six or more batteries. How will adding batteries affect electric current in the circuit? Write your hypothesis in the form *"If you add batteries to a circuit, then . . ."*

Test Your Hypothesis

Design an experiment to investigate how the number of batteries affects current in a circuit. Write out the materials you will need and the steps you will follow. Record your results and observations.

Draw Conclusions

Did your results support your hypothesis? Why or why not?

Inquiry Open

What else can you learn about circuits and how they work? For example, how do batteries and light bulbs change the electric current in parallel circuits? Design your own investigation to answer your question.

Remember to follow the steps of the scientific process.

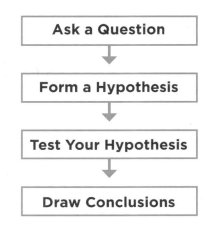

| Ask a Question |
| Form a Hypothesis |
| Test Your Hypothesis |
| Draw Conclusions |

4 IE 6.c. Formulate and justify predictions based on cause-and-effect relationships. • 4 IE 6.d. Conduct multiple trials to test a prediction and draw conclusions about the relationships between predictions and results.

Using Electrical Energy

Look and Wonder

What would your life be like if there were no electricity? How would you cook food or wash clothes? Could you use a computer or watch a movie? How do these appliances use electricity?

  4 PS 1.g. Students know electrical energy can be converted to heat, light, and motion.

What do appliances use electrical energy for?

Purpose

Appliances turn electrical energy into other kinds of energy. Find out what kinds of energy the appliances in your home produce.

toaster
heater
electric blanket

lamp
flashlight
television

fan
toy train
washing machine

Procedure

1 **Observe** Take a survey of the electrical devices in your home. Is there a fan? A toaster? A lamp? List all the appliances that use electricity.

2 **Classify** What type of energy does each device produce? Try to put them into groups that use electrical energy similarly. For example, a fan and a dryer both produce motion.

Draw Conclusions

3 What are some ways that appliances use electrical energy?

Explore More

Name some appliances that produce more than one kind of energy.

 4 IE 6.f. Follow a set of written instructions for a scientific investigation.

Read and Learn

► **Main Idea** 4 PS 1.g

Electrical energy can be converted to other forms of energy such as heat, light, and motion.

► **Vocabulary**

transformer, p. 312

circuit breaker, p. 314

fuse, p. 314

LOG ON ℮**-Glossary**
@ www.macmillanmh.com

► **Reading Skill**

Sequence

First

↓

Next

↓

Last

▲ Light bulbs resist the flow of electricity. Electrical energy is turned into light, another form of energy.

How is electrical energy used?

People depend on electrical energy to light rooms, to cook food, and to power computers and air conditioners. Electric currents carry the energy that people use. Electrical devices change this energy into other kinds of energy, such as heat, light, and motion.

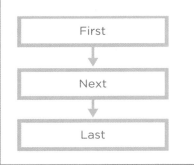

This train uses electrical energy to move. Motion is a form of energy.

Heat

Electrical energy can be converted into heat. This heat can be used to cook food and dry clothes. Some furnaces use electrical energy to heat homes. Inside a hair dryer, electric current passes through wires which have a lot of resistance. This causes the wire to heat air inside the hair dryer.

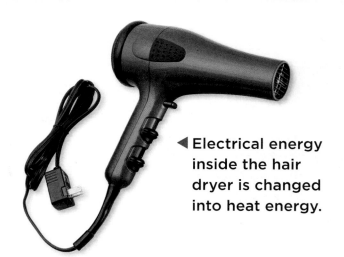

◄ Electrical energy inside the hair dryer is changed into heat energy.

Light

Electrical energy is used to light buildings, vehicles, and streets. An incandescent (in•kuhn•DES•uhnt) bulb produces heat and light. Inside an incandescent bulb is a thin wire called a *filament*. As the filament resists electric current, it heats up and glows. A fluorescent (flaw•RES•uhnt) bulb uses a gas to produce light. Electric current makes the gas glow. Fluorescent bulbs do not become as hot as incandescent bulbs.

Motion

Electric motors change electrical energy into motion. Electric motors are found in toys, washing machines, drills, and other tools. Electric motors are also used to run trains at speeds as high as 515 kilometers (320 miles) per hour.

✔ Quick Check

Sequence Electric current flows through a bulb's filament. What happens next?

Critical Thinking Eventually a filament will melt and break. When it breaks, what happens to the bulb?

How does electrical energy get to your home?

Power plants produce electrical energy. An electric current carries the energy from a power plant to homes and businesses. The electric current travels in a circuit through wires and transformers. **Transformers** are used to change the voltage of electric current.

Electric current leaves a power plant with a strength of about 25,000 volts. This is too low to be carried efficiently by power lines. At a higher voltage, more current can flow through a cable. A step-up transformer is used to boost the voltage.

◀ Step-down transformers change the voltage of electric current so it can be used in your home.

The Path of Energy

1. Electrical energy is produced at a power plant.

2. A transformer increases the voltage of electric current.

3. A transformer lowers the voltage of current.

4. Another transformer lowers the voltage so it is safe for your home.

5. Electrical cables carry the electric current back to the power plant.

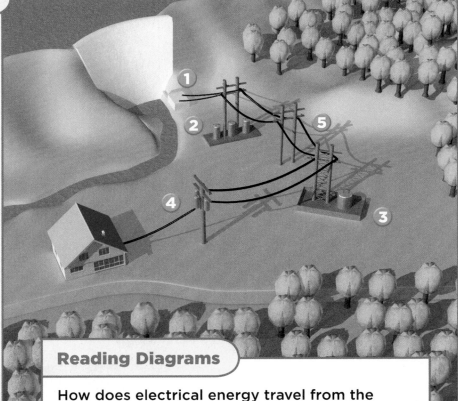

Reading Diagrams

How does electrical energy travel from the power plant to the home?

Clue: Follow the wires leaving the power station.

Electric current from the power plant enters the transformer. Electric current leaves the transformer with a strength of about 400,000 volts.

Before the electric current reaches a home or business, it must be changed again to a lower voltage. A step-down transformer is used to decrease the voltage. Most homes use an electric current at 240 volts. Appliances in your home usually run on 120- or 240-volt circuits. Factories, on the other hand, use from 11,000 to 33,000 volts.

In your home, some electrical energy is turned into light, heat, and motion. The current then leaves your home through different wires. Transformers change the voltage again as current travels back to the power plant.

Quick Check

Sequence Tell what happens to electric current as it travels between your home and a power plant.

Critical Thinking Why do wires carry the electric current back to the power plant? Would current flow without these wires?

Quick Lab

How much electrical energy do you use?

1 **Observe** List the major electrical appliances that your family uses each day, such as a clothes washer, dryer, computer, and so on.

Appliance	Watts	Appliance	Watts
refrigerator	725	microwave	900
television	120	radio	150
computer	270	vacuum cleaner	1,200
toaster	1,000	clothes washer	425
hair dryer	1,500	clothes dryer	3,400

2 **Use Numbers** Look up each appliance in the table. Multiply the value in the table by how many hours you use it. For example, if your family uses a computer about four hours per day:

270 watts x 4 hours = 1080 watt•hours

3 Then, add the amounts to find the total electrical energy used.

4 Think of some things you can do in your home to conserve electricity. Share ideas with your classmates.

How can homes use electrical energy safely?

Electrical energy can be very useful. However, it can also be dangerous. A short circuit might happen when the insulation on a wire frays. The bare wire touches a conductor, such as metal or another wire. Since this connection has very little resistance, it draws a large amount of electric current. The short circuit can heat up the wire and cause a fire.

Plugging too many devices into one outlet can also cause too much current to go through a wire. If this happens, the wire can overheat and may start a fire. To prevent this, most homes have many outlets that are connected to different circuits. No circuit carries too much current.

Circuit breakers and fuses also protect against dangerous amounts of electric current. A **circuit breaker** stops the flow of charges by switching off the current if it gets too high. A **fuse** melts if the electric current in the circuit gets too high. This causes an open circuit.

✔ Quick Check

Sequence How can a short circuit happen?

Critical Thinking Surge protectors break the circuit if too much electric current flows through it. How does this protect electrical devices and you?

▲ When a fuse melts and breaks, it must be replaced with a new fuse.

▲ When a circuit breaker breaks a circuit, it can be reset and used again.

◀ Surge protector

Lesson Review

Summarize the Main Idea

Electrical energy can be **converted to** other forms of energy, such as light, heat, and motion. (pp. 310–311)

Electrical energy **travels from** a source such as a power plant through wires to your home. (pp. 312–313)

Fuses and circuit breakers are **safety devices** that protect against dangerous amounts of electric current. (p. 314)

Make a FOLDABLES™ Study Guide

Make a three-tab book. Use it to summarize what you learned.

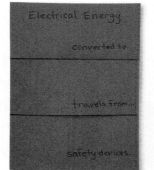

Think, Talk, and Write

1 **Main Idea** In what ways can you use electrical energy?

2 **Vocabulary** What does a transformer do?

3 **Sequence** Explain how electrical energy travels from a power plant to your home.

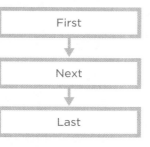

First

Next

Last

4 **Critical Thinking** Suppose an incandescent light bulb and a fluorescent light bulb produce the same amount of light. The incandescent bulb uses more energy. Why?

5 **Test Practice** Which changes electrical energy into motion?

  A a paper airplane

  B a toaster

  C an electric fan

  D a lamp

 Writing Link

Write a Safety Ad
Electric current does great things. But it can also be dangerous. Write an advertisement telling how to safely use electric current.

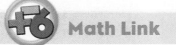 **Math Link**

Multiplying Voltage
Electric current enters a step-up transformer at 240 volts. The current leaving the transformer is 30 times stronger. What is the new voltage?

I'd Like to Make a Toast!

Breakfast is the most important meal of the day. Toast is a part of many students' breakfasts. Making toast is quick and easy.

Choose your favorite kind of bread. First, slide a slice of bread into each slot in the top of the toaster. Next, push down the lever on the side of the toaster. The bread slices should drop down inside. Inside the toaster, electric current causes wire coils to heat up and toast the bread.

When the bread is toasted, the slices pop up from the slots. Remove the toast and place it on a plate. Be careful, the toast might be hot! Spread butter or jam over the toast and enjoy.

Good explanatory writing

► explains how to complete a certain task

► gives step-by-step directions in an order that makes sense

► gives details that are easy to follow

► uses time-order words, such as *first*, *next*, *then*, and *finally*, or spatial words, such as *over* or *across*

 Write About It

Explanatory Writing Think of an electrical device that you use every day. Write an essay that explains how you use it. Use time-order words and spatial words to make your directions easy to follow.

 LOG ON ⓔ **-Journal** Write about it online @ **www.macmillanmh.com**

ELA W 4.1.3. Use traditional structures for conveying information (e.g., chronological order, cause and effect, similarity and difference, posing and answering a question).

Math in Science

Lighten Up

Suppose that you are decorating for a party and want to hang strings of lights. How many bulbs would you need? How much electrical power would they use?

Electrical power is measured in units called *watts*. One string of lights with 8 bulbs uses 40 watts of electrical power. You probably wouldn't use just one string of lights for decoration, though.

The table shows how many bulbs and how much power various numbers of strings use.

Number Patterns

For different numbers of strings you can recognize a pattern.

1 string x 8 bulbs per string = 8 bulbs

2 strings x 8 bulbs per string = 16 bulbs

3 strings x 8 bulbs per string = 24 bulbs

Each time you add a string, you add 8 to the previous number. You can also find the number of watts used.

2 strings x 40 watts per string = 80 watts

number of strings	1	2	3	4	5	10	20
number of light bulbs	8	16	24		40		
power used (watts)	40	80	120			400	

 Solve It

Copy the chart, and fill in the blank spaces.

 MA NS 4.3.3. Solve problems involving multiplication of multidigit numbers by two-digit numbers. •MA MR 4.2.3. Use a variety of methods, such as words, numbers, symbols, charts, graphs, tables, diagrams, and models, to explain mathematical reasoning.

Hybrid POWER

▲ Hybrid engines use both gasoline and electrical energy to move the car.

In cities like Los Angeles and Sacramento, millions of people drive cars. Most of the cars run on gasoline. There is a limited supply of gasoline in the world, however, and our cars make us very dependent on it. Also, the more gasoline the cars burn, the more they pollute the air. Pollution from cars contributes to a cloud of smog that sometimes covers a city like a blanket.

How can we become less dependent on gasoline and cut down on air pollution? One way is to build better cars. Car companies have been working to develop hybrid cars. *Hybrid* is a word that describes something that is a mix of two different things. Hybrid cars use two different power sources: gasoline fuel and electrical energy.

In a traditional car, the gasoline engine runs all the time. But when the car is stopped at a light, sitting in traffic, or slowing down, power from the gasoline engine is not needed at all. At these times, the fuel that is used to keep the engine running is just being wasted.

AMERICAN MUSEUM Ö NATURAL HISTORY

ELA R 4.2.2. Use appropriate strategies when reading for different purposes (e.g., full comprehension, location of information, personal enjoyment)

A hybrid car is designed so that it uses much less fuel than a traditional car. It combines a gas-powered engine with an electric motor powered by batteries. When the car is stopped or slowing down, the gas-powered engine shuts off. The battery-powered motor takes over to keep the lights, air conditioning, and radio working. The batteries get recharged when the car slows to a stop. The car changes its energy of motion into electrical energy.

The gasoline engines in hybrid cars can be smaller and more energy efficient and still provide enough power to keep the car cruising on the freeway. This makes us less dependent on gasoline—and makes for a cleaner environment!

◀ Burning fossil fuels to power cars produces smog.

▲ Hybrid cars can help to reduce the amount of air pollution.

Main Idea

▶ The main idea is the focus of the entire article.

▶ Details support and explain the main idea.

Write About It

Main Idea Reread the article. Then answer these questions. How do hybrid cars help people and the environment? How does a hybrid car produce electrical energy?

LOG ON **e-Journal** Write about it online @ **www.macmillanmh.com**

Summarize the Main Ideas

Some matter is electrically charged. Electrical charges attract or repel one another. (pp. 286–293)

Electric current, or flow of electrical charges, will only flow through a complete circuit. There are two basic types of circuits, series and parallel. (pp. 298–305)

Electrical energy can be converted to other forms of energy, such as light, heat, and motion. Fuses and circuit breakers keep your home safe when you use electrical energy. (pp. 310–315)

Make a FOLDABLES™ Study Guide

Tape your lesson study guides to a piece of paper as shown. Use your study guide to review what you have learned in this chapter.

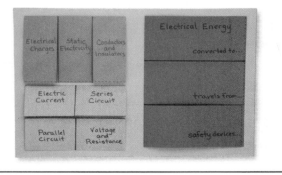

Fill each blank with the best word from the list.

circuit, p. 299

conductor, p. 292

electric current, p. 298

fuse, p. 314

parallel circuit, p. 302

resistance, p. 304

series circuit, p. 300

static electricity, p. 288

1. A buildup of electrical charge is called _____. 4 PS 1.e

2. When there is too much current in a circuit, a _____ will melt and break the circuit. 4 PS 1.g

3. Copper is a good _____ of electrical charges. 4 PS 1.e

4. The amount of electric current in a circuit depends on voltage and _____. 4 PS 1.a

5. A complete path in which electric current can flow is a _____. 4 PS 1.a

6. If one light bulb in a _____ burns out, none of the other bulbs in the circuit will shine. 4 PS 1.a

7. If one bulb in a _____ burns out, the other bulbs in the circuit will still shine. 4 PS 1.a

8. A flow of electrical charges through a circuit is called _____. 4 PS 1.a

Answer each of the following in complete sentences.

9. Main Idea How do people use electrical energy? 4 PS 1.g

10. Explanatory Writing How could you build a series circuit? How do series circuits work? 4 PS 1.a

11. Analyze Data Dina tested how long 1 D cell battery will power light bulbs in a parallel circuit. She recorded her data in the table below.

D Cell Battery Power	
# of bulbs	minutes the bulbs were lit
1	240
2	120
4	60

How long do you think a D cell battery would power eight bulbs in a parallel circuit? 4 PS 1.a

12. Critical Thinking Rubbing a balloon with plastic wrap gives the balloon a positive charge. What kind of charge does the plastic wrap receive? Explain how this happens. 4 PS 1.e

How do we use electricity?

CHAPTER 6

Design an Alarm System

Design a simple electrical alarm system. Assume that you can use an arrangement of power sources, wires, series and parallel circuits, and switches in your system. Assume that your system would also include devices that could sense when an intruder moved into an area.

- First, draw a diagram of your system.

- Then, describe how your system would work. For example, how would you turn the system on and off? What would happen when an intruder entered the property?

Key
= battery
= wire
= door
= switch
= window
= speaker

1 Electrical energy can be converted into all of the following *EXCEPT* 4 PS 1.g

A heat.

B light.

C motion.

D darkness.

2 What happens when lightning strikes? 4 PS 1.e

A Electricity flows from Earth to lakes.

B Electricity is released from Earth.

C Electricity flows from the clouds to Earth.

D Electricity is released from lakes.

3 A student made the circuit in the drawing below.

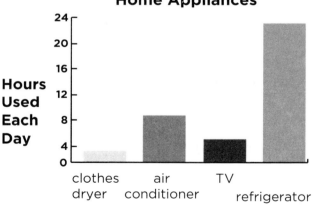

What does the student need to add to the circuit to make it work? 4 PS 1.a

A another bulb

B another battery

C a switch

D another wire

4 Which of the following *best* describes an electric current? 4 PS 1.a

A a series of electrical wires

B a flow of electrical charges

C a surge of electrical power

D a chain of electrical batteries

5 Five light bulbs are connected to one D cell battery. When one bulb burns out, the others continue to shine. The bulbs are part of 4 PS 1.a

A a parallel circuit.

B a series circuit.

C an open circuit.

D a circuit breaker.

6 This graph shows the amount of time some appliances are used daily.

Home Appliances

Hours Used Each Day

24, 20, 16, 12, 8, 4, 0

clothes dryer   air conditioner   TV   refrigerator

Which appliance is *always* in use according to the graph? 4 IE 6.e

A clothes dryer

B television

C air conditioner

D refrigerator

7 If you rub two balloons with wool, 4 PS 1.e

A the balloons will attract each other.

B the balloons will not affect each other.

C the balloons will repel each other.

D the balloons will pop.

8 A student tested various materials to see if they conduct electricity. She made a chart.

Conducts Electricity	Does Not Conduct Electricity
copper wire	cork
paper clip	toothpick
dime	rubber band
spoon	comb

Which of the following is an inference? 4 IE 6.a

A Four of the objects conducted electricity.

B Metal objects conduct electricity.

C The toothpick did not conduct electricity.

D The spoon might conduct electricity.

9 All of the following protect people from electric current *EXCEPT* 4 PS 1.g

A circuit breakers.

B fuses.

C insulators.

D short circuits.

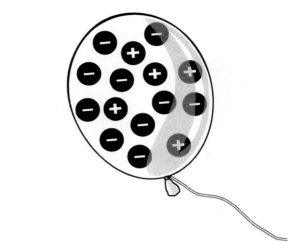

10 If a balloon has more negative charges than positive charges, 4 PS 1.e

A it is neutral.

B it is positively charged.

C it is negatively charged.

D it has no overall charge.

11 A transformer is used to change 4 PS 1.g

A the voltage of electric current.

B the resistance of electric current.

C electrical energy into light.

D light into electrical energy.

12 Which of the following is a good conductor of electricity? 4 PS 1.e

A rubber

B copper

C wood

D glass

Magnetism

How do we use magnets?

 4 PS 1. Electricity and magnetism are related effects that have many useful applications in everyday life.

Literature
Magazine
Article

ELA R 4.2.2. Use appropriate strategies when reading for different purposes (e.g., full comprehension, location of information, personal enjoyment). ELA W 4.2.3. Write information reports.

Maglev train

From *Scholastic SuperScience*

Cruising on Air

Boy, can this train fly! The Japanese Maglev train at left zoomed in for a world train speed record at 550 km per hour (342 mph)—without ever touching the tracks.

What's the secret? It's not magic, but magnets. Maglev stands for magnetic levitation (LEV-i-tay-shun) vehicle. Magnets on the train and track repel (push away) each other. That makes the train hover 10 cm (4 in.) above the ground. Magnets also work together to push and pull the train along at superfast speeds.

Scientists will "test-drive" Maglev for about a year. A Maglev train system could be ready for Japanese travelers by 2010!

 ## Write About It

Response to Literature In this article, you learned that Maglev trains use magnets to travel at very fast speeds. What are some ways you use magnets? Write a report about uses of magnets. Include facts and details from this article and your experience to support your writing.

LOG ON ⓔ-**Journal** Write about it online @ **www.macmillanmh.com**

Magnets

star

explore

N

S

moon

flower

GROCERY LIST

Salt
Cer
Gr
Ri
Juice

ead
ggs
utter
Apples
Spinach
Broccoli

Look and Wonder

What is the invisible force that holds a magnet to a refrigerator? How do magnets work? Do they always attract things?

4 PS 1.b. Students know how to build a simple compass and use it to detect magnetic effects, including Earth's magnetic field.

• **4 PS 1.f.** Students know that magnets have two poles (north and south) and that like poles repel each other while unlike poles attract each other.

How do magnets interact?

Make a Prediction

What happens when one magnet is near another magnet? How do different parts of magnets interact?

Test Your Prediction

1 **Experiment** Bring the north pole of one magnet close to the north pole of another magnet. Record what happens. Then try it again.

2 **Predict** What do you think will happen if you bring the south poles of the magnets near each other?

3 **Experiment** Try it and record the result.

4 **Experiment** Bring the north pole of one magnet close to the south pole of the other magnet. Record what happens. Try it again.

Draw Conclusions

5 **Analyze Data** What happens when like poles (south-south or north-north) of two magnets are brought together? What happens when unlike poles (south-north) are brought together?

Explore More

Experiment Are certain parts of the magnets stronger than other parts? How could you find the strongest parts of a horseshoe or disc magnet? Make a plan and try it.

4 IE 6.d. Conduct multiple trials to test a prediction and draw conclusions about the relationships between predictions and results.

Materials

- **2 bar magnets with the poles marked**

Step **1**

Step **4**

4 PS 1.b
4 PS 1.f

► **Main Idea**

Like magnetic poles repel each other and unlike poles attract each other. Compasses use magnets to tell direction.

► **Vocabulary**

magnet, p. 330

poles, p. 331

magnetic field, p. 334

compass, p. 336

LOG ON ℮-Glossary
@ www.macmillanmh.com

► **Reading Skill**

Predict

My Prediction	What Happens

SCIENCE QUEST Explore magnetism on Science Island.

▲ Magnets come in many shapes and sizes. This horseshoe magnet is a permanent magnet. It always has magnetic force.

What is a magnet?

You may have played with magnets and watched them snap together or push apart. Magnets can also make some objects move or even fly through the air. A magnet can affect an object without even touching it.

When you bring two magnets close together, they will either repel or attract each other. The force that pushes magnets apart or pulls them together is called *magnetic force*. A **magnet** is any object with magnetic force.

Magnetic Poles

The parts of a magnet where the magnetic force is strongest are called the magnetic **poles**. All known magnets have two poles—a north pole and a south pole. When two magnets are brought together, a north pole and a south pole attract each other. Like poles (north-north or south-south) repel each other.

Magnets that are far apart do not pull or push enough to move each other. The magnetic force between two magnets is weak when magnets are far apart. The magnetic force gets stronger as the magnets are brought closer together.

Refrigerator Magnets

Refrigerator magnets are made of tiny strips of magnets placed next to each other. The way these tiny strips are arranged makes the magnetic force strong on one side and very weak on the other. That's why only one side of the magnet sticks to a refrigerator. If you carefully slide a bar magnet over a refrigerator magnet, you will notice that some areas attract and other areas repel.

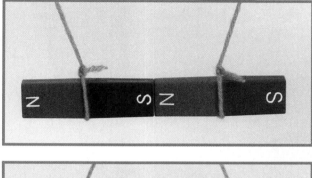

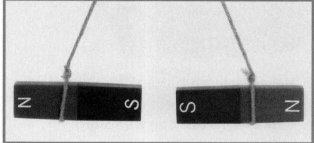

▲ Magnetic force pulls opposite poles together and pushes like poles apart.

✓ Quick Check

Predict You hold the south pole of a bar magnet against the south pole of a horseshoe magnet. What will happen when you let go?

Critical Thinking A pole of one magnet is attracted to a pole of another magnet. Are the poles the same or different? How do you know?

▲ Magnetite is a natural permanent magnet containing iron. Magnetite can be found in California's Mojave Desert.

How do magnets attract?

Magnets can attract some metal objects, such as paper clips. How? When you bring a magnet near certain metal objects, the metal will become magnetic. The objects actually become magnets!

Most magnets are made of metal. Metals, like all matter, are made of tiny particles. Those particles are like tiny magnets. Inside a magnet, these tiny magnetic particles are lined up. The north poles face one direction, and the south poles face the other. The particles push and pull in the same directions.

In objects made of metals like iron, nickel, and cobalt, those tiny magnetic particles push and pull in all different directions. When a permanent magnet is brought near the objects, however, the particles turn around and line up. The metal becomes a temporary magnet. It can attract other magnets.

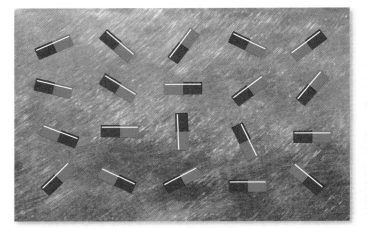

▲ Metals are made up of tiny magnetic particles. Normally, the particles point in different directions.

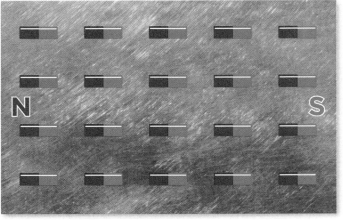

▲ When all the magnetic particles line up, the metal becomes a magnet.

If you take the permanent magnet away, the magnetic particles usually move around again. The north and south poles no longer line up. Sometimes, though, the particles stay lined up, and the metal becomes a permanent magnet. Computer hard drives store information this way. Computers use a magnet to write on hard disks by making some metal on the disk magnetic.

Reading Photos

What kinds of materials are attracted to the magnet? What kinds of materials are not attracted?

Clue: Look at the objects on and below the magnet.

Quick Lab

What Does a Magnet Attract?

1 Predict Many foods, such as cereals, contain iron. Can a magnet attract the iron from these foods?

2 Pour some iron-fortified cereal into a plastic bag. Seal the bag, then crush the cereal.

3 Experiment Rub the magnet over the plastic bag. What happens?

4 Infer What do you think the tiny bits attracted to the magnet are? Explain.

5 How could you determine which cereal has the most iron?

✔ Quick Check

Predict Would a magnet attract a coin made of pure nickel?

Critical Thinking What happens to an iron nail when it is brought near a magnet? What happens when the magnet is taken away?

What is a magnetic field?

To pull a wagon and push a merry-go-round, you have to touch them. Magnets can attract or repel objects without touching them. How?

Every magnet has a magnetic field around it. A **magnetic field** is the area of magnetic force around a magnet. When one magnet enters the magnetic field of another magnet, it is either attracted or repelled. This can happen even if the magnets are not touching. A magnet's magnetic field is strongest near the magnet's poles. The magnetic field is weaker farther away from the poles.

Did you know our planet is actually a giant magnet? Much of the inside of Earth is made up of melted iron. This iron creates a magnetic field that surrounds our planet.

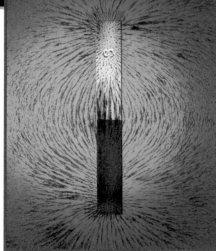

▲ Iron filings can be used to show the magnetic field of a bar magnet. Magnetic field lines curve from one pole to the other.

◄ The aurora australis is a display of lights near the South Pole. Charged particles from the Sun become caught in Earth's magnetic field and give off light.

Earth's Magnetic Field

Reading Diagrams

Where is Earth's magnetic field the strongest?

Clue: Look at the places where the field lines come together.

Earth spins around its *axis*, an imaginary line through the center of Earth. The *geographic* (jee•uh•GRAF•ik) North Pole is located at one end of this axis. The geographic South Pole is at the other end. Earth has one magnetic pole near its geographic North Pole. There is another magnetic pole near the geographic South Pole.

Long ago people noticed that one end of a magnet turned to point north. They called this end the north-seeking pole. The other end was named the south-seeking pole, because it pointed south. Today those names are shortened to just the north and south poles of a magnet.

✓ Quick Check

Predict If you hung a magnet on a piece of string, what would it do?

Critical Thinking The north poles of magnets are attracted to Earth's magnetic pole in the Arctic. Is that pole a magnetic north or south pole?

Quick Lab

Make a Compass

1. Fill a dish or cup with water.

2. Magnetize a craft needle by rubbing it many times with a permanent magnet. Drag the magnet from the eye of the needle to the point. Then put the magnet away.

3. Push the magnetized needle through a piece of foam.

   ⚠️ **Be Careful!** Do not stick yourself!

4. Place the needle and foam into the dish. They should float on the surface of the water.

5. **Predict** Which direction will the needle point?

6. **Observe** Test your prediction. If you move it, does it turn back to this position?

▲ Ancient sailors used compasses to navigate the seas when they could not see land or stars.

What is a compass?

Pretend you are on a boat at night. No land is in sight. The sky is cloudy. Ancient sailors could become lost on such nights until the compass was invented.

A **compass** is an instrument that uses Earth's magnetic field to help people find directions. A compass needle is actually a thin magnet. The needle points north because it lines up with Earth's magnetic field.

Since a compass needle points north, the compass can be used to tell north, east, south, and west, and other directions in between.

✔ Quick Check

Predict If you held the south pole of a magnet next to a compass, what would happen?

Critical Thinking Would an astronaut need a compass in space? Why or why not?

Lesson Review

Summarize the Main Idea

 All magnets have **two poles**. Like poles **repel** each other, and unlike poles **attract** each other. (pp. 330–333)

 A **magnetic field** is the region of magnetic force around a magnet. (pp. 334–335)

 A **compass** needle is attracted to Earth's magnetic poles, so it can be used to find which way is north. (p. 336)

Make a FOLDABLES™ Study Guide

Make a four-door book. Use it to summarize what you learned about magnets.

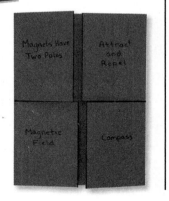

Think, Talk, and Write

1 **Main Idea** What happens to a metal paper clip when you bring it near a magnet?

2 **Vocabulary** What is a compass? Why does a compass needle point north?

3 **Predict** What will happen if you slowly bring the north pole of one magnet toward the south pole of another magnet?

My Prediction	What Happens

4 **Critical Thinking** How can you use a bar magnet and a length of string to make a compass?

5 **Test Practice** As you get closer to a magnet, its magnetic field

A stays the same

B becomes stronger

C becomes weaker

D disappears

 Writing Link

Write a Travel Brochure
Make a travel brochure for a trip to the North or South Pole. What would travelers need? How would they find the exact magnetic pole?

Health Link

Animals Using Magnets
Bees, birds, and other animals have natural magnets inside their bodies. How might these magnets help the animal? (Hint: Think of a compass.)

Draw Conclusions

When people do an experiment, they are trying to answer a question. They make observations and study the results of the experiment in order to draw a conclusion. When you **draw conclusions**, you interpret the results of an experiment to answer a question. Your conclusions help explain things you observe. They can help you make predictions in future experiments.

① Learn It

When you **draw conclusions**, you have to look at all the facts before you can decide on an answer. It is a good idea to record your observations and facts on a chart. That way you will have all the facts in one place to help you draw your conclusions.

② Try It

Scientists use observations and information that they know to **draw conclusions**. You can, too.

▶ Make a clay base with one flat side. Stick a pencil in the clay. Place the clay on a table or desk. Make sure it holds the pencil upright and steady.

▶ Place two ring magnets on the pencil. Try different ways of stacking the magnets. Flip one of them over or change their order. Record your observations.

▶ Next, arrange three magnets on the pencil in different ways. Record what happens.

Now use your observations to draw conclusions. Why do some of the magnets float? Why do the others stick together? How could you make one of the magnets float?

③ Apply It

Now **draw conclusions** on your own by experimenting and collecting data.

▶ Add more magnets above the rings on the pencil so that the magnets float.

▶ Push down on the top magnet, squeezing the magnets together. Then let go.

▶ Draw conclusions about how magnets behave. What happened when you let go? Why?

 4 IE 6.a. Differentiate observation from inference (interpretation) and know scientists' explanations come partly from what they observe and partly from how they interpret their observations.

Electromagnets

Look and Wonder

This magnet is so strong that it can lift huge chunks of metal into the air! It uses an electric current to produce a magnetic field. How do electric currents interact with magnets?

4 PS 1.c. Students know electric currents produce magnetic fields and know how to build a simple electromagnet. **• 4 PS 1.d.** Students know the role of electromagnets in the construction of electric motors, electric generators, and simple devices, such as doorbells and earphones.

How does an electric current affect a magnet?

Make a Prediction

Can an electric current move a magnet?

Test Your Prediction

1. Wrap fine wire around a compass in several loops.

2. Turn the compass so its needle stays lined up with the coils of wire.

3. **Observe** Connect the wire ends to the battery to make a circuit. What change do you notice in the compass?

4. **Experiment** Open and close the circuit. What does the compass needle do?

Draw Conclusions

5. **Infer** What happened to the compass needle when electric current was flowing? Why did this happen?

6. Did you detect a magnetic field around the wire when there was no current?

Explore More

Experiment Reverse the wires on the battery. What happens? Explain the result.

 4 IE 6.a. Differentiate observation from inference (interpretation) and know scientists' explanations come partly from what they observe and partly from how they interpret their observations.

Materials

- **fine wire, about 40 cm**
- **compass**
- **D cell battery**
- **battery holder**

Step 1

Step 3

▶ **Main Idea** 4 PS 1.c
4 PS 1.d

An electric current produces a magnetic field. Electromagnets are used in many common household items.

▶ **Vocabulary**

electromagnet, p. 343

loudspeaker, p. 344

microphone, p. 345

LOG ON ⓔ-Glossary
@ www.macmillanmh.com

▶ **Reading Skill**

Problem and Solution

Problem

↓

Steps to Solution

↓

Solution

▲ Electric current in the wires turns this curved metal bar into a magnet.

What is an electromagnet?

In the 1820s and 1830s, scientists such as Michael Faraday and Joseph Henry made some amazing discoveries about electric currents and magnets. They found that electric currents make magnetic fields and that magnets could *generate*, or make, an electric current.

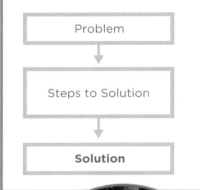

◀ Michael Faraday taught himself science from books. He eventually became a famous scientist.

When an electric current flows through a wire, it creates a magnetic field around the wire. Increasing the current makes the magnetic field stronger. You can also make the magnetic field stronger by winding the wire into a long coil. Each loop of wire is like a little magnet that has its own magnetic force. The loops all push and pull in the same direction.

Electromagnets can make even stronger magnetic fields. An **electromagnet** is a coil of wire wrapped around a metal core, such as an iron bar. When an electric current flows through the coil, it creates a magnetic field. This magnetic field causes particles inside the metal core to line up. The metal core becomes magnetic. When the current stops, the metal core is no longer magnetic.

 Quick Check

Problem and Solution How could you make the magnetic field of an electromagnet stronger?

Critical Thinking When electric currents flow in the same direction through two wires, the wires attract each other. Why?

Quick Lab

Make an Electromagnet

1. Wind a 50-cm piece of wire around a nail about 20 times.

2. Attach the wire ends to a D cell battery. Test to see if your electromagnet will pick up paper clips.

   ⚠️ **Be Careful!** The wire may become warm.

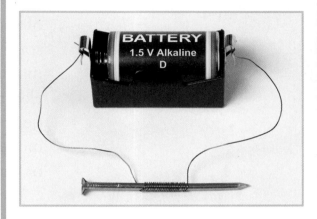

3. **Predict** How could you use a permanent magnet to find the poles of the electromagnet?

4. **Observe** Hold the north pole of a permanent magnet to one end of the nail. Then hold it to the other end. What happens?

5. **Experiment** Switch the wire connections on the battery. This makes the electric current run in the opposite direction through the wire. Repeat step 4. What difference do you notice?

6. **Infer** What can you infer about the poles of an electromagnet?

Headphones are small loudspeakers with tiny electromagnets. ▼

How does a loudspeaker work?

Electromagnets are important parts of the loudspeakers in radios, televisions, and headphones. A **loudspeaker** is a device that changes electrical energy into sound. Sounds are produced when objects vibrate, or move back and forth quickly.

A device, such as a stereo, sends electric current to an electromagnet in the loudspeaker. The electromagnet is attached to a *diaphragm* (DIGH•uh•fram). The diaphragm is the part of the loudspeaker that vibrates to create sound. The loudspeaker also has a permanent magnet. When electric current flows, the electromagnet is pushed and pulled by the permanent magnet. As the electromagnet moves, so does the diaphragm. The motion of the diaphragm produces sound.

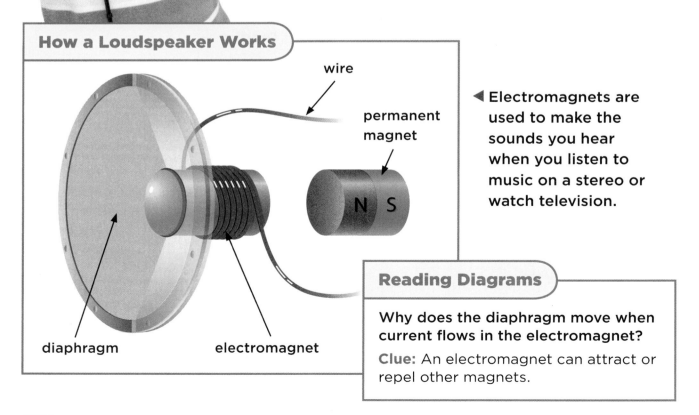

How a Loudspeaker Works

wire

permanent magnet

N S

diaphragm

electromagnet

◀ Electromagnets are used to make the sounds you hear when you listen to music on a stereo or watch television.

Reading Diagrams

Why does the diaphragm move when current flows in the electromagnet?

Clue: An electromagnet can attract or repel other magnets.

Telephones

Telephones also rely on electromagnets. A telephone receiver is actually a tiny loudspeaker. When a friend calls you on the telephone, his or her voice is changed into electrical signals. Those signals travel as an electric current through telephone lines. When the signals reach your telephone, the receiver uses an electromagnet to change the signals back into sound.

A telephone mouthpiece is like a loudspeaker in reverse. Some contain a microphone (MIGH•kruh•fohn). A **microphone** is a device that uses a magnet to convert sound into electrical signals. When you speak into the mouthpiece, a diaphragm vibrates. As the diaphragm moves, a magnet generates electrical signals in a wire connected to the diaphragm. Those signals are sent to your friend's phone through telephone lines.

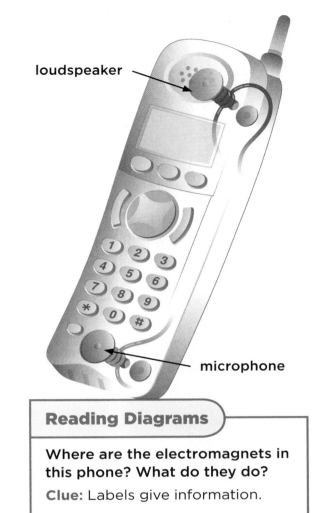

loudspeaker

microphone

Reading Diagrams

Where are the electromagnets in this phone? What do they do?

Clue: Labels give information.

✓ *Quick Check*

Problem and Solution Suppose you call a friend on the telephone. You can hear him, but he cannot hear you. What part of the phone might be broken?

Critical Thinking How is a loudspeaker like a microphone? How are they different?

Telephones use magnets to turn electrical signals into sound and sound into electrical signals. ▶

How else are electromagnets used?

Electromagnets are often more useful than ordinary permanent magnets. An electromagnet can be switched on and off by turning the electric current on and off. Also, by changing the current, the magnetic field can be made stronger or weaker.

Today, electromagnets are found in hundreds of devices from electric guitars to power plant generators (JEN•uh•ray•tuhrz). They are used in the electric motors that power some trains and toy cars. They are used in transformers that increase or decrease the voltage of electric currents. They are also found in many common appliances, such as doorbells, vacuum cleaners, and dishwashers.

An electric current flows through the electromagnet inside the doorbell. The magnetic field pulls a metal hammer to strike a bell. ▶

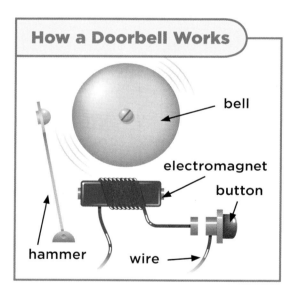

How a Doorbell Works

bell

electromagnet

button

hammer   wire

✔ *Quick Check*

Problem and Solution If you dropped a box of needles, would you rather pick them up with a permanent magnet or an electromagnet? Why?

Critical Thinking Most devices that change electrical energy into motion use electromagnets. List some devices that you used today that might have an electromagnet.

Lesson Review

Summarize the Main Idea

An **electric current** flowing through a wire produces a **magnetic field** around the wire. (pp. 342–343)

Electromagnets are used in **loudspeakers** to make sound. (pp. 344–345)

Electromagnets are used in many household **appliances and toys**. (p. 346)

Make a FOLDABLES™ Study Guide

Make a trifold book. Use it to summarize what you learned about electromagnets and their uses.

Electromagnets

Think, Talk, and Write

1. **Main Idea** Compare electromagnets to permanent magnets.

2. **Vocabulary** How does an electromagnet work?

3. **Problem and Solution** Workers in junkyards use huge electromagnets to lift heavy objects. Why is an electromagnet better in this case than a permanent magnet?

Problem

↓

Steps to Solution

↓

Solution

4. **Critical Thinking** Why does adding an iron core to a wire make a stronger magnet? Would a wooden core work?

5. **Test Practice** If an electromagnet receives more current, it

   A becomes stronger
   B becomes weaker
   C does not change
   D turns off

Writing Link

Writing That Compares
Would you want an electromagnet for a refrigerator magnet? When is an electromagnet necessary or more useful? When is a permanent magnet the better choice?

Music Link

Current and Volume
Most concerts and performances today wouldn't be the same without speakers and microphones. How do you think changing the volume affects the electric current inside a loudspeaker?

Be a Scientist

Materials

fine wire, at least 60 centimeters

nail

D cell battery

battery holder

50 paper clips

How do wire loops affect an electromagnet?

Form a Hypothesis

Electromagnets are created from coiling wire around a metal core and running electric current through the wire. How do these coils affect the metal core? How does changing the number of coils affect the electromagnet? Write your hypothesis in the form, *"If you increase the number of wire coils on an electromagnet, then . . ."*

Test Your Hypothesis

1. Wind wire around the nail five times to make an electromagnet.

2. Put the battery in the battery holder. Connect one end of the wire to each terminal of the battery holder.

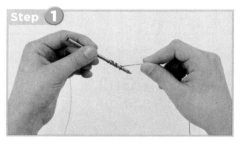

3. **Experiment** Hold one end of the electromagnet near a pile of paper clips. Record how many paper clips the electromagnet picked up.

   ⚠ **Be Careful!** Wires can become hot.

4. **Use Variables** Disconnect one wire from the battery holder. Then wrap the wire five more times around the nail. Reconnect the wire to the battery holder.

5. **Experiment** Repeat Steps 3 through 5 several times, and record how many paper clips the electromagnet attracts.

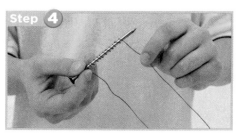

Draw Conclusions

6 **Analyze Data** How did changing the number of wire loops change the number of paper clips the electromagnet attracted? Make a graph to show your results.

7 **Infer** Did adding wire loops make the magnet stronger or weaker? How could you tell?

Inquiry Guided

How does distance affect a magnet's strength?

Form a Hypothesis

Did you have to hold the electromagnet close to the paper clips to pick them up? How does distance affect the pull of an electromagnet? Write your answer as a hypothesis in the form, "*If you move an electromagnet farther from an object, then . . .*"

Test Your Hypothesis

Design an experiment to investigate how distance affects magnetic force. Write out the steps you will follow. Record your results and observations.

Draw Conclusions

Did your experiment support your hypothesis? Why or why not? Compare your results with a classmate's results.

Inquiry Open

What else can you learn about how electromagnets work? For example, how can different numbers of batteries affect an electromagnet? Design an investigation to answer your question.

Remember to follow the steps of the scientific process.

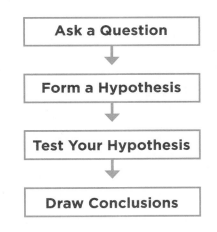

| Ask a Question |
| Form a Hypothesis |
| Test Your Hypothesis |
| Draw Conclusions |

 4 IE 6.d. Conduct multiple trials to test a prediction and draw conclusions about the relationships between predictions and results. • **4 IE 6.e.** Construct and interpret graphs from measurements.

349
EXTEND

Motors and Generators

wind turbines, Tehachapi Pass, California

Look and Wonder

Magnets can turn the power of wind into electrical energy. Magnets can also change electrical energy into motion. How can you use magnets to produce motion?

 4 PS 1.d. Students know the role of electromagnets in the construction of electric motors, electric generators, and simple devices, such as doorbells and earphones.

How can you use magnets to produce motion?

Purpose

To observe how magnets can be used to turn electrical energy into motion.

Procedure

1. Straighten one turn of each paper clip, making one long end. Insert the long ends into the terminals of the battery holder.

2. Make a coil by wrapping the wire around the battery many times. A few centimeters of wire should stick out from each side. Slide the coil off the end of the battery.

3. Tape the loops together so that they hold their shape. Bend the ends of the wire out. Then use a marker to color the top half of one of the wire ends.

4. Fit the battery into the battery holder. Place the coil ends inside the paper clips.

5. **Experiment** Put a magnet under the coil. Push the coil to start the motion.

Draw Conclusions

6. What is making the wire loop turn? Where is the energy to turn the loop coming from?

Explore More

How can you make your motor go faster?

 4 IE 6.f. Follow a set of written instructions for a scientific investigation.

Materials

- **2 metal paper clips**
- **100-cm wire**
- **D cell battery**
- **adhesive tape**
- **waterproof marker**
- **battery holder**
- **strong magnet**

Step 3

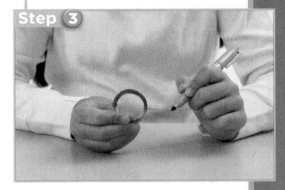

Step 5

Main Idea 4 PS 1.d

Electric motors convert electrical energy into motion. Electric generators change the energy of motion into electrical energy.

Vocabulary

motor, p. 352

generator, p. 354

alternating current, p. 356

direct current, p. 356

LOG ON e-Glossary
@ www.macmillanmh.com

Reading Skill

Summarize

Summary

What is an electric motor?

Electric motors are used in everyday devices such as refrigerators, air conditioners, and electric trains. An electric **motor** is a device that changes electrical energy into *mechanical energy* (muh•KAN•i•kuhl EN•ur•gee), or motion. Electric motors power tools, toys, and other machines.

A simple electric motor has a power source, a permanent magnet, a rotating loop of wire, and a motor shaft. The *shaft* is a rod that can spin and move. An electric current runs through the wire loop, making a magnetic field. The permanent magnet pushes and pulls on the wire loop. This causes the wire loop to spin. The wire loop then turns the motor shaft, which might turn a wheel or a gear.

An electric motor makes the mechanical energy that spins the car's wheels. ▼

How a Motor Works

The motor in a power drill changes electrical energy into the spinning motion of the drill bit.

wire loop

shaft

permanent magnet

N

S

Reading Diagrams

What causes the wire loop to spin?

Clue: Look at the magnetic poles around the wire loop.

In larger motors, the loop of wire is made into a coil that is wound hundreds of times around an iron cylinder. This makes a strong electromagnet. It has a much stronger magnetic field than a single wire loop. The electromagnet feels more push and pull from the permanent magnets. The motor might use this stronger force to move something heavy or spin faster.

Quick Check

Summarize How does a simple electric motor work?

Critical Thinking How might an electric train use the spinning motion produced by the motor?

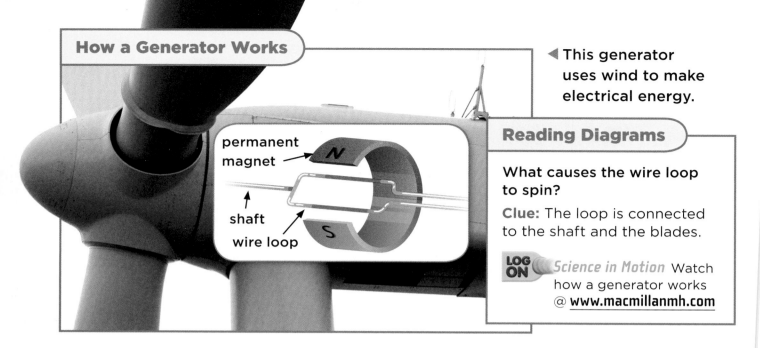

◀ This generator uses wind to make electrical energy.

permanent magnet

N

shaft

wire loop

S

Reading Diagrams

What causes the wire loop to spin?

Clue: The loop is connected to the shaft and the blades.

LOG ON *Science in Motion* Watch how a generator works @ **www.macmillanmh.com**

What is a generator?

An electric **generator** turns motion into electrical energy. The opposite of a motor, it changes mechanical energy into electrical energy. We depend on electric generators to produce nearly all of our electrical energy.

A simple generator has many of the same parts as a motor. Mechanical energy turns the wire loop between two magnetic poles. The magnetic field produces an electric current in the wire. As the wire gets closer to the magnetic poles, electrical charges are pushed through the wire. The moving electrical charges make an electric current.

Sources of Energy

Different power plants use different sources of energy to spin turbines. Some use heat to produce steam. Others use moving water or wind. The mechanical energy from a turbine is then used to produce electrical energy.

Fossil Fuels
Oil, coal, and natural gas can be burned to heat water, producing steam.

Nuclear Energy
Nuclear power plants split atoms that contain large amounts of energy.

Electrical energy can also be generated by spinning a magnet inside a coil of wire. The more loops of wire in the coil, the more electrical energy is produced.

The mechanical energy for a generator is provided by a *turbine*. A simple turbine looks like an electric fan. Steam, water, or air is used to turn the fan blades. The spinning blades are attached to a shaft which spins the wire loop or magnet inside the generator.

✔ **Quick Check**

Summarize How does a simple generator work?

Critical Thinking What do simple generators and simple electric motors have in common?

Quick Lab

Make a Generator

1. Push a nail through a cardboard tube. Place a lump of clay on the nail inside the tube. Stick a disc magnet on each side of the clay.

2. Wrap wire 50 times around the tube near the nail. Wrap the extra wire around a compass several times. Twist the ends of the wire together.

3. Turn the compass so that the needle lines up with the wire.

4. **Infer** Spin the nail so that the magnets spin inside the tube. What does the compass needle do? Is electric current flowing?

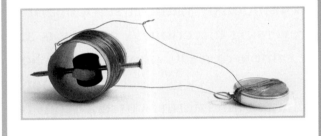

Geothermal Energy
Geothermal plants use the heat inside Earth to produce steam.

Hydropower
Flowing water can turn turbines and create electrical energy.

Wind
Wind can be changed into electrical energy using a generator.

What kinds of electric current are there?

Most generators that make electrical energy produce an alternating current (AC). **Alternating current** flows in one direction and then flows in the opposite direction. The electrical charges continuously flow back and forth. Electrical wall outlets, such as those in your home and school, use alternating current.

When the flow of a current is always in one direction, it is called a **direct current** (DC). In a DC circuit, electric current flows continuously without stopping or reversing direction. A battery is an example of a DC power source. Some electrical devices, such as computers, change alternating current from the wall outlet into direct current.

▲ The electric current from a wall outlet in your home is alternating current.

✓ Quick Check

Summarize What is the difference between alternating current and direct current?

Critical Thinking What devices have you used today that use direct current? Alternating current?

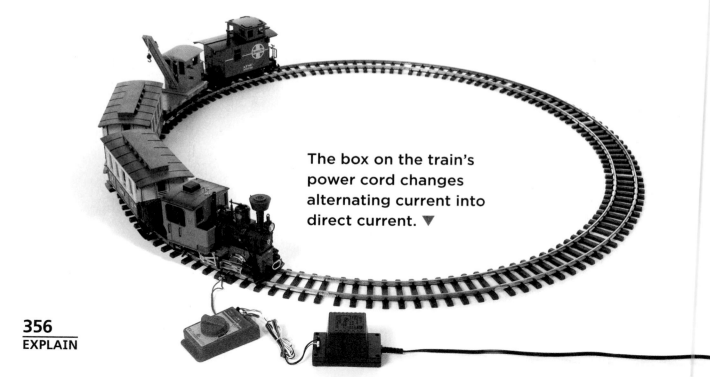

The box on the train's power cord changes alternating current into direct current. ▼

Lesson Review

Summarize the Main Idea

Electric motors convert electrical energy into motion. (pp. 352–353)

Electric generators change the energy of motion into electrical energy. (pp. 354–355)

Alternating current continuously switches direction. **Direct current** always flows in one direction. (p. 356)

Make a FOLDABLES™ Study Guide

Make a three-tab book. Use it to summarize what you learned about motors and generators.

Electric Motors

Electric Generators

AC and DC

Think, Talk, and Write

1 **Main Idea** How does an electric motor work?

2 **Vocabulary** Compare alternating current and direct current.

3 **Summarize** How does a generator produce electric current?

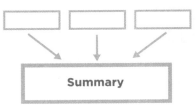

Summary

4 **Critical Thinking** An alternator uses the motion of the car's engine to make electric current. Is an alternator a motor or a generator?

5 **Test Practice** A motor changes electrical energy into

A light
B heat energy
C motion
D static electricity

Writing Link

Writing That Compares
Power plants produce electricity using fossil fuels, hydroelectricity, wind, geothermal power, or nuclear power. Research all of these energy sources. What are the advantages of each? What are the disadvantages?

Math Link

Multiply Mileage
Heidi's gasoline-powered car can drive about 20 km using 1 liter of gasoline. Juan's hybrid car can go about 26 km using 1 liter. Both cars start with 60 liters of gasoline. How much farther can Juan's car travel?

LOG ON **e-Review** Summaries and quizzes online @ **www.macmillanmh.com**

Maggie's Magnet

During the summer, Maggie would help her parents in their hardware store. One day, Maggie's father asked her, "Will you put these boxes of nails on the shelves?"

"Sure," Maggie answered. As she was putting the boxes on a shelf, one fell open. Nails spilled all over the floor. "Oh no!" Maggie said. There were 200 nails in each box. Maggie knew it would take a long time to pick up all 200 nails.

Suddenly, she had an idea. She took a horseshoe magnet from a shelf and passed it over the floor. The nails stuck to the magnet's poles. Maggie pulled them off and dropped them into their box. She stacked the box on the shelf and smiled, knowing she had done a good job.

A good story

▶ has characters, a setting, and a plot with a problem to solve

▶ has an interesting beginning, middle, and end

▶ often uses the third-person point of view (*he* or *she*)

▶ uses dialogue to make the story come alive

 **Write About It**

Fictional Narrative Write a story about a special way that a character uses a magnet.

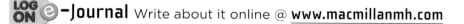

LOG ON e–Journal Write about it online @ **www.macmillanmh.com**

ELA W 4.2.1. Write narratives: a. Relate ideas, observations, or recollections of an event or experience. b. Provide a context to enable the reader to imagine the world of the event or experience. c. Use concrete sensory details. d. Provide insight into why the selected event or experience is memorable.

Using Graphs

The data table and graph show three different electromagnets and the number of paper clips they picked up.

You can see that adding batteries allows an electromagnet to pick up more paper clips.

To make a graph

▶ label the bottom of the graph with one variable

▶ label the left side of the graph with the second variable

▶ draw a vertical bar to represent each number from the second variable

Number of D cell Batteries	Number of Paper Clips
1	21
2	37
3	53

Solve It

This data table shows how many paper clips an electromagnet picked up from different distances. Make a bar graph of the data.

1. At what distance did the electromagnet pick up the most paper clips? The fewest paper clips?
2. What can you conclude about the strength of the magnetic field as you move away from the electromagnet?

Distance from Magnet (cm)	Number of Paper Clips
20	31
10	46
30	24
5	65
15	36

MA SDAP 4.1.3 Interpret one- and two-variable data graphs to answer questions about a situation.

Motors at Work

Refrigerators, vacuum cleaners, hair dryers, and fans have one thing in common. They all have a motor. You can use those motors today because of people such as Joseph Henry and Michael Faraday. In 1831 these two scientists discovered how to use electromagnets to turn electrical energy into motion.

A few years later, Thomas Davenport, a blacksmith in Vermont, learned about electromagnets and built the first simple motor. He used the device to separate iron from iron ore.

1888 The electric car, or "horseless carriage," is invented.

1831 Michael Faraday and Joseph Henry each produce motion using electromagnets.

1834 Thomas Davenport builds motors for his tools, as well as an electric model train.

AMERICAN MUSEUM OF NATURAL HISTORY

ELA R 4.2.1. Identify structural patterns found in informational text (e.g., compare and contrast, cause and effect, sequential or chronological order, proposition and support) to strengthen comprehension.

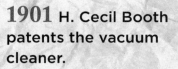
1901 H. Cecil Booth patents the vacuum cleaner.

1891 Electric fans are sold by Westinghouse Electric & Manufacturing Company.

It wasn't long before people started inventing new devices that used motors. Washing machines, invented in the early 1900s, use a motor to turn and wash your clothes. Another motor in a washing machine turns the water faucet on and off. Some of the first automobiles ran on electrical energy. Today many new cars use electric motors in addition to gasoline engines. Motors are useful for a lot of things! Can you think of any other machines that use electric motors?

1908 Washing machines use motors to spin and clean clothes.

Problem and Solution

▶ A problem is something that needs to be solved.

▶ A solution is a plan that helps you solve a problem.

 Write About It

Problem and Solution How did Thomas Davenport first use his motor? Write about a problem you have had, like a messy room or a really hot summer day. How did an electric motor help you solve it?

LOG ON **e-Journal** Write about it online @ **www.macmillanmh.com**

Summarize the Main Ideas

Like magnetic poles repel each other and unlike poles attract each other. A magnetic field is the region of magnetic force around a magnet. (pp. 328–337)

An electric current produces a magnetic field. Electromagnets are used in many common household items. (pp. 340–347)

An electric motor converts electrical energy into motion. An electric generator changes the energy of motion into electrical energy. (pp. 350–357)

Make a FOLDABLES™ Study Guide

Tape your lesson study guides to a piece of paper as shown. Use your study guide to review what you have learned in this chapter.

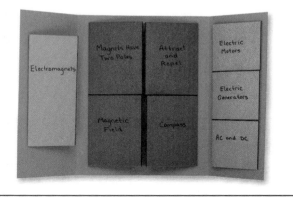

Fill each blank with the best word from the list.

compass, p. 336   **magnet**, p. 330

electromagnet, p. 343   **magnetic field**, p. 334

generator, p. 354   **motor**, p. 352

loudspeaker, p. 344   **pole**, p. 331

1. Electrical energy is produced by a _____. 4 PS 1.d

2. Electrical energy is changed into sound in a _____. 4 PS 1.d

3. Electric current produces a magnetic field in an _____. 4 PS 1.c

4. The area of magnetic force around a magnet is called its _____. 4 PS 1.c

5. Electrical energy is turned into mechanical energy or motion by a _____. 4 PS 1.d

6. Every magnet has a north and a south _____. 4 PS 1.f

7. Earth's magnetic field causes a _____ to point north. 4 PS 1.b

8. Any object that has magnetic force is called a _____. 4 PS 1.f

Answer each of the following in complete sentences.

9. Problem and Solution Dwayne built a generator with a hand crank. When he turns the crank, it produces electrical energy. How can Dwayne make it produce more energy? 4 PS 1.d

10. Narrative Writing Write a story in which the main character uses a motor to solve a problem. 4 PS 1.d

11. Draw Conclusions Suppose astronauts land on Planet Z. Planet Z does not have a magnetic field. Will the astronauts be able to use a compass to find direction? Why or why not? 4 PS 1.b

12. Critical Thinking Why do magnets stick to a refrigerator door? What happens to the metal in the door? 4 PS 1.e

How do we use magnets?

CHAPTER 7

Zoom Zoom

As Earth's supply of fossil fuels runs out, people are looking for other ways to power cars, trains, and airplanes. Design an electric car that you would like to drive some day.

- Draw a diagram to show how you can use electric motors to power the wheels of your car.

- Would your car use batteries or a generator to produce electrical energy?

- How else would your car use electrical energy? Would it have headlights? A radio?

- How else could your car use magnets?

- Make a poster that shows a detailed drawing of your car. Explain in detail how your car would work.

1 The drawing below shows a horseshoe magnet and a disc magnet.

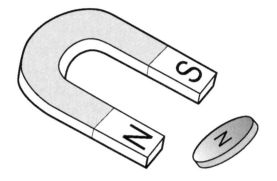

What will happen when the north pole of the horseshoe magnet is placed against the north pole of the disc magnet? 4 IE 6.c

A They will attract each other.

B They will repel each other.

C Nothing will happen.

D They will vibrate.

2 Earth can be thought of as a giant magnet because it 4 PS 1.b

A orbits around the Sun.

B has a magnetic field.

C rotates on its axis.

D has a moon.

3 Magnetic force becomes stronger when magnets are 4 PS 1.f

A both metal.

B farther apart.

C different sizes.

D closer together.

4 The ruler measures the distance between two objects.

About how far apart are the magnet and the paper clip in the picture? 4 IE 6.b

A 6 cm

B 4 cm

C 25 cm

D 12 cm

5 What does an electric motor do? 4 PS 1.d

A changes magnetic fields

B changes the voltage of electric current

C produces electric current

D changes electrical energy into motion

6 What causes the wires in a generator to spin? 4 PS 1.d

A heat energy

B electrical energy

C light energy

D mechanical energy

7 **What happens when a magnet is brought near an iron nail?** 4 PS 1.f

  A The magnet repels the nail.

  B The nail repels the magnet.

  C The nail becomes magnetic.

  D Nothing will happen.

8 **Iron filings were sprinkled around a magnet.**

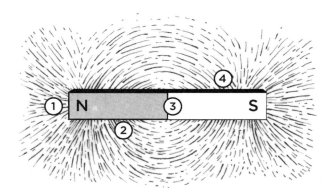

Where is the magnetic force strongest? 4 PS 1.f

  A 1

  B 2

  C 3

  D 4

9 **A loudspeaker uses electromagnets to** 4 PS 1.d

  A turn electrical energy into sound.

  B turn electrical energy into light.

  C turn motion into electrical energy.

  D turn sound into electrical energy.

10 **All of the following are true about permanent magnets EXCEPT** 4 PS 1.f

  A they have two poles.

  B they are surrounded by magnetic fields.

  C they have magnetic force.

  D they can be turned on and off.

11 **The electric current produced by a battery is an example of** 4 PS 1.d

  A alternating current.

  B direct current.

  C open current.

  D static electricity.

12 **Look at the simple electromagnet below.**

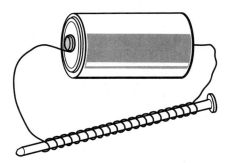

How can you make the electromagnet's magnetic field stronger? 4 PS 1.c

  A Remove the iron nail.

  B Use a wooden nail instead of an iron nail.

  C Wrap more coils of wire around the nail.

  D Wrap fewer coils of wire around the nail.

N

W   E

S

Magnetic Migration

Suppose that you are going on a trip. How will you know which way to go? You might ask for directions. You could follow someone who knows the way. Maybe you would look at a map or watch for road signs. You might use a compass to keep track of whether you are heading north, south, east, or west.

Now suppose you are a bird. Winter is on the way. It's time to migrate south. But you hatched just this summer. You have never taken this trip before. Of course you don't have a map! How will you know how to get there?

Many Canada geese spend the winter in California's Central Valley. ▶

Every year, birds make amazing journeys thousands of miles long. Some travel in groups with birds that have already made the trip. Others go alone. Some travel by day and seem to use the position of the Sun or special landmarks to find their way. Others travel at night and might navigate by the stars. But some travel even when clouds hide the Sun and stars. How is this possible?

For a long time, people didn't know the answer to this question. Then scientists discovered an interesting fact. Some birds have tiny bits of a mineral called magnetite in their heads. Magnetite is the most magnetic of all minerals. It is like a compass needle. These birds have a built-in compass! That's how they find their way!

▲ Flying in the shape of a *V* helps these birds stay together and fly farther.

4 PS 1. Electricity and magnetism are related effects that have many useful applications in everyday life.

367

Careers in Science

Electrician

Have you ever experienced a blackout? This is when electric current stops flowing to your home. When this happens, electricians are the ones who fix the problem. Electricians work in homes, offices, and buildings of every type. They install and repair electrical alarms, switches, wiring—you name it! Electricians need to be skilled with tools and to know a lot about electricity. You can learn these skills from high school, military training, junior college classes, or an apprentice program. Afterward you will have the skills and knowledge to become an electrician.

▲ Electricians install wires, switches, and outlets into new homes.

Electrical Engineer

Suppose that you are building a new stadium. The lights, retractable roof, and scoreboard all run on electrical energy. So does the heating, cooling, and security systems. All of these features are designed by an electrical engineer. Electrical engineers plan and construct all kinds of electrical systems. To become an electrical engineer you need to be an excellent math and science student. The best electrical engineers go through four-year programs in college. After the training, get ready for an exciting career!

▲ Electrical engineers design electrical systems and keep them working.

Reference

▶ **A hand lens is a tool scientists use.**

Science Content Standards

Physical Sciences

1. **Electricity and magnetism are related effects that have many useful applications in everyday life. As a basis for understanding this concept:**

   a. *Students know* how to design and build simple series and parallel circuits by using components such as wires, batteries, and bulbs.

   b. *Students know* how to build a simple compass and use it to detect magnetic effects, including Earth's magnetic field.

   c. *Students know* electric currents produce magnetic fields and know how to build a simple electromagnet.

   d. *Students know* the role of electromagnets in the construction of electric motors, electric generators, and simple devices, such as doorbells and earphones.

   e. *Students know* electrically charged objects attract or repel each other.

   f. *Students know* that magnets have two poles (north and south) and that like poles repel each other while unlike poles attract each other.

   g. *Students know* electrical energy can be converted to heat, light, and motion.

Life Sciences

2. **All organisms need energy and matter to live and grow. As a basis for understanding this concept:**

   a. *Students know* plants are the primary source of matter and energy entering most food chains.

   b. *Students know* producers and consumers (herbivores, carnivores, omnivores, and decomposers) are related in food chains and food webs and may compete with each other for resources in an ecosystem.

   c. *Students know* decomposers, including many fungi, insects, and microorganisms, recycle matter from dead plants and animals.

3. **Living organisms depend on one another and on their environment for survival. As a basis for understanding this concept:**

   a. *Students know* ecosystems can be characterized by their living and nonliving components.

   b. *Students know* that in any particular environment, some kinds of plants and animals survive well, some survive less well, and some cannot survive at all.

   c. *Students know* many plants depend on animals for pollination and seed dispersal, and animals depend on plants for food and shelter.

   d. *Students know* that most microorganisms do not cause disease and that many are beneficial.

Earth Sciences

4. **The properties of rocks and minerals reflect the processes that formed them. As a basis for understanding this concept:**

  a. *Students know* how to differentiate among igneous, sedimentary, and metamorphic rocks by referring to their properties and methods of formation (the rock cycle).

  b. *Students know* how to identify common rock-forming minerals (including quartz, calcite, feldspar, mica, and hornblende) and ore minerals by using a table of diagnostic properties.

5. **Waves, wind, water, and ice shape and reshape Earth's land surface. As a basis for understanding this concept:**

  a. *Students know* some changes in the earth are due to slow processes, such as erosion, and some changes are due to rapid processes, such as landslides, volcanic eruptions, and earthquakes.

  b. *Students know* natural processes, including freezing and thawing and the growth of roots, cause rocks to break down into smaller pieces.

  c. *Students know* moving water erodes landforms, reshaping the land by taking it away from some places and depositing it as pebbles, sand, silt, and mud in other places (weathering, transport, and deposition).

Investigation and Experimentation

6. **Scientific progress is made by asking meaningful questions and conducting careful investigations. As a basis for understanding this concept and addressing the content in the other three strands, students should develop their own questions and perform investigations. Students will:**

  a. Differentiate observation from inference (interpretation) and know scientists' explanations come partly from what they observe and partly from how they interpret their observations.

  b. Measure and estimate the weight, length, or volume of objects.

  c. Formulate and justify predictions based on cause-and-effect relationships.

  d. Conduct multiple trials to test a prediction and draw conclusions about the relationships between predictions and results.

  e. Construct and interpret graphs from measurements.

  f. Follow a set of written instructions for a scientific investigation.

Measurement

Units of Measurement

Temperature

▶ The temperature on this thermometer reads 86 degrees Fahrenheit. That is the same as 30 degrees Celsius.

Length and Area

▶ This student is 3 feet plus 9 inches tall. That is the same as 1 meter plus 14 centimeters.

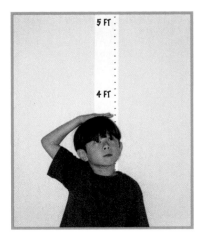

Mass

▶ You can measure the mass of these rocks in grams.

Volume of Fluids

▶ This bottle of water has a volume of 1 liter. That is a little more than 1 quart.

Weight/Force

▶ This pumpkin weighs 7 pounds. That is a force of 31.5 newtons.

Rate

▶ This student can ride her bike 100 meters in 50 seconds. That means her speed is 2 meters per second.

Table of Measurements	
SI (International System) of Units	**English System of Units**
Temperature Water freezes at 0 degrees Celsius (°C) and boils at 100°C.	**Temperature** Water freezes at 32 degrees Fahrenheit (°F) and boils at 212°F.
Length and Distance 10 millimeters (mm) = 1 centimeter (cm) 100 centimeters = 1 meter (m) 1,000 meters = 1 kilometer (km)	**Length and Distance** 12 inches (in.) = 1 foot (ft) 3 feet = 1 yard (yd) 5,280 feet = 1 mile (mi)
Volume 1 cubic centimeter (cm³) = 1 milliliter (mL) 1,000 milliliters = 1 liter (L)	**Volume of Fluids** 8 fluid ounces (fl oz) = 1 cup (c) 2 cups = 1 pint (pt) 2 pints = 1 quart (qt) 4 quarts = 1 gallon (gal)
Mass 1,000 milligrams (mg) = 1 gram (g) 1,000 grams = 1 kilogram (kg)	**Weight** 16 ounces (oz) = 1 pound (lb) 2,000 pounds = 1 ton (T)
Area 1 square kilometer (km²) = 1 km x 1 km 1 hectare = 10,000 square meters (m²)	**Rate** mph = miles per hour
Rate m/s = meters per second km/h = kilometers per hour	
Force 1 newton (N) = 1 kg x 1m/s²	

Measurement

Measure Time

You use timing devices to measure how long something takes to happen. Some timing devices you use in science are a clock with a second hand and a stopwatch. Which one is more accurate?

Comparing a Clock and a Stopwatch

1. Look at a clock with a second hand. The second hand is the hand that you can see moving. It measures seconds.

2. Get an egg timer with falling sand. When the second hand of the clock points to 12, tell your partner to start the egg timer. Watch the clock while the sand in the egg timer is falling.

3. When the sand stops falling, count how many seconds it took. Record this measurement. Repeat the activity, and compare the two measurements.

4. Look at a stopwatch. Click the button on the top right. This starts the time. Click the button again. This stops the time. Click the button on the top left. This sets the stopwatch back to zero. Notice that the stopwatch tells time in hours, minutes, seconds, and hundredths of a second.

5. Repeat the activity in steps 2 and 3, but use the stopwatch instead of a clock. Make sure the stopwatch is set to zero. Click the top right button to start timing. Click the button again when the sand stops falling. Do this twice.

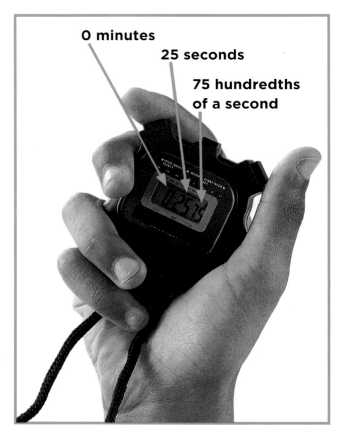

0 minutes

25 seconds

75 hundredths of a second

More About Time

1. Use the stopwatch to time how long it takes your heart to beat 100 times. Then run in place for 3 minutes. How long does it take for your heart to beat 100 times now?

2. Estimate how long it would take you to walk 100 meters. Then time yourself and try it.

Measure Length

You measure length to find out how long something is or how far away something is.

Find Length with a Ruler

1 Look at the ruler below. Each number represents 1 centimeter (cm). Each centimeter is divided into 10 millimeters (mm). How long is the beetle?

2 The length of the beetle is 1 centimeter plus 9 millimeters. You can write this length as 1.9 centimeters.

3 Place a ruler on your desk. Lay a pencil against the ruler so that one end of the pencil lines up with the 0 on the ruler. Record the length of the pencil in centimeters.

4 Measure the length of another object in centimeters. Then ask a partner to measure the same object.

5 Compare your measurements. Explain how two scientists can record slightly different measurements even if the item measured is the same.

Measure Area

Area is the amount of surface something covers. To find the area of a rectangle, multiply the rectangle's length by its width. For example, the rectangle here is 3 centimeters long and 2 centimeters wide. Its area is 3 cm x 2 cm = 6 square centimeters. You write the area as 6 cm^2.

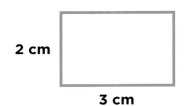

2 cm

3 cm

Find Area with a Ruler

1 Find the area of your science book. Measure the book's length to the nearest centimeter. Measure its width.

2 Multiply the book's length by its width. Remember to put the answer in cm^2.

Measurement

Measure Mass

Mass is the amount of matter an object has. You use a balance to measure mass. To find the mass of an object, you balance it with objects whose masses you know.

Measure the Mass of a Box of Crayons

1. Place the balance on a flat, level surface.

2. The pointer should point to the middle mark. If it does not, move the slider a little to the right or left to balance the empty pans.

3. Gently place a box of crayons on the left pan. Add gram masses to the right pan until the pans are balanced.

4. Count the numbers on the masses that are in the right pan. The total is the mass of the box of crayons in grams.

5. Record this number. After the number, write a *g* for "grams."

More About Mass

What would happen if you replaced the box of crayons with a paper clip or a pineapple? You may not have enough masses to balance the pineapple. It has a mass of about 1,000 grams. That's the same as 1 kilogram, because *kilo* means "1,000." Measure other objects and record your measurements.

Measure Volume

Have you ever used a measuring cup? Measuring cups measure the volume of liquids. Volume is the amount of space something takes up. In science you use special measuring cups called beakers and graduated cylinders. These containers are marked in milliliters (mL).

Measure the Volume of a Liquid

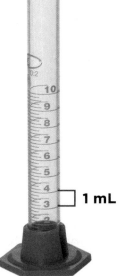

1 mL

1. Fill a beaker and a graduated cylinder so they are each half full with water.

2. The surface of the water in the graduated cylinder curves up at the sides. You measure the volume by reading the height of the water at the flat part. Compare the height of the water to the marks on the measuring device. What is the volume of water in the graduated cylinder? How much water is in the beaker?

▲ **This graduated cylinder can measure volumes up to 10 mL. Each number on the cylinder represents 1 mL.**

3. Pour 50 mL of water from a pitcher into a graduated cylinder. The water should be at the 50-mL mark on the graduated cylinder. If you go over the mark, pour a little water back into the pitcher.

4. Pour the 50 mL of water into a beaker.

5. Repeat steps 3 and 4 using 30 mL, 45 mL, and 25 mL of water.

6. Measure the volume of water you have in the beaker. Do you have about the same amount of water as your classmates?

▲ A beaker is a tool you can use to measure volume.

Measurement

Measure Weight/Force

You use a spring scale to measure weight. An object has weight because the force of gravity pulls down on the object. Therefore, weight is a force. Like all forces, weight is measured in newtons (N).

Measure the Weight of an Object

1 Look at a spring scale to see how many newtons it measures. See how the measurements are divided. The spring scale shown here measures up to 20 N. It has a mark for every 0.5 N.

2 Hold the spring scale by the top loop. Put a small object on the bottom hook. If the object will not stay on the hook, place it in a net bag. Then hang the bag from the hook.

3 Let go of the object slowly. It will pull down on a spring inside the scale.

4 Wait for the spring to stop moving. Read the number of newtons next to the tab. This is the object's weight.

More About Spring Scales

You probably weigh yourself by standing on a bathroom scale. This is a spring scale. The weight of your body stretches a spring inside the scale. The dial on the scale is probably marked in pounds—the English unit of force. One pound is equal to about 4.5 newtons.

The scale in a grocery store is also a spring scale. ▶

Measure Temperature

Temperature is how hot or cold something is. You use a thermometer to measure temperature. A thermometer is made of a thin tube with colored liquid inside. When the liquid gets warmer, it expands and moves up the tube. When the liquid gets cooler, it contracts and moves down the tube. You may have seen most temperatures measured in degrees Fahrenheit (°F). Scientists measure temperature in degrees Celsius (°C).

Read a Thermometer

1. Look at the thermometer shown here. It has two scales—a Fahrenheit scale and a Celsius scale. Every 20 degrees on the Celsius scale has a number. Every 40 degrees on the Fahrenheit scale has a number.

2. What is the temperature shown on the thermometer? Give your answers in °F and in °C.

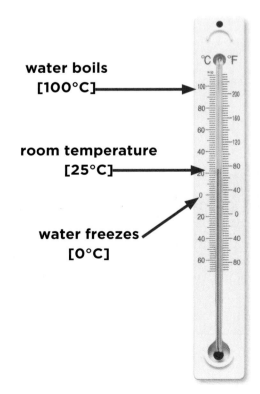

water boils [100°C]

room temperature [25°C]

water freezes [0°C]

How Is Temperature Measured?

1. Fill a large beaker about half full of cool water. Put the thermometer in the water. Do not let the thermometer bulb touch the beaker. Use a clamp if necessary.

2. Wait until the liquid in the thermometer stops moving— about a minute. Read and record the temperature. Record the temperature scale you used.

3. Remove the thermometer. Place the beaker on a hot plate and warm the beaker for two minutes. Be careful of the hot plate and warm water.

4. Put the thermometer in the water. Record the temperature of the water. Use the same temperature scale you chose in Step 2.

Collect Data

Use a Hand Lens

You use a hand lens to magnify an object or make the object look larger. With a hand lens, you can see details that would be hard to see without the hand lens.

Magnify a Rock

1. Look at a rock carefully. Draw a picture of it.

2. Hold the hand lens so that it is just above the rock. Look through the lens, and slowly move it away from the rock. The rock will look larger.

3. Keep moving the hand lens until the rock begins to look blurry. Then move the lens a little closer until you can see the rock clearly.

4. Draw a picture of the rock as you see it through the hand lens. Fill in details that you did not see before.

5. Repeat this activity using objects you are studying in science. They might include a plant, some soil, a seed, or something else.

Use a Microscope

Hand lenses make objects look several times larger. A microscope, however, can magnify an object to look hundreds of times larger.

Examine Salt Grains

1 Place the microscope on a flat surface. Always carry a microscope with both hands. Hold the arm with one hand, and put your other hand beneath the base.

2 Look at the photo to learn the different parts of the microscope.

3 Move the mirror so that it reflects light up toward the stage. Never point the mirror directly at the Sun or a bright light. Bright light can cause permanent eye damage.

4 Place a few grains of salt on a slide. Put the slide under the stage clips on the stage. Be sure that the salt grains are over the hole in the stage.

5 Look through the eyepiece. Turn the focusing knob slowly until the salt grains come into focus.

6 Draw what the grains look like through the microscope.

7 Look at other objects through the microscope. Try a piece of leaf, a strand of hair, or a pencil mark.

8 Draw what each object looks like through the microscope. Do any of the objects look alike? If so, how? Are any of the objects alive? How do you know?

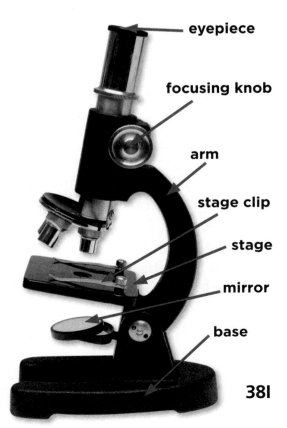

eyepiece

focusing knob

arm

stage clip

stage

mirror

base

381

Use Technology

Use Calculators: Add and Subtract

Sometimes after you make measurements, you have to add or subtract your numbers. A calculator helps you do this.

Add and Subtract Rainfall Amounts

The table shows the amount of rain that fell in a town each week during the summer.

Week	Rain (cm)
1	3
2	5
3	2
4	0
5	1
6	6
7	4
8	0
9	2
10	2
11	6
12	5

1. Make sure the calculator is on. Press the ON key.

2. To add the numbers, enter a number and press +. Repeat until you enter the last number. Then press =. Your total should be 36.

3. What if you found out that you made a mistake in your measurement? Week 1 should be 2 cm less, week 6 should be 3 cm less, week 11 should be 1 cm less, and week 12 should be 2 cm less. Subtract these numbers from your total. You should have 36 displayed on the calculator. Press −, and enter the first number you want to subtract. Repeat until you enter the last number. Then press =.

Use Calculators: Multiply and Divide

Sometimes after you make measurements, you have to multiply or divide your measurements to get other information. A calculator helps you multiply and divide, especially if the numbers have decimal points.

Multiply Decimals

What if you are measuring the width of your classroom? You discover that the floor is covered with tiles and the room is exactly 32 tiles wide. You measure a tile, and it is 22.7 centimeters wide. To find the width of the room, you can multiply 32 by 22.7.

1. Make sure the calculator is on. Press the ON key.
2. Press 3 and 2.
3. Press X.
4. Press 2, 2, ·, and 7.
5. Press =. Your total should be 726.4. That is how wide the room is in centimeters.

Divide Decimals

Now what if you wanted to find out how many desks placed side by side would be needed to reach across the room? You measure one desk, and it is 60 centimeters wide. To find the number of desks needed, divide 726.4 by 60.

1. Turn the calculator on.
2. Press 7, 2, 6, ·, and 4.
3. Press ÷.
4. Press 6 and 0.
5. Press =. Your total should be about 12.1. This means you can fit 12 desks across the room with a little space left over.

Suppose the room was 35 tiles wide. How wide would the room be? How many desks would fit across it? Use a calculator to multiply and divide.

Use Technology

Use Computers

A computer has many uses. The Internet connects your computer to many other computers around the world, so you can collect all kinds of information. You can use a computer to show this information and write reports. Best of all, you can use a computer to explore, discover, and learn.

You can also get information from compact discs (CDs) and digital videodiscs (DVDs). They are computer disks that can hold large amounts of information. You can fit a whole encyclopedia on one DVD.

Use Computers for a Project

Here's a project that uses computers. You can do the project in a group.

1. Use a collecting net to gather a soil sample from a brook or stream. Collect pebbles, sand, and small rocks. Keep any small plants also. Return any fish or other animals to the stream right away.

2. After the sample has dried, separate the items in the sample. Use a camera to photograph the soil, pebbles, small rocks, and plants.

3. Each group can use one of the photos to help them start their research. Try to find out what type of rocks or soil you collected.

4. Use the Internet for your research. Find a map and mark your area on it. Identify the type of soil. What types of plants grow well in that type of soil?

5 Find Web sites from an agency such as the Department of Environmental Protection. Contact the group. Ask questions about samples you collected.

6 Use DVDs or other sources from the library to find out how the rocks and soil in your sample formed.

7 Keep the information you have gathered in a folder. Review it with your group and use it to write a group report about your sample.

8 Each group will present and read a different part of the report. Have an adult help you to record your reports on a video recorder. Show your photographs in the video and explain what each represents. If you'd like, use music or other sounds to accompany the voices on the video recorder.

9 Make a list of computer resources you used to make your report. List Web sites, DVD titles, or other computer resources. Show or read the list at the end of your presentation.

10 Discuss how the computer helped each group to do their report. What problems did each group encounter using the computer? How were the problems solved?

Represent Data

Make Graphs

Graphs can help organize data. Graphs make it easy to notice trends and patterns. There are many kinds of graphs.

Bar Graphs

A bar graph uses bars to show information. For example, what if you are growing a plant? Every week you measure how high the plant has grown. Here is what you find.

The bar graph at the bottom right organizes the measurements so you can easily compare them.

Week	Height (cm)
1	1
2	4
3	7
4	10
5	17
6	20
7	22
8	23

1. Look at the bar for Week 2. Put your finger at the top of the bar. Move your finger straight over to the left to find how many centimeters the plant grew by the end of Week 2.

2. Between which two weeks did the plant grow most?

3. Look at the 0 on the graph. Is it just a label on a scale or does it have a meaning in the graph? Explain.

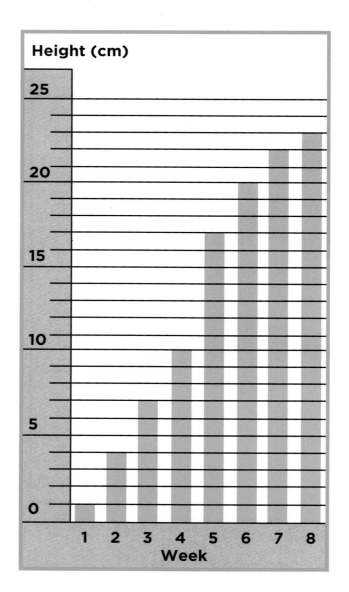

386

Pictographs

A pictograph uses symbols, or pictures, to show information. What if you collect information about how much water your family uses each day? Here is what you find.

Water Used Daily (liters)	
drinking	10
showering	100
bathing	120
brushing teeth	40
washing dishes	80
washing hands	30
washing clothes	160
flushing toilet	50

You can organize this information into a pictograph. In the pictograph below each bucket means 20 liters of water. A half bucket means half of 20, or 10 liters of water.

1. Which activity uses the most water?

2. Which activity uses the least water?

Water Used Daily	
drinking	▯
showering	▯▯▯▯▯
bathing	▯▯▯▯▯▯
brushing teeth	▯▯
washing dishes	▯▯▯▯
washing hands	▯▯
washing clothes	▯▯▯▯▯▯▯▯
flushing toilet	▯▯▯

▯ = 20 liters of water

Line Graphs

A line graph shows how information changes over time. What if you measure the temperature outdoors every hour starting at 6 A.M.? Here is what you find.

Time	Temperature (°C)
6 A.M.	10
7 A.M.	12
8 A.M.	14
9 A.M.	16
10 A.M.	18
11 A.M.	20

Now organize your data by making a line graph. Follow these steps.

1. Make a scale along the bottom and side of the graph. Label the scales.

2. Plot points on the graph.

3. Connect the points with a line.

4. How do the temperatures and times relate to each other?

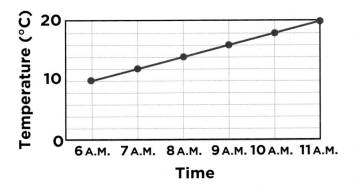

387

Represent Data

Make Maps

Locate Places

A map is a drawing that shows an area from above. Most maps have numbers and letters along the top and side. What if you wanted to find the Crocker Art Museum on the map below? It is located at D2. Place a finger on the letter D along the side of the map and another finger on the number 2 at the top. Then move your fingers straight across and down the map until they meet. The art museum is located where D and 2 meet.

1. What building is located at B4?

2. The U.S. District Court is located two blocks west and one block north of the library. What is its number and letter?

3. Make a map of an area in your community. It might be a park or the area between your home and school. Include numbers and letters along the top and side. Use a compass to find north, and mark north on your map. Exchange maps with a classmate.

Idea Maps

The map on the left shows how places are connected to each other. Idea maps, on the other hand, show how ideas are connected to each other. Idea maps help you organize information about a topic.

Look at the idea map below. It connects ideas about water. This map shows that Earth's water can be fresh water or salt water. The map also shows three sources of fresh water. You can see that there is no connection between "rivers" and "salt water" on the map. This reminds you that salt water does not flow in rivers.

Make an idea map about a topic you are learning in science. Your map can include words, phrases, or even sentences. Arrange your map in a way that makes sense to you and helps you understand the connection between ideas.

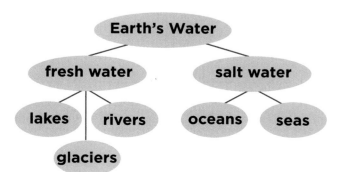

Make Tables

Tables help to organize data during experiments. Most tables have columns that run up and down, and rows that run across. The columns and rows have headings that tell you what kind of data go in each part of the table.

A Sample Table

What if you are going to do an experiment to find out how long different kinds of seeds take to sprout? Before you begin the experiment, you should set up your table. Follow these steps.

1. In this experiment you will plant 20 radish seeds, 20 bean seeds, and 20 corn seeds. Your table must show how many of each kind of seed sprouted on days 1, 2, 3, 4, and 5.

2. Make your table with columns, rows, and headings. You might use a computer. Some computer programs let you build a table with just the click of a mouse. You can delete or add columns and rows if you need to.

3. Give your table a title. Your table could look like the one here.

Types of Seeds	Number of Seeds that Sprout				
	Day 1	Day 2	Day 3	Day 4	Day 5
radish seeds					
bean seeds					
corn seeds					

Make a Table

Plant 20 bean seeds in each of two trays. Keep each tray at a different temperature and observe the trays for seven days. Make a table to record, examine, and evaluate the information of this experiment. How do the columns, rows, and headings of your table relate to one another?

Represent Data

Make Charts

A chart is simply a table with pictures as well as words. Charts can be useful for recording information during an experiment. They are also useful in communicating information.

Make a Chart

Make a chart that shows the information from the bean seed experiment on page 405. Make your chart with columns and rows. Remember to include labels.

Change	Living Thing	What Might Happen	Why
warmer climate	 saber-toothed cat	becomes extinct	unable to find food; unable to survive in warm climate
volcanic eruption	 short-tailed albatross	survives	flies to new environment
colder climate	 bear	survives	grows thicker fur

▲ This chart shows how changes can affect living things. It provides information using both pictures and words.

by Dinah Zike

Folding Instructions

So how do you make a Foldables study guide? The following pages offer step-by-step instructions—where and when to fold, where to cut—for making 11 basic Foldables study guides. The instructions begin with the basic shapes, such as the hot dog fold.

Half-Book

Fold a sheet of paper ($8\frac{1}{2}''$ x 11") in half.
1. This book can be folded vertically like a hot dog or …
2. … it can be folded horizontally like a hamburger.

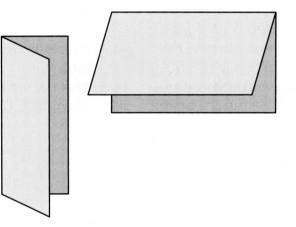

Folded Book

1. Make a Half-Book.
2. Fold in half again like a hamburger. This makes a ready-made cover and two small pages inside for recording information.

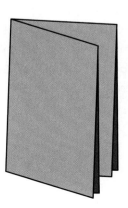

Trifold Book

1. Fold a sheet of paper ($8\frac{1}{2}$" x 11") into thirds.
2. Use this book as is, or cut into shapes.

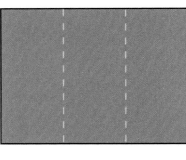
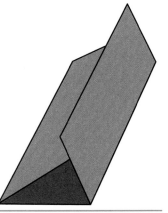

Shutter Fold

1. Begin as if you were going to make a hamburger, but instead of creasing the paper, pinch it to show the midpoint.
2. Fold the outer edges of the paper to meet at the pinch, or midpoint, forming a Shutter Fold.

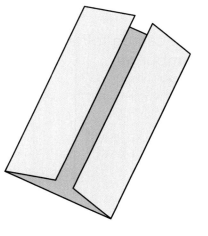

Pocket Book

1. Fold a sheet of paper ($8\frac{1}{2}$" x 11") in half like a hamburger.
2. Open the folded paper and fold one of the long sides up two inches to form a pocket. Refold along the hamburger fold so that the newly formed pockets are on the inside.
3. Glue the outer edges of the two-inch fold with a small amount of glue.

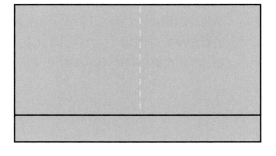

Two-Tab Book

Take a Folded Book and cut up the valley of the inside fold toward the mountain top. This cut forms two large tabs that can be used on the front and back for writing and illustrations.

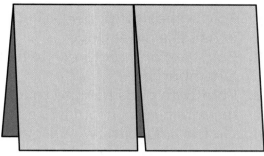

Three-Tab Book

1. Fold a sheet of paper like a hot dog.
2. With the paper horizontal and the fold of the hot dog up, fold the right side toward the center, trying to cover one half of the paper.
3. Fold the left side over the right side to make a book with three folds.
4. Open the folded book. Place one hand between the two thicknesses of paper and cut up the two valleys on one side only. This will create three tabs.

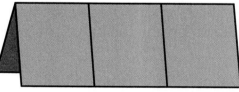

Layered-Look Book

1. Stack two sheets of paper ($8\frac{1}{2}$" x 11") so that the back sheet is one inch higher than the front sheet.
2. Bring the bottoms of both sheets upward and align the edges so that all of the layers or tabs are the same distance apart.
3. When all the tabs are an equal distance apart, fold the papers and crease well.
4. Open the papers and glue them together along the valley, or inner center fold, or staple them along the mountain.

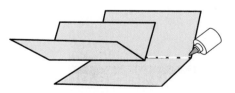

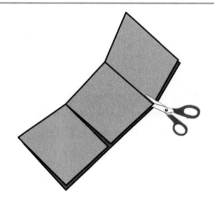

Four-Tab Book

1. Fold a sheet of paper ($8\frac{1}{2}''$ x 11″) in half like a hot dog.
2. Fold this long rectangle in half like a hamburger.
3. Fold both ends back to touch the mountain top or fold it like an accordion.
4. On the side with two valleys and one mountain top, make vertical cuts through one thickness of paper, forming four tabs.

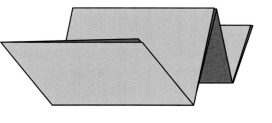

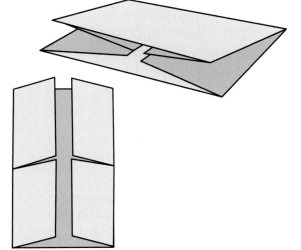

Four-Door Book

1. Make a Shutter Fold using 11″ x 17″ or 12″ x 18″ paper.
2. Fold the Shutter Fold in half like a hamburger. Crease well.
3. Open the project and cut along the two inside valley folds. These cuts will form four doors on the inside of the project.

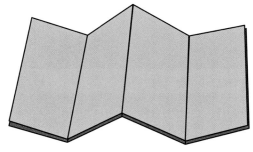

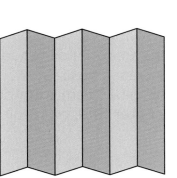

Folded Table or Chart

1. Fold the number of vertical columns needed to make the table or chart.
2. Fold the horizontal rows needed to make the table or chart.
3. Label the rows and columns.

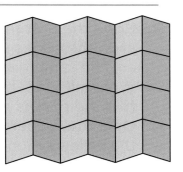

Glossary

Use this glossary to learn how to pronounce and understand the meanings of Science Words used in this book. The page number at the end of each definition tells you where to find that word in the book.

abiotic factor (ā′bī ot′ik fak′tər) A nonliving part of the ecosystem. (p. 85) *Hot temperatures and rainfall are abiotic factors in the desert ecosystem.*

abrasion (ə brā′zhən) The peeling or scraping away of an outer layer. (p. 195) *Wind abrasion is a form of physical weathering that wears down rock.*

accommodation (ə kä′mə dā′shən) An individual organism's response to a change in the ecosystem. (p. 108) *One type of accommodation is a change in the type of food an organism eats.*

active volcano (ak′tiv vol cā′nō) A volcano that still erupts from time to time. (p. 265) *Mt. Saint Helens is an active volcano.*

adaptation (a′dap′tā′shən) A special trait that helps an organism survive in its environment. (p. 116) *A fish's gills are an example of adaptation.*

algae (al′jē) A plant-like producer in a water environment. (pp. 46, 67) *Algae usually float on the surface of ponds and lakes.*

alternating current (ôl′tər nā ting kûr′ənt) Electrical current that flows through a circuit, first in one direction, then in the opposite direction. (p. 356) *Most generators that make electrical energy produce an alternating current, or AC.*

Pronunciation Key
The following symbols are used throughout the Macmillan McGraw-Hill Science Glossaries.

a	**a**t	e	**e**nd	o	h**o**t	u	**u**p	hw	**wh**ite	ə	**a**bout
ā	**a**pe	ē	m**a**	ō	**o**ld	ū	**u**se	ng	so**ng**		tak**e**n
ä	f**a**r	i	**i**t	ôr	f**or**k	ü	r**u**le	th	**th**in		penc**i**l
âr	c**are**	ī	**i**ce	oi	**oi**l	u̇	p**u**ll	th	**th**is		lem**o**n
ô	l**a**w	îr	p**ier**ce	ou	**ou**t	ûr	t**ur**n	zh	mea**s**ure		circ**u**s

′ = primary accent; shows which syllable takes the main stress, such as **kil** in **kilogram** (kil′ e gram′).
′ = secondary accent; shows which syllables take lighter stresses, such as **gram** in **kilogram**.

amoeba (əmē′ bə) A type of protist that acts like an animal in some ways. (p. 67) *An amoeba can change its shape to catch food.*

analyze data (an′ə līz da′tə) To use information that has been gathered to answer a question or solve a problem. (p. 11) *You can analyze data to find how daylight hours change throughout the year.*

anthracite (an′thrə sīt) A hard, natural type of coal. (p. 177) *Anthracite burns cleaner and longer than soft coal.*

attract (ə trakt) To pull or draw towards. (p. 287) *An object with positive electrical charge will attract an object with negative electrical charge.*

axis (ak′sis) A real or imaginary line through the center of a rotating object. (p. 335) *The geographic North and South poles of Earth are located at the ends of the planet's axis.*

bacteria (bak tîr′ē ə) Microorganisms that have cell membranes but no nuclei. (p. 65) *Bacteria can be both helpful and harmful to humans.*

barrier island (ba′rē′ər ī′lənd) A long, narrow strip of land formed along the ocean shore by deposition. (p. 219) *Ocean waves constantly reshape barrier islands.*

biomass (bī′ō mas′) A measure of the amount of living things in an environment. (p. 32) *Plants make up most of the biomass in many environments.*

biotic factor (b ot′ik fak′tər) A living part of the ecosystem. (p. 84) *Fish are biotic factors in the ocean.*

blubber (blə′bər) A thick layer of fat found in large mammals. (p. 122) *Whale blubber allows the animal to stay warm in cold waters.*

branch (branch) In a parallel circuit, one of the paths that electric current can follow. (p. 302) *The branches of a parallel circuit divide the current between them.*

buildup (bild′əp) Having more of one kind of charge than the other. (p. 288) *Rubbing a balloon will lead to a buildup of electrical charge.*

C

camouflage (kam'ə fläzh') An adaptation that allows an animal to blend into its surroundings. (p. 117) *Camouflage allows some animals to hide from predators.*

canopy (ka'nə pē') The part of a forest just below the uppermost branches of the tallest trees. (p. 88) *Most rain-forest animals live in the canopy because of the sunlight and food found there.*

canyon (kan'yən) A deep, narrow valley with steep sides. (p. 215) *Canyons are the results of river erosion.*

carbon dioxide (kär'bən dī ok'sīd) A gas in the air. (p. 28) *Plants need carbon dioxide to live.*

carbonic acid (kär bä'nik a'səd) A weak acid that forms when carbon dioxide reacts with water. (p. 197) *Carbonic acid can wear away limestone and create caves.*

carnivore (kär'nə vôr') An animal that eats other animals. (p. 42) *Hawks that eat mice are carnivores.*

cell (sel) The smallest unit of life. (p. 64) *Your body is made up of trillions of cells.*

chaparral (sha'pə ral') An area with dense thickets of small shrubs and trees. (p. 112) *A chaparral environment is usually very dry and warm.*

chemical weathering (kem'i kəl weth'ər ing) The process in which rocks break down due to chemical changes to the minerals. (p. 196) *When oxygen reacts with iron and forms rust, chemical weathering occurs.*

chlorophyll (klôr'ə fil') A material in plants that helps them take in sunlight. (p. 28) *Chlorophyll gives plants their green color.*

cinder-cone volcano (sin'dər kōn vol cā'nō) A volcano shaped like a cone. (p. 266) *The magma in a cinder-cone volcano is usually quite thick.*

circuit (sər'kət) The path along which electric current flows. (p. 299) *A simple circuit has a power soure, connectors, and a switch.*

circuit breaker (sər'kət brā'kər) Something that switches off a circuit when the current gets too high. (p. 314) *A circuit breaker can help prevent electric shock or fire hazards.*

classify (klas'əfī) To place similar materials together in a group. (p. 5) *The periodic table classifies elements that share the same properties.*

cleavage (klē′vij) The way a mineral splits or breaks along flat surfaces. (p. 142) *The cleavage of quartz is uneven.*

climate (klī′mit) The typical weather patterns of a region. (p. 85) *Most pond animals need a rainy climate.*

closed circuit (klōzd sər′kət) A complete, unbroken electrical circuit. (p. 299) *A closed circuit allows electric current to flow.*

communicate (kə mū′ni kāt′) To share information. (p. 13) *Recording your data helps you to communicate your observations to others.*

compass (kəm′pəs) An instrument that tells direction using Earth's magnetic forces. (p. 336) *A compass needle is a thin magnet that lines up with Earth's magnetic field and points north.*

competition (kom′pi tish′ən) The struggle among living things for the same resources. (p. 53) *There is great competition for mice as food in a woodland food chain.*

composite volcano (käm pä′zət vol cā′nō) A volcano made up of layers of lava and ash. (p. 267) *A composite volcano usually forms during periods of alternating quiet and explosive eruptions.*

conductor (kən duk′tər) A material through which heat or electricity flows easily. (p. 292) *Metals such as copper and silver are good conductors.*

conglomerate (kən′glom′ər it) A substance formed from rocks that have been lumped together. (p. 165) *Conglomerate is usually coarse and chunky.*

conserve (kən sərv′) To save or protect. (p. 208) *When you conserve resources, you try to use less of them.*

consumer (kən sü′mər) An organism that eats other organisms. (p. 38) *Consumers cannot make their own food.*

contour plowing (kän′tùr plou′ing) A farming method that cuts into the soil across a hillside rather than up and down the hillside. (p. 208) *Contour plowing helps farmers reduce erosion.*

crater (krā′tər) A cup-like shape in the earth. (p. 266) *On a volcano, a crater often forms around the vent.*

creep (krēp) A slow movement of plates along a fault. (p. 250) *Plate movement due to creep does not usually lead to earthquakes.*

crust (krəst) The outermost layer of Earth.(pp. 214, 248) *Earth's crust is made up of huge, moving slabs of rocks called plates.*

crystal (kris′təl) The geometric shape a mineral forms when its atoms and molecules are in fixed patterns. (p. 141) *Some crystal shapes can be like cubes or hexagons.*

decomposer (dē′kəm pōz′ər) An organism that breaks down other organisms. (p. 39) *Decomposers return an organism's nutrients to the soil.*

delta (del′tə) An area of land caused by deposition at the mouth, or end, of a river. (p. 217) *Most deltas are composed of sediment.*

deposition (dep′əzish′ən) The dropping off of weathered rock at the end of erosion. (p. 205) *Deposition may leave sand and soil miles away from its original location.*

desert (de′zərt) An ecosystem with few plants and little water. (p. 86) *Animals in the desert must be adapted to dry conditions.*

diaphragm (dī′ə fram′) The part of a loudspeaker that vibrates and produces sound waves. (p. 344) *The diaphragm on most loudspeakers is made of either paper or plastic.*

direct current (di rekt′ kûr′ənt) Electrical current that flows through a circuit in just one direction. (p. 356) *Most batteries produce a direct current, or DC.*

discharge (dis′chärj) A release of electrical energy from one object to another. (p. 290) *Static electricity will discharge from a charged object to a lesser charged object.*

dormant volcano (där′mənt vol cā′nō) A volcano that is quiet and no longer erupts. (p. 265) *Hawaii's oldest island Kauai is a dormant volcano.*

draw conclusions (drô kən klü′zhənz) To arrive at possible answers based on information you have gathered. (p. 13) *After you analyze the data from an experiment, you can draw conclusions about what you observed.*

drought (drout) A long period with little or no rain. (p. 104) *A drought can have deadly effects on an ecosystem.*

dynamo (dī′nə mō) Something that generates a great amount of energy. (p. 283) *Dynamos can produce electricity for many homes.*

earthquake (ərth′kwāk) A sudden shaking or trembling in Earth's crust. (p. 249) *Earthquakes can be caused by volcanoes or sudden shifts of Earth's plates.*

ecosystem (ek′ō sis′təm) All the living and nonliving things that interact in an environment. (p. 84) *The forest and the ocean are different ecosystems.*

electrical charge (i lek′trik əl chärj) A property of matter that tells whether something has a positive or negative charge. (p. 286) *Something with a positive electrical charge will repel an object with the same property.*

electrical engineer (i lek′trik əl en′jənir) A person who plans and constructs electrical systems. (p. 368) *An electrical engineer might figure out how to power all the lights and air conditioning in a shopping mall.*

electric current (i lek′trik kûr′ənt) A flow of electrical charges. (p. 298) *Electric current moves in one direction like a river.*

electrician (i lek tri′shən) A person who works with electrical power. (p. 368) *An electrician might install wiring throughout a house.*

electromagnet (i lek′trō mag′nit) A magnet formed when electric current flows through wire coiled around an iron rod. (p. 343) *When the current stops in an electromagnet, the iron bar is no longer magnetic.*

element (el′ə mənt) A basic building block of all matter. (p. 274) *Oxygen, carbon, and iron are all elements.*

emergent (i mər′jənt) A tree that rises above the forest around it. (p. 88) *The tops of the tallest trees form the emergent layer of the rain forest.*

endangered (en dān′jərd) Close to extinction. (p. 109) *When very few of a kind of animal exist, it becomes an endangered species.*

energy pyramid (en′ər jē pir′əmid) A diagram that shows the amount of energy at each level of the food web in an ecosystem. (p. 58) *Humans are usually at the top of the energy pyramid; insects are near the bottom.*

environment (en vī′rən mənt) All the living and nonliving things that surround an organism. (p. 32) *Plants need an environment in which they can get sunlight, water, carbon dioxide, and other nutrients.*

erosion (i'rō'zhən) The transportation of weathered rock from one place to another. (p. 204) *Erosion can be caused by rainfall, waves, and wind.*

eruption (i rəp'shən) A violent outburst or outpouring. (p.262) *The eruption of a volcano forces melted rock, gases, and rock out of the vent.*

euglena (yü glē'nə) A type of protist that behaves like both a plant and an animal. (p. 67) *Euglena is also classified as a kind of algae.*

exfoliation (eks'fō lē ā'shən) A kind of physical weathering in which layers of rock peel off. (p. 195) *Rocks that are partly buried may show signs of exfoliation on the exposed surfaces.*

experiment (ek sper'ə ment') An organized test designed to support or disprove a hypothesis. (p. 9) *Most experiments are designed and carried out very carefully.*

extinct (ek stingkt') All dead; no more left alive on Earth. (p. 109) *Animals that cannot adapt to changes in their ecosystem may become extinct.*

extrusive (eks trü'siv) A kind of igneous rock formed when magma cools and hardens above Earth's surface. (p. 153) *Extrusive igneous rock may form in a matter of hours.*

fault (folt) A break or crack in Earth's crust where two plates come together. (p. 249) *Earthquakes are common along faults.*

filament (fi'lə mənt) A thin wire. (p. 311) *The filament in an incandescent light heats up and glows as it resists electric current.*

flood (fləd) The flow of water over the banks of a body of water and across land. (p. 240) *Large amounts of rainfall can cause floods along rivers.*

food chain (füd chān) The path that energy takes from one organism to another in the form of food. (p. 38) *A food chain shows how energy goes from the Sun to a plant to an insect to a bird.*

food web (füd web) The food chains that link together in an environment. (p. 52) *A food web shows that some animals are part of more than one food chain.*

forester (fôr'est ər) Someone who takes care of a forest or wilderness area. (p. 132) *A forester might interact with hikers, campers, and hunters.*

forest floor (fôr'əst flôr) The ground level of a forest ecosystem. (p. 89) *Not many plants grow on the forest floor because of the lack of sunlight that reaches it.*

fossil (fos'əl) The remains of a living thing from many years ago. (p. 164) *Most fossils are found in sedimentary rock.*

fungus (fung'gəs) n. sing., **fungi** (fun'jī) pl. A plant-like organism that breaks down dead or dying plants. (p. 164) *Fungi are one kind of decomposers in a woodland environment.*

fuse (fūz) A device that melts if too much electric current is flowing through a circuit. (p. 314) *When a fuse melts, it must be replaced to restore power to the circuit.*

gem (jem) A mineral valued for its beauty. (p. 146) *Diamonds, rubies, and emeralds are gems.*

generate (jen'ər rāt') To create or produce. (p. 342) *Magnets can be used to generate electricity.*

generator (jen'ər rā'tər) A device that creates alternating current when an electric coil spins between the poles of a magnet. (p. 354) *An electric generator changes motion into electrical energy.*

genetics (je'ne'tiks) The study of how organisms pass along traits over periods of time. (p. 117) *Genetics helps to explain why the necks of giraffes are so long.*

geologist (jə ol'ə jist) A scientist who studies rocks to learn about Earth's history. (pp. 178, 278) *Geologists use the properties of rocks to classify them.*

glacier (glā'shər) A large mass of moving ice. (p. 222) *Glaciers cut into landforms and create valleys over time.*

gneiss (nīs) A type of metamorphic rock. (p. 173) *Gneiss is formed when granite is heated under great pressure.*

gravity (gra'vi tē) The pulling force between two objects. (p. 238) *The gravity between your body and Earth prevents you from floating into space.*

hardness (härd'nis) A property of minerals that tells how well it resists scratching. (p. 144) *Diamond has the highest degree of hardness.*

herbivore (hûr′bə vôr′) An animal that eats mainly plants. (p. 40) *Deer, rabbits, and cows are all herbivores.*

horizon (hə rī′zən) A layer of soil that is distinct from the layers above and below it. (p. 198) *Each horizon has its own properties.*

hot spot (hot spot) A place where magma has partially melted through Earth's crust. (p. 264) *Plates moving over hot spots may give rise to volcanoes.*

humus (hū′məs) Decayed plant or animal material in soil. (p. 198) *Each layer of soil has different amounts of rock and humus.*

hybrid (hī′brid) Having two or more different things mixed together. (p. 318) *A hybrid car uses both gasoline and electricity as power sources.*

hypothesis (hī poth′ə sis) A suggested statement or explanation that can be tested to answer a question. (p. 7) *An experiment can help you to test a hypothesis.*

igneous rock (ig′nē əs rok) A type of rock formed when melted rock cools and hardens. (p. 152) *Igneous rock, such as granite, can be found near a volcano.*

insulator (in′sə lā tər) Something that slows or stops the flow of energy, such as heat, electricity, or sound. (p. 292) *Wood, rubber, and glass are good insulators.*

intrusive (in trü′siv) A kind of igneous rock formed when magma cools and hardens below Earth's surface. (p. 153) *Intrusive igneous rock may take thousands of years to form.*

kelp (kelp) A type of seaweed. (p. 54) *Kelp is usually large and brown in color.*

kidney (kid′nē) A bean-shaped organ that filters water and waste materials out of the blood. (p. 119) *In some animals, the kidneys can help store water for later use.*

L

landform (land′fôrm) A natural feature on Earth's surface. (p. 214) *Plains, mountains, and valleys are all landforms.*

landslide (land′slīd) The rapid, downhill movement of large amounts of rock, soil, and other material. (p. 238) *An earthquake might cause landslides in mountainous areas.*

lapis lazuli (la′pəs la′zə lē) A type of metamorphic rock formed from limestone. (p. 176) *Lapis lazuli is a deep blue color and used to make jewelry.*

lava (lä′və) Magma that reaches Earth's surface. (pp. 152, 263) *Lava often flows when a volcano erupts.*

lava rock (lä′və rok) Another name for pumice, an extrusive igneous rock. (p. 155) *Lava rock is very light in weight with many tiny holes.*

leaf (lēf) The part of a plant that collects light from the Sun. (p. 27) *The leaves of most plants are green.*

levitation (le′vi tā′shən) The act of lifting something or being lifted off the ground. (p. 327) *Maglev trains use magnets for levitation above the ground.*

lightning (līt′ning) A large spark caused by the discharge of static electricity in a thunderhead. (p. 290) *Lightning can jump from one cloud to another or from a cloud to the ground.*

loudspeaker (loud′spē′kər) A device that changes electrical energy into sound. (p. 344) *Headphones are small loudspeakers with tiny electromagnets that make them work.*

luster (lus′tər) The way light reflects off a mineral's surface. (p. 142) *Luster is one of several properties of minerals.*

magma (mag′mə) Hot, molten rock below Earth's crust. (pp. 152, 262) *Magma flows like liquid even though it is rock.*

magnet (mag′net) An object that can attract iron and produce a magnetic field. (p. 330) *When you bring two magnets together, they will either attract or repel each other.*

magnetic field (mag net′ik fēld) The region of positive and negative attractive forces surrounding a magnet. (p. 334) *Earth has a magnetic field similar to a bar magnet.*

malaria (mə ler′ē ə) A disease that causes high fever. (p. 72) *Malaria is caused by microorganisms in the blood.*

measure (mezh′ər) To find the size, volume, area, mass, weight, or temperature of an object, or to find how long an event occurs. (p. 11) *When you measure something, you gather data or information about it.*

mechanical energy (mi ka′ni kəl en′ər jē) Motion, or the energy in moving objects. (p. 352) *A motor can produce mechanical energy in power tools, toys, and cars.*

metallic (mə ta′lik) Shiny and reflective. (p. 142) *Some minerals have a metallic luster.*

metamorphic rock (met′ə môr′fik rok) Rock whose form has been changed by heat or pressure. (p. 172) *Under pressure, limestone becomes the metamorphic rock marble.*

microbiologist (mī′krō bī ä′ləjist) A person who studies microorganisms. (p. 72) *A microbiologist might study the small organisms that cause disease.*

microorganism (mī′krō ôr′gə niz′əm) An organism that is too small to see without a microscope. (p. 64) *Protists and bacteria are microorganisms.*

microphone (mī′krə fōn′) A device that converts sound into electrical signals. (p. 345) *Magnets in a microphone turn your voice into signals that can be sent to other locations.*

microscope (mī′krə skōp′) A tool that makes small objects appear larger. (p. 64) *You can see bacteria using a microscope.*

mimicry (mim′i krē) When one organism imitates the traits of another. (p. 117) *Some insects use mimicry to look like other insects and fool predators.*

mineral (min′ər əl) A natural, nonliving substance. (p. 140) *Some minerals are the building blocks of rocks.*

Moh's hardness scale (mōz härd′nis skāl) A table that shows the hardness of minerals. (p. 144) *On the Mohs hardness scale, talc has a value of 1 and diamond has a value of 10.*

mold (mōld) A type of fungi. (p. 68) *Many foods grow mold over time if left alone.*

motor (mō′tər) A device that changes electrical energy into mechanical energy. (p. 352) *Electric motors are used in everyday devices such as refrigerators, air conditioners, and electric trains.*

mudslide (mud′slīd) Land that becomes too full of water and slides down a slope. (p. 241) *Mudslides may occur after a period of heavy rain.*

N

nectar (nek′tər) A sweet liquid found inside flowers. (p. 99) *The nectar attracts animals that help flowers pollinate.*

neutral (nü′trəl) Having no overall electrical charge. (p. 287) *In a neutral object, the positive and negative electrical charges cancel each other out.*

normal fault (nôr′məl folt) The crack or line between two plates that are pulling apart. (p. 250) *Rocks above a normal fault move down.*

O

observe (əb zûrv′) To use one or more of your senses to identify or learn about an object or event. (p. 5) *You conduct an experiment to observe what happens in a controlled situation.*

omnivore (om′nə vôr′) An animal that eats both plants and animals. (p. 43) *Most humans are omnivores.*

open circuit (ō′pən sər′kət) An electrical circuit with breaks or openings. (p. 299) *Electric current cannot flow in an open circuit.*

ore (ôr) A mineral or rock containing a useful property or substance. (p. 146) *Hematite is an ore that contains iron.*

organism (ôr′gə niz′əm) A living thing. (p. 28) *All organisms carry out five basic life functions.*

oxygen (ok′sə jən) A gas that most plants and animals need to live. (p. 26) *The air that we breathe contains oxygen.*

P

parallel circuit (par′ə lel′ sər′kət) A circuit in which the electrical current follows more than one path. (p. 301) *Each branch of a parallel circuit has its own electric current.*

photographer (fə tä′grə fər) A person who takes pictures with a camera. (p. 132) *Nature photographers work in many outdoor places like jungles and oceans.*

photosynthesis (fō′tō sin′thə sis) The process by which plants turn sunlight into food. (p. 28) *Most photosynthesis takes place in the summer.*

physical weathering (fiz′i kəl weth′ər ing) The processes that change the size and shape of rocks without changing them chemically. (p. 194) *Extreme high and low temperatures can lead to physical weathering.*

pistil (pis′təl) The parts of a plant that produce the female sex cells. (p. 98) *The ovary is part of the plant's pistil.*

plain (plān) A large, flat stretch of land. (p. 214) *The Great Plains are located in the middle of the United States.*

plate (plāt) An extremely large, moving slab of rock that forms Earth's crust. (p. 248) *The movement of plates can cause earthquakes.*

pole (pōl) The part of a magnet where the magnetic force is strongest. (p. 331) *When two magnets are brought together, the north pole will attract the south pole.*

pollen (pol′ən) The powder-like grains in a flower that contain the male sex cells. (p. 99) *During pollination, pollen is transferred from stamen to pistil.*

pollination (pol′ə nā′shən) The process in which the male and female cells of plants come together. (p. 98) *After pollination a seed develops that lets the plant reproduce.*

population (pop′yə lā′shən) All the members of a single type of living thing in an environment. (p. 54) *When one population changes, it affects other populations in the same food web.*

predator (pred′ə tər) An animal that hunts another animal for food. (p. 41) *Sharks are the ocean's fiercest predators.*

predict (pri dikt′) To state likely results of an event or experiment. (p. 9) *You might be able to predict the weather by looking at clouds in the sky.*

pressure (pre′shər) A squeezing force that pushes things together. (p. 172) *Pressure deep in the Earth can form new kinds of rock from old kinds.*

prey (prā) An animal that is hunted by another animal for food. (p. 41) *Mice are prey to hawks.*

primary consumer (prī′mer ē kən sü′mər) The first consumer in a food chain. (p. 40) *Herbivores, such as deer or rabbits, are often the primary consumers in their food chains.*

producer (prə dü′sər) An organism that makes its own food. (p. 38) *Green plants are producers that make their own food from water, carbon dioxide, and sunlight.*

protist (prō′tist) A microorganism that lives in water. (p. 65) *Many harmful protists are found in ponds and lakes.*

repel (ri pel′) To push away. (p. 287) *An object with positive electrical charge will repel another object with positive electrical charge.*

reproduce (rē′prədüs′) To make new living things like the original. (p. 28) *Not all organisms reproduce the same way.*

resistance (ri zis′təns) The ability of a substance to stop or slow down electric current. (p. 304) *Resistance allows electrical energy to be changed into other forms of energy, such as heat or light.*

reverse fault (rə vərs′ folt) The crack or line between two plates that are pushing together. (p. 250) *Rocks above a reverse fault move upward.*

rift volcano (rift vol cā′nō) A volcano that forms where Earth's plates move apart. (p. 264) *Most rift volcanoes form along the ocean floor.*

rock cycle (rok sī′kəl) The series of processes that show how rocks change from one into another. (p. 180) *Over time, all rocks melt and harden in the rock cycle.*

rock-forming minerals (rok-fôrm ing min′ər əlz) The types of nonliving substances common to rocks. (p. 141) *Quartz and feldspar are two common rock-forming minerals.*

root (rüt) The part of a plant that gets water and food from the soil. (p. 27) *Some roots reach far underground.*

sand dune (sand dün) Hill-like deposit of sand left behind by wind erosion. (p. 221) *Winds off the ocean create sand dunes along the shore.*

sediment (sed′ə ment) Small pieces of material normally carried and deposited by water or wind. (p. 162) *Some sediments are tiny particles of rocks and minerals or bits of bone and shell.*

sedimentary rock (sed′ə men′tər ē rok) A type of rock that forms when sediments are pressed together in layers. (p. 162) *Limestone is an example of sedimentary rock.*

seed dispersal (sēd di spər′səl) The process of spreading seeds that allow plants to reproduce. (p. 100) *Animals play an important role in seed dispersal.*

series circuit (sîr′ēz sər′kət) A circuit in which all the electrical charges flow along the same path. (p. 300) *If any part of a series circuit is broken, no electric current will flow.*

shaft (shaft) A pole or rod that spins or moves. (p. 352) *A motor shaft might turn a gear or a wheel.*

shield volcano (shēld vol cā'nō) A volcano with sides that are wide and flat. (p. 267) *The Hawaiian Islands are examples of shield volcanoes.*

short circuit (shôrt sər'kət) A path of electric current with almost no resistance. (p. 304) *A short circuit can create dangerous levels of heat in the rest of the circuit.*

solar energy (sō'lər en'ər jē) Energy that comes from the Sun. (p. 28) *Most plants rely on solar energy to grow.*

stamen (stā'mən) The part of the plant that holds the male cells for reproduction. (p. 98) *The stamen is part of the plant's anther.*

static electricity (sta'tik i lek'tri'sə tē) A buildup of electrical charge on an object. (p. 288) *Objects rubbing against one another in a clothes dryer create static electricity.*

stem (stem) The part of a plant that holds it upright. (p. 27) *A plant's stem also carries food and water.*

stomata (stō'mə tə) n. pl., **stoma** (stō'mə) sing. Holes on the bottoms of leaves through which air and water pass. (p. 29) *Carbon dioxide enters a plant through its stomata.*

streak (strēk) A property of minerals that tells the color of powder left behind when the mineral is scratched along a white tile (p. 143) *Not all minerals leave a streak that is the same color as the mineral itself.*

strike-slip fault (strīk slip folt) The crack or line between two plates that are sliding past each other in different directions. (p. 251) *California's San Andreas Fault is a strike-slip fault.*

strip farming (strip fär'ming) Planting alternating rows of grasses and food crops in an area. (p. 208) *Strip farming slows down soil erosion.*

submersible (sub mər'sə bəl) Something that can work underwater. (p. 271) *Scientists use vehicles called submersibles to study the bottom of the ocean.*

survey technician (sər'vā tek ni'shən) A person who creates maps and locates boundaries of land. (p. 278) *A survey technician might use a special instrument to calculate large distances.*

switch (swich) A device that can make, break, or change the flow of electric current in a circuit. (p. 299) *Most switches turn the electric current on or off.*

transformer (trans fär′mər) Something that changes the voltage of electric current. (p. 312) *Some transformers increase voltage as electric current leaves a power plant, then others decrease the voltage before it enters a home.*

tsunami (sü nä′mē) A giant ocean wave. (p. 252) *A tsunami is usually caused by an earthquake in the ocean.*

turbine (tər′bīn) A type of engine that provides the mechanical energy for a generator. (p. 355) *A simple turbine looks like an electric fan that moves when steam, water, or air pushes against the blades.*

understory (ən′dər stôr′ē) The area in a forest between the canopy and the ground. (p. 89) *Leopards, frogs, and many insects live in the understory.*

valley (va′lē) An area of low land between hills or mountains. (p. 216) *Rivers can cut away at landforms and create valleys.*

vent (vent) The central opening in a volcano. (p. 263) *During eruption, lava and rocks are forced out of the volcano's vent.*

volcano (vol cā′nō) A mountain that builds up around an opening in Earth's crust. (p. 262) *When trapped energy is released from a volcano, there may be an explosive eruption.*

voltage (vōl′tij) The strength of a power source. (p. 304) *A power source with more voltage can produce more electric current.*

volt (vōlt) A unit of measurement of the strength of a power source. (p. 304) *Most wall outlets have 120 volts.*

warning (wôr′ning) In weather, a term used to report that something is occurring or will occur soon. (p. 242) *A flood warning means that water is rising over the banks of rivers or lakes.*

watch (wäch) In weather, a term used to report that a weather event is possible. (p. 242) *A flood watch means that conditions are good for a flood in the near future.*

watt (wot) A unit of measure that tells how much electrical power is used. (p. 317) *Light bulbs that use more watts generally provide more light.*

weathering (weth'ər ing) The natural processes that break down rocks without transporting them. (p. 194) *Freezing, wind, and pressure can lead to weathering.*

wind abrasion (wind əbrā'zhən) A kind of physical weathering in which blowing sand wears away the rock. (p. 195) *A sandstorm can cause a high level of wind abrasion.*

Index

Q

R

S

Credits

(t) David Sieren/Visuals Unlimited; (b) Photodisc/Getty Images. 278: (t) David Mendelsohn/Masterfile; (b) Carsten Peter/NGS Images. 279: (tl) Kelly-Mooney Photography/CORBIS; (tr) Richard Megna/Fundamental Photographs; (b) Matthias Breiter/Minden Pictures. 280-281: Kelly-Mooney Photography/CORBIS. 281: (tr) Miles Ertman/Masterfile; (cr) Boden/Ledingham/Masterfile; (br) BananaStock/PunchStock. 282-283: Scott Stulberg/Alamy. 283: Royalty-free/CORBIS. 284-285: Miles Ertman/Masterfile. 288: (t) Dylan Collard/Getty Images. 290: (tl) Chris Cheadle/Getty Images. 292: (t) Lester Lefkowitz/CORBIS; (b) David Hebden/Alamy. 293: (b) Lester Lefkowitz/CORBIS. 294: (t) Photodisc/Getty Images. 296-297: Boden/Ledingham/Masterfile. 298: (t) Daryl Benson/Masterfile; (b) Dynamic Graphics Group/Creatas/Alamy. 304: David Chasey/Getty Images. 305: (t) Daryl Benson/Masterfile; (bl) David Chasey/Getty Images. 308-309: BananaStock/PunchStock. 309: (cl) Photodisc; (c, cr) Photodisc/Getty Images. 310: (t) Richard Hamilton Smith/CORBIS. 310-311: Craig Lovell/Eagle Visions Photography/Alamy. 311: (tr) Siede Preis/Getty Images. 312: (l) Peter Casolino/Alamy. 314: (tr) Paul Silverman/Fundamental Photographs; (cr) Steve Cole/Getty Images; (bl) David Young-Wolff/PhotoEdit. 315: (t) Richard Hamilton Smith/CORBIS; (bl) Paul Silverman/Fundamental Photographs. 316: Image Source/Alamy. 318: Toshifumi Kitamura/AFP/Getty Images. 318-319: (inset) Mark Richards/PhotoEdit. 319: Marty Lederhandler/AP/Wide World Photos. 320: (tl) Miles Ertman/Masterfile; (cl) Boden/Ledingham/Masterfile; (bl) BananaStock/PunchStock. 321: (bl) Kelly-Mooney Photography/CORBIS. 324-325: Richard Megna/Fundamental Photographs. 325: (cr) Jeremy Walker/Photo Researchers; (br) EJ West/Index Stock. 326-327: Bernd Mellmann/Alamy. 327: Kevin Foy/Alamy. 331: (tr) Andrew Lambert/Leslie Garland Picture Library/Alamy. 332: (tl) Sinclair Stammers/Photo Researchers; (bl, br) The Studio Dog/Getty Images. 334: (cl) Yoav Levy/Phototake. 334-335: (l to r) NASA JSC/Getty Images. 336: (t) Comstock/SuperStock. 337: (cl) Yoav Levy/Phototake; (bl) Comstock/SuperStock. 340-341: Jeremy Walker/Photo Researchers. 342: (t) DK Limited/CORBIS; (b) NRM/Pictorial Collection/SSPL/The Image Works. 344: (tl) BananaStock/age fotostock. 345: (br) Rob Lewine/CORBIS. 346: (l) C Squared Images/Getty Images. 347: (tl) DK Limited/CORBIS; (tc) BananaStock/age fotostock. 350-351: EJ West/Index Stock. 352: Peter Parks/AFP/Getty Images. 353: Stockbyte. 354: (tl) Chris Laurens/Alamy; (bl) SuperStock; (br) AbleStock/Index Stock. 355: (bl) David Halpern/Photo Researchers; (bc) Richard Cummins/SuperStock; (br) age fotostock/SuperStock. 357: (cl) age fotostock/SuperStock. 360: (tr) Topham/The Image Works; (bl) DK Limited/CORBIS. 360-361: (bkgd) Wetzel and Company. 361: (tl) Reven TC Wurman/Alamy; (tr) SSPL/The Image Works; (cr) Schenectady Museum/Hall of Electrical History Foundation/CORBIS. 362: (cl) Jeremy Walker/Photo Researchers; (bl) EJ West/Index Stock. 363: (tr) Koichi Kamoshida/Getty Images; (bl) Richard Megna/Fundamental Photographs. 366: Nicholas Eveleigh/Iconica/Getty Images. 366-367: John Warden/Stone/Getty Images. 367: (tr) Frans Lanting/Minden Pictures. 368: (t) A. Ramey/PhotoEdit; (b) Jeff Greenberg/PhotoEdit. 372: (tl) David Young-Wolff/Photo Edit; (bl) Randy Faris/Corbis; (c) Getty Images; (cr) Ingram Publishing; (br) PhotoLink/Getty Images. 373: (r) BananaStock/PunchStock. 375: (l) Creatas/PunchStock; (b) Amos Morgan/Getty Images. 377: (b) Stockbyte/PunchStock. 378: (b) Rim Light/PhotoLink/Getty Images. 381: (l) image100 Ltd; (r) Getty Images. 382: TRBfoto/Getty Images. 382-383: (b) Tony Watson/Alamy. 384-385: (c) Stockbyte/PunchStock; (b) Siede Preis/Getty Images.

Acknowledgments

"Benjamin Franklin" from *A Book of Americans* by Rosemary and Stephen Vincent Benét. Copyright © 1933 by Rosemary and Stephen Vincent Benét, copyright renewed, 1961, by Rosemary Carr Benét. Published by Holt, Rinehart and Winston.

"California's Weather Woes" from *TIME for Kids*. Copyright © 2005 by Time, Inc. Published by Time, Inc. All rights reserved.

"Cruising on Air" from *Scholastic SuperScience*. Copyright © 1998. Published by Scholastic, Inc.

"Rock Secrets" by Betsy James from *Click Magazine*. Copyright © 2005 by Click Magazine. Published by Carus Publishing.

"Sierra" by Diane Siebert. Text copyright © 1991 by Diane Siebert. Published by HarperCollins Publishers.

"The Story Goes On" by Aileen Fisher. Text copyright © 2002 by Aileen Fisher. Published by Roaring Brook Press. All rights reserved.

"Welcome to the Seas of Sand" by Jane Yolen. Text copyright © 1996 by Jane Yolen. Published by Penguin Putnam Books for Young Readers. All rights reserved.